"*The Exegetical Process* by Dr. Aída Spencer is an ind[...] [...]s and anyone venturing into the intricate world of co[...] [...]. With precision and clarity, Dr. Spencer has skillfully create[...] [...] [...]rs pragmatic strategies, illuminating insights, and a systematic approach to masterfully interpreting and presenting the treasures of the New Testament.

"This guide presents a unique approach that promises to revolutionize the process of writing New Testament exegesis papers. Dr. Spencer's meticulous organization and lucid explanations make it an essential companion for both novice scholars and experienced researchers. The book is thoughtfully divided into focused chapters, each dedicated to an essential facet of the exegesis process, facilitating readers' seamless engagement with the content.

"Central to the guide's methodology is its emphasis on establishing a rock-solid foundation for exegesis. Key concepts such as historical context, literary genres, and theological themes are introduced with precision. Dr. Spencer's clarity, supplemented with practical examples, equips readers with the essential tools to navigate the complexities of New Testament texts confidently. The standout feature of this guide lies in its hands-on approach. Dr. Spencer focuses on the practical application of interpretive principles rather than inundating readers with theoretical debates. The guide perfectly balances providing succinct methodologies and avoiding information overload. This approach fosters critical thinking and promotes a holistic understanding by introducing readers to diverse interpretive lenses, ranging from historical-critical analysis to literary and theological exploration.

"A noteworthy aspect of this guide is its integration of real-world case studies and tangible examples. Dr. Spencer adeptly demonstrates how interpretive principles can be effectively employed to dissect specific passages, thereby illuminating the intended essence of the text. These real-life illustrations seamlessly bridge theory and practicality, elevating the learning experience and rendering the concepts immediately applicable. The guide's meticulous attention to detail is commendable. It features invaluable study aids, such as glossaries, recommended further readings, and reflective questions at the end of each chapter. These resources not only facilitate active learning but also empower readers to embark on a comprehensive exploration of the subject matter.

"*The Exegetical Process* is an essential tool for seminary students and individuals embarking on the journey of crafting impactful exegesis papers. With its pragmatic approach, insightful guidance, and comprehensive coverage, this guide equips readers with the necessary tools to approach New Testament texts with precision and depth. Dr. Aída Spencer's exceptional work balances scholarly rigor and accessibility, establishing this guide as an invaluable asset for honing exegesis skills."

—Mark A. Arnold,
Adjunct Professor,
Gordon-Conwell Theological Seminary

"Teaching people to handle the Scriptures correctly is the aim of *The Exegetical Process*. The principles and tools in this book will help any preacher, teacher, or serious student of God's Word. Last year I specifically inquired about using Dr. Spencer's instruction sheet 'How to Write a New Testament Exegesis Paper' (which reads like an outline of this book) so that I could use it in my class as a rubric for grading exegesis papers. The systematic process of going from the wider context (historical, cultural) to the immediate context (literary, grammatical, semantic, stylistic analysis, and word study) and then to secondary sources (beginning with contemporaries of the biblical era to early church fathers and mothers) has proven invaluable to me as a pastor and professor. What's more, Dr. Spencer is not content with mere head knowledge but consistently sees the hermeneutical process through to life application so readers will not only be hearers but doers of the Word. Her hermeneutics of respect and adherence to the Scripture's authority for matters of faith and life shine through the exegetical process."

—Grace Y. May,
Vice Provost of Academic Affairs,
Director of the Women's Institute, Associate Professor of Biblical Studies,
William Carey International University

"My spiritual life as well as my mind benefited from exegesis. Ever since taking interp with _____ and a New Testament course with _____ I looked at studying Scripture as a purely technical science in which one employs sentence flows and parsing guides to dissect the Bible but, unfortunately, in the process, turned the text into a corpse. Studying Luke with you, however, has been a totally different experience. You insisted that we familiarize ourselves with Luke by reading and rereading it. Only after successive readings, outlining the book or letter for ourselves and researching the historical background, did you permit us to go on to the next step of analyzing a particular pericope in great detail. While all of this preliminary work involved quite a bit of legwork in the library and many hours poring through Scripture, the dividends were unbelievable! I have never gotten more from a book study in my entire life. . . . Throughout the course, you also showed us how to bring the tools and techniques of good exegesis to bear in our study and ultimately our ministry. You revealed the purpose of wading through all the dense textual apparatus and even showed me new ways of using textual criticism. . . . You introduced me to the church fathers when none of my other exegesis professors did. You encouraged me to . . . read the text and appreciate how the Holy Spirit uses a human medium like language to communicate truth. . . . You also made it readily apparent how important knowing the Jewish and Hellenistic background is in understanding the meaning of the New Testament in its day. . . . While you demanded a lot, you never assigned superfluous or inordinate amounts of work. . . . You also underscored the importance of original work. . . . Thanks for motivating me to dig hard and drink deeply of God's *living* Word. . . . I'm convinced that the better equipped I am to mine Scripture, the better off I'll be in whatever ministry situation God puts me in. After all, this is the stuff that eternal life is made of and what I want to proclaim to others as best as I know how."

—Grace Y. May,
Earlier comments while a student and teaching assistant
at Gordon-Conwell Theological Seminary

"I'm glad to hear that you are preparing your notebook for publication. As a student, I found your material extremely helpful. Your thorough, step-by-step manual makes the process of writing an exegesis paper clear (and less daunting) for the student. In particular, I found your annotated sample paper to be helpful both for myself and for other students. It will be helpful to have access to an electronic version once it is published, as print resources are not always available in the part of the world where I teach. I hope eventually to be able to use your exegesis manual here as a textbook to teach Interpreting the New Testament and New Testament Exegesis at some future point."

—Jen Creamer,
Faculty,
University of the Nations

"I have noticed that students, after having learned the general principles of interpretation, need an extra skill, the ability to write the paper. We might call it the gap between general knowledge and writing knowledge, the writing gap. . . .

"I took two classes, Exegesis of Luke and Exegesis of the Pastoral Epistles (1 Timothy), with Dr. Spencer at seminary. I found out the manual *How to Write an Exegesis Paper* written by Dr. Spencer is a great resource to write an exegesis paper in the right way. The manual provides checklists and tracks that guide you through steps and instructions Dr. Spencer suggests. Thorough step-by-step instruction helps you do exegesis research on a New Testament passage, providing valuable guidance for anyone who is new to exegesis study like myself. These are some of the most helpful features of the manual:

- It provides a sample paper for the exegesis study.
- It focuses on the primary source for studying the historical context of the Bible passage rather than jumping into the secondary source early on.
- It helps the user diagram each passage to understand sentence flow.
- It provides a detailed section for conducting text critical study through textual variants using a template.

"I have adopted the exegesis approach in the *Exegetical Process* provided by Dr. Spencer for assignments in the New Testament exegesis classes. A similar exegesis approach can be applicable to the exegesis process of Old Testament passages. This manual is a good handbook for students who want to do exegesis study and pastors who study and preach the Word of God."

—J. B. Jiabing Wang,
Teacher,
China

"One of the daunting experiences of seminary students who take a New Testament class is the requirement to write an exegesis paper. How do you begin? What elements should be included in the paper? How do you use primary source documents? How do you draw out the author's intended meaning for those original recipients, and how does that meaning speak to this generation? These are all questions that new exegetes have when attempting to write an exegesis paper. *The Exegetical Process* answers these questions and will help to remove the uncertainty and fear of fulfilling this requirement for New Testament students. It provides careful step-by-step instruction for completing all the elements of an exegesis paper. In addition, the author includes a completed exegesis paper, a sentence flow chart, an outline of a New Testament letter, and other resources that will help students become skilled exegetes."

—Darin Poullard,
Pastor,
Fort Washington Baptist Church

"The impetus behind my enrollment at Gordon-Conwell Theological Seminary in the United States, despite leaving my home in South Korea, was to gain a comprehensive and accurate understanding of the Bible to accurately convey its teachings to fellow believers. During my studies in Professor Spencer's New Testament exegesis course, I came across her guidebook and was convinced that God had prepared this institution for me.

"This guidebook presents numerous advantages, and I will list five based on my own experience as one of Dr. Spencer's students. First, the guidebook blends Dr. Spencer's profound respect for the Bible by emphasizing the need to submit to its authority. This challenges the critical approach to the Word that has been dominant in contemporary Western Christianity that prioritizes human reasoning over God's authority. Second, the guidebook is highly systematic and practical, presenting the essential elements of the exegetical method with appropriate examples, making it accessible for readers to understand and apply the suggested methods in their own readings. Third, it encourages readers to focus on the Bible itself and demonstrates how the text can address many questions that can be raised in relation to contexts and topics. Fourth, the guidebook provides principles for applying the meanings of the past to our present reality, divided into personal, pastoral, and academic applications, allowing readers to adapt the guidelines to their needs. Last, it provides a systematic method and process for writing an exegetical paper, making it particularly valuable for students and professors.

"This book inspires readers to listen to God's Word, fostering a desire for the Word itself while also presenting practical guidelines for studying it with humility and faithfulness. I highly recommend it."

—Jihyung Kim,
Pastor, PhD candidate,
McMaster Divinity College

"I have been honored and privileged to study several New Testament exegesis courses with Dr. Aída Spencer. For each course, I used Dr. Spencer's manual *The Exegetical Process*. Dr. Spencer's goal is to help her students learn how to study the Bible well enough not to rely on secondary sources while staying true to the biblical text. The comprehensive manual includes all the elements necessary to write an excellent exegesis paper.

"I studied under Dr. Spencer decades ago, and to this day, I still remember and apply what I learned in her courses. More than anything, I love studying God's Word, and this manual prepared me well to do so whether for teaching or preaching."

—Leslie McKinney Attema,
Pastor and Spiritual Director,
Georgia

"I am so happy to hear that Dr. Spencer finally decided to publish her amazing manual. I was overjoyed to hear my three-hole binder format of *The Exegetical Process*, which I kept for a decade since my seminary years, is now a published book at last. As a seminary student and Dr. Spencer's teaching assistant, I was blessed to use this step-by-step guide not only for writing New Testament exegesis papers but also for exegeting original biblical texts for personal study. Anyone who wants to master biblical exegesis would want this invaluable treasure."

—Young Kwon Kim,
Pastor, Psychotherapist, PhD student

THE EXEGETICAL PROCESS

How to Write a
New Testament
Exegesis Paper
Step-by-Step

AÍDA BESANÇON SPENCER

The Exegetical Process: How to Write a New Testament Exegesis Paper, Step-by-Step
© 2025 by Aída Besançon Spencer

Published by Kregel Academic, an imprint of Kregel Publications, 2450 Oak Industrial Dr. NE, Grand Rapids, MI 49505-6020.

All rights reserved. No part of this book may be reproduced, stored in a retrieval system, or transmitted in any form or by any means—electronic, mechanical, photocopy, recording, or otherwise—without written permission of the publisher, except for brief quotations in printed reviews.

All Scripture quotations, unless otherwise indicated, are the author's own translation.

Scripture quotations marked ESV are from the ESV® Bible (The Holy Bible, English Standard Version®), copyright © 2001 by Crossway, a publishing ministry of Good News Publishers. Used by permission. All rights reserved.

Scripture quotations marked GNT are from the Good News Translation © 1994 published by the Bible Societies/HarperCollins Publishers Ltd., UK Good News Bible © American Bible Society 1966, 1971, 1976, 1992. Used with permission.

Scripture quotations marked HCSB are from the Holman Christian Standard Bible®. Copyright © 1999, 2000, 2002, 2003 by Holman Bible Publishers. Used by permission.

Scripture quotations marked KJV are from the King James Version.

Scripture quotations marked NASB are taken from the (NASB®) New American Standard Bible®, Copyright © 1960, 1971, 1977, 1995, 2020 by The Lockman Foundation. Used by permission. All rights reserved. www.lockman.org

Scripture quotations marked NIV are taken from the Holy Bible, New International Version®, NIV® 1973, 1978, 1984, 2011 by Biblica, Inc.™ Used by permission of Zondervan. All rights reserved worldwide. www.zondervan.com The "NIV" and "New International Version" are trademarks registered in the United States Patent and Trademark Office by Biblica, Inc.

Scripture quotations marked NLT are from the Holy Bible, New Living Translation, copyright © 1996, 2004, 2007 by Tyndale House Foundation. Used by permission of Tyndale House Publishers, Inc., Carol Stream, Illinois 60188. All rights reserved.

Scripture quotations marked NRSV are from the New Revised Standard Version Bible, copyright © 1989 by the National Council of the Churches of Christ in the United States of America. Used by permission. All rights reserved worldwide. https://www.friendshippress.org/pages/nrsvue-quick-faq

Scripture quotations marked REB are from the Revised English Bible, copyright © 1989 Oxford University Press and Cambridge University Press. All rights reserved.

Scripture quotations marked RSV are from the Revised Standard Version of the Bible, copyright © 1946, 1952, and 1971 by the National Council of the Churches of Christ in the U.S.A. Used by permission. All rights reserved.

Scripture quotations marked TEV are from the Today's English Version. Copyright © 1966, 1971, 1976, 1992 by American Bible Society. Used by permission. All rights reserved.

Library of Congress Cataloging-in-Publication Data

Names: Spencer, Aída Besançon author
Title: The exegetical process : how to write a New Testament exegesis paper step by step / Aída Besançon Spencer.
Description: First edition. | Grand Rapids, MI : Kregel Academic, [2025] | Includes bibliographical references and index.
Identifiers: LCCN 2025004552 (print) | LCCN 2025004553 (ebook)
Subjects: LCSH: Bible. New Testament—Hermeneutics—Handbooks, manuals, etc.
Classification: LCC BS2331 .S64 2025 (print) | LCC BS2331 (ebook) | DDC 225.601—dc23/eng/20250515
LC record available at https://lccn.loc.gov/2025004552
LC ebook record available at https://lccn.loc.gov/2025004553

ISBN 978-0-8254-4916-1

Printed in the United States of America

25 26 27 28 29 / 5 4 3 2 1

Words of Light

1. *Your word is like a searchlight at my feet*
   And it lights up my way.
   So I might not stumble and fall,
   But I will get through every day.
   Words of light, words of light,
   Teach me a better way.
   Deep within my heart,
   I will recall,
   Wisdom to guide me today.

2. *Your word is like a scalpel in my soul.*
   And it pares the dross away,
   Like cutting right where bone and marrow meet,
   Revealing all I do and all I say.
   Words of light, words of light,
   Teach me a better way.
   Deep within my heart,
   I will recall,
   Wisdom to guide me today.

3. *Your word is like a treasury of grace,*
   Like a bank of the good.
   It notes the way to pay the debt of bad I've done
   And do and say the things I really should.
   Words of light, words of light,
   Teach me a better way.
   Deep within my heart,
   I will recall,
   Wisdom to guide me today.

4. *Your word tells me that Jesus paid that debt:*
   What I owe for my sin,
   To bring me back to where I ought to be,
   So I can now begin my light again.
   Words of light, words of light,
   Teach me a better way.
   Deep within my heart,
   I will recall,
   Wisdom to guide me today.
   Deep within my heart, I will recall,
   Wisdom to guide me today.

(Words and music © William David Spencer, March 14, 2017)

This book is dedicated to my colleague in marriage and ministry with whom I search God's words of light.

CONTENTS

Acknowledgments // 14

Introduction // 15

    Foundations for Approach // 15

        Figure 0.1. Priority of context // 19

    Explanation of Study // 21

Part 1: Study of the Literary and Historical Contexts of the Text

    Chapter 1: Discern the Wider Context // 25

        Introduction // 27

        Read the Book // 28

        Study the Historical Context of the Book // 30

            Who Wrote the Book or Letter? // 30

            To Whom Was the Book or Letter Written? // 31

            When Was the Book or Letter Written? // 32

            From Where Was the Book or Letter Written? // 33

            Why Was the Book or Letter Written? // 33

            Significance of Historical Context // 33

            Practice // 34

            Historical Context of Philemon: First Version // 34

            Further Thoughts in the Midst of Doing the Draft of the Paper // 35

            Historical Context Cover Sheet // 36

            Further Thoughts After Doing the First Draft of the Historical Context Study // 38

            Historical Context of Philemon: Final Version // 41

        Thematic Summary of the Book // 43

            Purpose // 44

            General Message of a Book or Letter // 45

            Scope of a Book or Letter // 45

            Keyword or Phrase // 47

            General Comments on Doing a Thematic Summary // 47

        Outline the Book or Letter // 49

            Thematic Summary and Outline Cover Sheet // 50

            Thematic Summary of 2 Timothy // 53

            Outline of 2 Timothy // 53

            Outline of the Gospel of Mark // 54

Practice   //   55

Thematic Summary of Philemon   //   55

Outline of Philemon   //   56

Suggestions for Doing a Thematic Summary and Outline   //   56

How the Wider Context Relates to the Text   //   57

How to Avoid Common Errors   //   58

Part 2: Preparation for the Study of the Text

Chapter 2. Choose the Text and Its Immediate Context   //   59

Figure 2.1. Priority of context (pyramid)   //   61

Choose the Text   //   62

Figure 2.2. Priority of context (circle)   //   63

Overview: Elements in an Exegesis Paper   //   66

Communicate Your Findings   //   69

Overview: Presentation of an Exegesis Paper   //   71

Figure 2.3 Paper Quest   //   72

Figure 2.4. How to write an exegesis paper   //   73

Exegesis Paper Cover Sheet   //   74

How to Avoid Common Errors   //   76

Appendix: How to Interpret a Narrative Passage   //   77

Chapter 3. Discover the True Text   //   79

Introduction   //   80

Procedure for Choosing the True Text   //   81

Figure 3.1. Map of text types   //   84

One Variation Unit: Philemon 6   //   86

One Variation Unit: Blank   //   88

Basic Criteria for Evaluating Variant Readings   //   90

Summary Evaluation of Variation Unit: Philemon 6   //   91

Summary Evaluation of Variation Unit: Blank   //   92

How to Avoid Common Errors   //   92

Appendix: Important Witness for the New Testament: Papyri,
Uncials, Versions   //   94

Part 3: In-Depth Study of the Text

**Chapter 4. Seek a Translation and Understand the Grammar
of the Text**   //   101

Introduction   //   102

Basic Grammatical Categories   //   103

Greek Parts of Speech   //   104

How to Study the External Structure of Words:
A Sentence Flow (Part 1)   //   105

Steps in Doing a Sentence Flow   //   106

How to Study the External Structure of Words:
A Sentence Flow (Part 2) // 111

Example: Doing a Sentence Flow of Philemon 4–6 // 111

Analyze the Relation of the Sentences to One
Another (Part 3) // 114

Comparing Different Translations with the Greek:
2 Corinthians 11:16–12:13 // 116

How to Avoid Common Errors // 117

Appendices: Grammatical Helps // 118

How to Study the Eternal Structure of Words:
A Sentence Flow (Parts 1, 2, 3) // 118

Sentence Flow of Philemon 4–6 // 119

Sentence Flow with Parsing and Lexical Forms: Philemon 4–6 // 120

Semantic Structural Analysis: Philemon 4–6 // 123

Grammatical Diagram: Philemon 4–6 // 124

Grammatical Notes // 125

The Structural Relation of Clauses // 125

Summary of Key Types of Grammatical Forms: Cases, Infinitives,
Conditions, Participles // 128

Grammatical Information Sheet: Blank // 142

Grammatical Information Sheet of Philemon 4–6 // 143

Chapter 5. Understand the Meaning of the Words and Phrases // 147

Introduction // 149

Word Study References // 150

New Testament Concordances // 150

Parallel or Interlinear Bible References // 151

Greek-English Lexicons // 151

Old Testament Concordances // 151

Concordances to Greek Extrabiblical References // 152

Further Secondary Reading // 152

Example of How to Do a Word Study (Philemon 4–6) // 153

Word Study Notes: Philemon 4–6 // 154

How to Avoid Common Errors // 157

Appendices // 159

How to Study an Old Testament Quotation
in the New Testament // 159

Cover Sheet for Word Study // 160

Selected Writings in the *Thesaurus Linguae Graecae (TLG)*, Loeb
Classical Library, and Old Testament Pseudepigrapha // 162

Chapter 6. Understand the Meaning of the Text by a Stylistic Analysis // 167

Introduction // 168

Identify Unusual Word Order // 169

Identify Other Figures of Speech // 169

How to Avoid Common Errors // 174

Appendices // 174

    Greek Word and Clause Order // 174

    Sentence Changes in Philemon 4–6 // 175

    Definitions of Frequent New Testament Rhetorical Terms // 176

    Sentence Changes: Summary of Frequent Rhetorical Terms // 178

Chapter 7. Study Further Contextual Resources: Jewish and Greco-Roman Background // 179

Introduction // 180

Elements of Background // 181

Three Types of Literary Parallels // 184

References for the Study of Ancient Literatures // 185

    References for the Literature of the Ancient Jewish World // 185

    References for the Literature of the Ancient Greco-Roman World // 189

    References for the Literature of the Early Church // 191

    Study Further Contextual Resources: Foreground // 191

How to Avoid Common Errors // 193

    Cover Sheet for Cultural Background Study // 194

Appendices // 195

    Philemon: Examples of the Place of Slaves in the Rabbinic and Greco-Roman Worlds // 195

    Early Church Fathers and Mothers Who Wrote in the First Four Centuries // 198

    Bible Reading Plan That Highlights Chronological Order // 199

Chapter 8. Sample Exegesis Paper: Philemon 4–6 // 201

Introduction // 202

Exegesis of Philemon 4–6 // 203

    Historical Context // 204

    Literary Context // 205

    Textual Verification // 206

    Grammatic, Semantic, and Stylistic Analysis // 208

    Larger Historical and Literary Context // 214

    Summary // 215

    Bibliography // 216

Part 4: Application and Completion of Study

    Chapter 9. Make the Application to Life   //   221

        Introduction   //   223

        Types of Direct Application   //   226

            Personal Application   //   226

            Sermon Outline   //   228

            Lesson Plan   //   230

            Inductive Bible Study   //   231

            Artistic Creation   //   233

            Situational Application   //   234

            Theological Motifs   //   234

        How to Avoid Common Errors   //   237

        Appendices: Sample Application Outlines   //   238

            Sermon Outline of Philemon 4–6   //   238

            Lesson Plan of Philemon 1–7   //   239

    Chapter 10. Find Other Interpretations of Text   //   241

        Introduction   //   242

        Theories for Quotations   //   243

        Procedures for Finding Secondary References   //   248

            List of Commentary Series   //   249

        How to Avoid Common Errors   //   251

        Appendices   //   252

            Summary of Interpretations Paper of Philemon 4–6   //   252

            Summary of Interpretations Cover Sheet   //   257

Conclusion   //   259

Bibliography   //   261

ACKNOWLEDGMENTS

In many places the New Testament highlights thanksgiving. I too am truly thankful for the many people who have encouraged me in the teaching and exposition of God's powerful revelation. First of all, I am thankful for the students (and now graduates) at Gordon-Conwell Theological Seminary who encouraged me as I taught them. I have cited some of their appreciative words. I am also thankful to my colleagues Dr. Roy Ciampa and Dr. Edward Keazirian, who have graciously used my example passage (Philem. 4–6) as the basis for their own sample syntactical studies so I could use those studies in this book. These are included in chapter 4 (see "Semantic Structural Analysis: Philemon 4–6" and "Grammatical Diagram: Philemon 4–6" respectively). Ruth Martin, editorial assistant for the *Africanus Journal,* retyped parts of the appendix for chapter 4, "The Structural Relation of Clauses" and "Summary of Key Types of Grammatical Forms." I dreaded retyping all the Greek! Librarian Jim Darlack organized the Old Testament Pseudepigrapha in the appendix of chapter 5. He decided that the appendix would be even more helpful to students with this additional list. David Shorey and Adam Davis at Gordon-Conwell graciously enabled the printing of the chapters so I could proofread them.

I have dedicated this book to my wonderful husband, Rev. Dr. William David Spencer, who is my companion in searching God's Word. He read the first draft of this work and checked every page and every word, an excruciating process. I am also thankful to Kregel Publications, which aims "to develop and distribute—with integrity and excellence—trusted, biblically based resources that lead individuals to know and serve Jesus Christ." We are all on the same road, giving thanks for all the blessings God grants us as we journey into and apply God's words of light!

INTRODUCTION

What do you write when you expect to die? The apostle Paul's last letter, which he wrote while imprisoned in Rome, contains one of his most urgent commands to his disciple Timothy: to present himself approved by God, not ashamed, but "rightly handling the word of truth" (2 Tim. 2:15). It is so easy to look for approval from those who are unworthy of the effort, as Timothy might have been tempted to do before those who sounded authoritative but were not because they did not stand on God's authority. Rather, like Timothy, we ourselves, disciples two thousand years later, should learn to "cut" the word of truth in a "straight line" (*orthotomeō*) so that we can walk righteously and blamelessly in straight paths (cf. Prov. 11:5). Correct or "straight-cutting" interpretation will prepare us for correct or "straight-walking" action.[1]

FOUNDATIONS FOR APPROACH

This book is a training manual on how to interpret Scripture. The technical term is learning to do *exegesis* (from *exagō*, "to lead out"), that is, the process of leading out the truth of Scripture as intended for the original audience, rather than *eisegesis* (from *eisagō*, "to lead in"), the process of leading the Scripture into the interpreter's own inappropriate ideas into the text. The goal of exegesis is to encourage handling the Bible correctly. Many fine books have been written to spur disciples to understand the Bible through looking at its literary and historical contexts as a prelude to communicating that understanding to others. Our focus is the final, or payoff, stage of the process: writing down one's findings in a coherent, integrated, clear essay followed by an outline of one's application.

Why study the Bible? From my research in 2 Timothy, I came up with nine reasons:

1. The Bible provides a standard of wholesome, true principles to guide us and help us to teach others.[2]
2. The writers claim the messages are from God (2 Tim. 3:16).[3]
3. The Bible is relevant no matter our situation (2:9; 4:17).

---

1. See further Aída Besançon Spencer, *2 Timothy and Titus*, New Covenant Commentary Series (Eugene, OR: Cascade, 2014), 166–67.
2. 2 Tim. 1:13; 2:2, 18–19, 22; 16–17. Also Pss. 12:6; 119:160; Prov. 30:5–6; John 10:35; 14:26; 16:13–15; 17:17; Acts 4:25.
3. Also 1 Thess. 2:13; 2 Peter 1:20–21.

16 | Introduction

4. The Bible enables us neither to be deceived nor to deceive others (3:13).
5. We follow wise teachers (faithful parents, guardians, grandparents, Sunday school teachers, pastors, professors, mentors, etc.) who know the Bible (3:14).
6. We experience the Bible's effects in our lives by obtaining a wisdom that leads to salvation (3:15).
7. We are challenged to mature and change because the Bible exposes evil and restores (3:16–17).
8. The Bible prepares us for the judgment (4:1, 8, 18).
9. The Bible prepares us to minister to others (4:2).[4]

Paul defined Scripture as "God-breathed and advantageous for teaching, for reproof, for restoration, for guidance, for the one in righteousness, in order that God's person may be complete, being completed fully for every good work" (2 Tim. 3:16–17).[5] Paul highlighted two key characteristics of Scripture: its origin from God and its purpose to be helpful. "God-breathed" is a composite of two words: "God" and to "breathe forth" (*pneō*).[6] *Pneō* is often used literally of winds that blow, such as winds that blow down a house or a ship.[7] The Holy Spirit is analogous to the wind that "blows wherever it pleases" (John 3:8 NIV). The Spirit creates and keeps humans and animals alive.[8] Similar to breathing the breath of life into a mass of dirt and making Adam alive (Gen. 2:7), God has blown life into the Scriptures. The Scriptures are created by God and therefore are inspired by God. Human beings who receive God's revelation, mainly through the prophets and the apostles,[9] now have heard God Incarnate's message[10] recorded in God-breathed writings, true to his original message and, as God-breathed, standing forever (Isa. 40:8).

Therefore, the Scriptures are useful for four goals: teaching, reproof, restoration, and guidance (2 Tim. 3:16). Timothy was serving in Ephesus when Paul wrote him. Teaching (*didaskalia*) and learning were crucial concerns in Ephesus.[11] Scriptures cause the reader to learn.[12] They also reprove, bringing

---

4. Spencer, *2 Timothy and Titus,* 130–32.
5. All translations without a version listed are by the author. My goal is to render a literal but readable translation for Bible interpreters.
6. Henry George Liddell and Robert Scott, compilers, *A Greek-English Lexicon,* rev. Henry Stuart Jones (Oxford: Clarendon, 1996), 1425. Hereafter referred to as LSJ.
7. Matt. 7:25, 27; John 6:18.
8. Ps. 103:29–30 LXX. John C. Poirier, "Scripture and Canon," in *The Sacred Text: Excavating the Texts, Exploring the Interpretations, and Engaging the Theologies of the Christian Scriptures,* ed. Michael Bird and Michael Pahl (Piscataway, NJ: Gorgias, 2010), 92, agrees *theopneustos* is "life-giving," but Scripture not only "contains" the life-giving gospel; *all* of it is life-giving.
9. 2 Sam. 23:2; 2 Chron. 18:13; Jer. 1:9; Ezek. 3:4; 13:1.
10. John 3:33–34; 1 Cor. 2:10; Gal. 1:11–17; 1 Thess. 2:13; Rev. 21:5; 22:6.
11. See 1 Tim. 2:12; Titus 2:15.
12. LSJ, 371, 421. Also Rom. 15:4.

deeds and thoughts out in the open for clear and truthful analysis.[13] Readers may learn that some actions are sinful and thus reproved. The process does not end with reproof but continues on to restored "health." The Scriptures also help people to become "straight," restoring them to an "upright or a right state."[14] The Scriptures teach and restore or reform and are always available. Paul ended the list of goals with guidance (*paideia*, 3:16), the day-by-day instruction activity Timothy was to do in a righteous manner with his opponents (2 Tim. 2:24–25; 3:16).

Scripture's final goal is that God's followers may be complete, being prepared fully for every good work (3:17). To be complete (*artios*, 3:17) is to be "perfect of its kind, suitable, exactly fitted" to the purpose; "full-grown," "sound, of body and mind"; "prepared, ready."[15] Thus, as a result of studying Scripture, Timothy was completely prepared for every good work (3:17). All study of Scripture must be practical; otherwise its intended purpose is distorted. Learning without knowing and applying the truth (3:7) was inconceivable to Paul. He emphasized that learning Scripture while engaging in foolish arguments was contradictory (2:23). Studying Scripture was intended to prepare Timothy to be a vessel of the Lord for holy behavior (2:21). That same goal should spur us today to be vessels for the same great Lord with our own holy, God-pleasing behavior.

The key for all good interpreters is context, specifically, priority of context. "Context" refers to the parts of a sentence, paragraph, or discourse that occur just before and after a specified word or passage and determine its exact meaning. "Context" comes from the Latin *contexo*, to weave together, to entwine into a *textum*, a woven cloth or fabric.[16] In the same way that a thread is entwined in a cloth to make clothes, words are connected to their paragraphs to make a letter or a book.

For instance, "I can do all things." Does that mean I can jump from the tops of buildings without hurting myself? Can I speak before large crowds although I am agoraphobic? Can I be the wealthiest person in the world? Can I get an A on every test or paper I write? The context of Philippians 4:13 limits the meaning.

To begin, we have the most immediate context of the sentence: "I can do all things in the one who strengthens me." We can look at this sentence from

---

13. See 1 Tim. 5:20; Titus 1:13.
14. Joseph H. Thayer, *Thayer's Greek-English Lexicon of the New Testament,* unabridged (Marshallton, DE: National Foundation for Christian Education, 1889), https://www.blueletterbible.org/resources/lexical/thayers.cfm, 228.
15. LSJ, 249; Walter Bauer, Frederick William Danker, William T. Arndt, and F. Wilbur Gingrich, eds., *A Greek-English Lexicon of the New Testament and Other Early Christian Literature,* 3rd ed. (Chicago: University of Chicago Press, 2000), 136. Hereafter referred to as BDAG. For directions on how to use BDAG, see Gordon D. Fee, *New Testament Exegesis: A Handbook for Students and Pastors,* 3rd ed. (Louisville: Westminster John Knox, 2002), 84–89.
16. John C. Traupman, *The New College Latin and English Dictionary* (New York: Bantam, 1966), 311.

18 | Introduction

various aspects. What do the words mean? What light does assessing the grammatical structure add? What unusual stylistic elements are there? How does this idea fit within the whole letter to the Philippians? How might these words compare and contrast with the ancient Jewish or Greek and Roman contexts? How did the Philippian church regard Paul's thoughts? How might this idea relate to Paul's other letters at this time of imprisonment? How might the idea fit in Paul's own life? How might this idea compare and contrast with other New Testament and Old Testament writings? How was this idea interpreted in the early church? How do commentators today understand and apply this sentence? To what setting or audience do I plan to apply this text? Are they an analogous group? What aspects of the meaning do I want to emphasize as most appropriate for them?

If one can translate Koine Greek, one's foundation for interpretation is all the more accurate. If not, we should compare several translations to note where they agree and disagree. Do we have the best original Greek text?

Paul wrote literally "all things I am able," placing the direct object ("all things," *panta*) *before* the verb "I am able" or "I can do" (*ischyō*), emphasizing how many things he can do: "all." But then he limits the "all" by the words that follow: "in the one strengthening me." Who is that person who does the strengthening? It is *not* Paul himself, but "the Lord" who is mentioned earlier in the paragraph (v. 10). Paul's ideology is not Horatio Alger's self-help, but his empowering comes from the Lord, who earlier in the letter is described as very God born in human form (Phil. 2:6–8). Moreover, strengthening is done as a process since the verb employed is a participle ("strengthening"). It is continual. The part some readers ignore is the rest of the paragraph, which answers the question, what is "all" that Paul can do? What kind of strengthening is involved? The answer is, he can be flexible! He can accept poverty or wealth. Paul knew how to have little and to have much (4:12). Yet Paul still appreciated the material gift the Philippians sent to him while he was in prison (Phil. 1:12–14; 4:14–18).

Doing an exegetical study in which one seeks to draw out meaning from, not put meaning into, a text is a wonderful adventure. The questions and threads one traces are almost endless. To keep in mind the importance of context to determine meaning, I recommend that students draw out as much meaning from this one letter as possible, keeping in mind the priority of the immediate context. In other words, as interpreters, we try to import the least amount of meaning from outside the letter. After all, Paul wrote the sentence "I can do all things in the one strengthening me" to the Philippians, not to the Corinthians or the Colossians or the Romans. Once the sentence was understood in the letter to the Philippians, then it could be explained to the other churches. When the church at Philippi received the codex or scroll, it did not leap to the end of the manuscript and read just this one sentence. Neither should we. But, unfortunately, some of us do. We remember parts of sentences, and these parts of sentences get new contexts in our minds and then new applications not related to Paul's applications. Simply using our own contexts today for interpretation may mislead us. So what we are trying to do in an exegetical study is exercise common sense: to go back, to capture as much meaning as possible, with the aid of the same God who breathed life into these original words, as Paul intended when he wrote them, with the end result that we can make applications to analogous situations today.

Figure 0.1 is a diagram to remind us of the different rated aspects of context to determine the meaning of a text.

PRIORITY OF CONTEXT

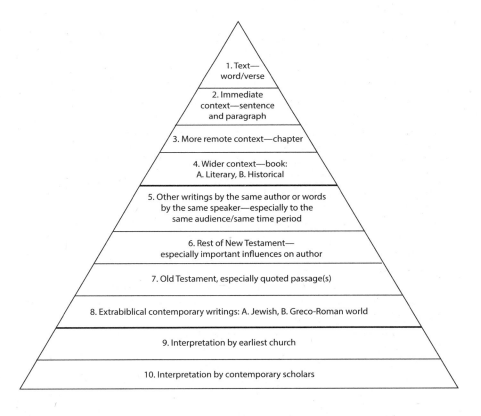

Rated Aspects of Context to Determine the Meaning of a Text

Figure 0.1. Priority of context

The diagram includes two bold lines separating the figure into three parts. The first four levels are the most important aspects of context, the literary and historical wider context—the literary one being the New Testament letter or

20 | Introduction

book itself. Sometimes these levels are sufficient. The next four levels (5–8) are often helpful. The importance of any of these additional levels varies with the passage. A formal exegetical paper will include all eight levels, but a lesson or sermon is limited by time or space, and the interpreter needs to discern which of the additional four levels are necessary. Sometimes interpreters begin at level 10, interpretation by contemporary scholars, but then their understanding of the meaning of a text becomes limited, like that of a horse with blinders, not seeing all traffic so as not to be startled. But we are seeking God's living breath infused into and communicated by the apostle Paul. C. S. Lewis commented on the importance of reading primary sources in his introduction to Athanasius's *The Incarnation of the Word of God*:

> There is a strange idea abroad that in every subject the ancient books should be read only by the professionals, and that the amateur should content himself with the modern books. Thus I have found as a tutor in English Literature that if the average student wants to find out something about Platonism, the very last thing he thinks of doing is to take a translation of Plato off the library shelf and read the *Symposium*. He would rather read some dreary modern book ten times as long, all about "isms" and influences and only once in twelve pages telling him what Plato actually said. The error is rather an amiable one, for it springs from humility. The student is half afraid to meet one of the great philosophers face to face. He feels himself inadequate and thinks he will not understand him. But if he only knew, the great man, just because of his greatness, is much more intelligible than his modern commentator. The simplest student will be able to understand, if not all, yet a very great deal of what Plato said; but hardly anyone can understand some modern books on Platonism. It has always therefore been one of my main endeavours as a teacher to persuade the young that first-hand knowledge is not only more worth acquiring than second-hand knowledge, but is usually much easier and more delightful to acquire.
>
> This mistaken preference for the modern books and this shyness of the old ones is nowhere more rampant than in theology.[17]

Yet in theology is where it is most important to meet God and God's spokesperson face-to-face. Sometimes interpreters begin at level 8, supposing that Paul, as a man of his times, could not mean anything incomprehensible to his own Jewish and Greco-Roman culture. Paul was indeed a man of his times; however, he was also a human being inspired by God's living Spirit. Sometimes interpreters begin at level 9, supposing the early church understood more than we do now about Paul's meaning. Yet some early believers

---

17. C. S. Lewis, "Introduction," in *The Incarnation of the Word of God*, by Athanasius (New York: Macmillan, 1946), 5.

were trained in Greek or Jewish philosophies that had alien aspects contradictory to biblical teachings. For these reasons, I recommend we begin at level 4: the wider context of the letter.

EXPLANATION OF STUDY

At the time of this writing, I have taught the New Testament more than forty-five years, including Interpreting the New Testament; Exegesis of Luke, Acts, 2 Corinthians, Ephesians, Philippians, 1 and 2 Timothy, Titus, James, 1 Peter; and New Testament Survey in English and Spanish, as well as other courses. For many years, I have also tutored successfully many students on how to pass the Presbyterian Church USA ordination examinations that include an exegesis paper. I continue to teach exegesis courses every fall at Gordon-Conwell Theological Seminary at its multicultural Boston campus. Probably the most helpful and appreciated tool I have created these many years is *The Exegetical Process* (in an earlier, unpublished version "How to Write a New Testament Exegesis Paper, Step-by-Step"). For decades the students have used it for my classes and for other professors' New Testament classes, buying it at our various campuses' bookstores, collected in a binder. I have received countless positive comments on the binder's helpfulness, including these:

> I gained new skills in doing exegesis work, familiarizing myself with a series of steps for exegesis of a text. Dr. Spencer's manual on the exegesis paper is an essential tool for me. (J. B.)

> It has been helpful to see how Dr. Spencer teaches these methods in addition to the way it was taught by [my former professor] in Interpreting the New Testament. There were clear similarities, but hearing it re-expressed and reading specifically from Dr. Spencer's "How to Write a New Testament Exegesis Paper" was very helpful in improving my exegetical skills and confidence. (Andy)

> The manual "How to Write a New Testament Exegesis Paper, Step-by-Step" was an invaluable resource in my studies as I wrote my New Testament exegesis paper. This excellent resource is comprehensive, well organized and guides the reader through each step of the exegesis process. There are many helpful guides and references as well as common errors to avoid when writing exegesis papers. This is a resource you will refer to again and again as you carefully and faithfully exegete God's word. (Phyllis)

> The binder on New Testament exegesis was great, and I'm sure I will be referencing it for a long time. (Amber)

I am so happy to hear that you finally decide to publish your amazing manual. (Paul)

Thank you so much, Dr. Spencer, for standing strong to continue to teach very important biblical exegesis method that seems to be diminishing more and more in our churches today. Every time I come to your class I am reminded how our own theology always needs to be laid before and under the Word of God. Thank you for your faithfulness. (Taekyun)

That is my goal for this book: to encourage believers to place their lives before and under God's Word.

Part 1 ("Study of the Literary and Historical Contexts of the Text") explains how to create original short studies that break open the New Testament book or letter. A historical context study answers from whom, to whom, when, from where, and why a letter was written. The thematic summary of the letter or book is a one-page original synopsis of a New Testament book or letter, followed by a one- to two-page analytical outline. I provide examples of each study and helpful aids for every exegetical step.

Part 2 explains the preparation for the study of the text (how to define the passage to be studied, choose the immediate context, and discover the original text).

Part 3 develops how to do an in-depth study of the text (understanding the grammar, word meanings, and style of the passage, and looking at the Jewish, Greco-Roman backgrounds). Chapter 8 provides an annotated sample exegesis paper.

Part 4 discusses how to make an application and find other interpretations of the passage, both now and in the early church. Chapter 10 ends with a second paper summarizing key contemporary perspectives of secondary studies on the same passage. All my sample studies are on the same passage: Philemon 4–6.

Philemon is a short book that can easily be used as a sample because it is rarely employed by itself for a term's study. Students can learn a technique from the Philemon study that they can transfer to whatever New Testament book or letter they are studying.

Every chapter in this book begins with an outline and an indication of whether the chapter is appropriate for those who can read Koine Greek or those who cannot. Through the years, I have collated the types of errors students have made and listed them at the end of each chapter. I close the book with a bibliography.

Part 1 can be done by using a variety of translations of the Bible. Some of parts 2–3 (chapters 3–4, 6) necessitates being able to work with Koine Greek for a more detailed understanding of the passage to be studied, but chapters 1–3, and 7–10 do not require any knowledge of Greek. Simply being acquainted with Greek letters will open up Greek lexicons. To derive a deeper understanding of a Bible text, and I have found the most helpful aids are studying the passage in light of its wider context and translating the passage from its original Greek (or Hebrew, for the Old Testament).

My father told me that for him to graduate from high school in the Netherlands, he had to be able to speak and read in four languages: Dutch, English, French, and German. The Netherlands is a relatively small country and known for hundreds of years for its citizens' traveling. We often hear of Spaniards sailing to Hispaniola in the late 1400s. But not until my last visit to the Dominican Republic did I learn that the Dutch were also there in those early years; their coins can be found there alongside Spanish coins. My father could speak in four languages, but then the Dutch company he worked for, the Curacao Trading Company, sent him to Latin America, and he had to learn to speak and read a fifth language, Spanish! If an average schoolboy has to learn four or five languages, is it too much to ask devout Christians to learn to read (not even to speak or write or listen to) two Bible languages? Reading in New Testament Greek cannot be required of every Christian, but we can urge those Christians who want a more precise understanding of the New Testament to make this effort. For those who have made the effort, their reward in a clearer understanding amply justifies the effort.

PART 1

STUDY OF THE LITERARY AND HISTORICAL CONTEXTS OF THE TEXT

CHAPTER 1

DISCERN THE WIDER CONTEXT

I. Seek a summary of the historical and literary contexts of the book or letter containing the text.
   A. Read the book or letter.
   B. Study the historical context.
   C. Compose the thematic summary and outline of the book or letter.
II. Study how the wider context relates to the text.

All steps can be done by both Greek and translation readers.

INTRODUCTION

A thematic summary and outline of a book or letter of the Bible is one of the most important and most interesting aspects of a study. Its aim is to capture the central meaning, the heart, of a book or letter, its characteristics.

In *How to Understand the Bible*, Martin Anstey suggested that one of the reasons for the decay of interest in study of the Bible is the old method, now reintroduced by contemporary scholars, of only reading the Bible in solitary verses instead of devoting the necessary time to grasp the scope and sweep of its majestic argument. He cited the example of an American layman:

> He had gone into the country to spend the Sabbath with his family on one occasion, taking with him a pocket copy of Ephesians, and in the afternoon, going out into the woods and lying down under a tree, he began to read it; he read it through at a single sitting, and finding his interest aroused, read it through again in the same way, and, his interest increasing, again and again. I think he added that he read it some twelve or fifteen times, and "when I arose to go into the house," said he, "I was in possession of Ephesians, or better yet, it was in possession of me, and

I had been lifted up to sit in heavenly places in Christ Jesus in an experimental sense in which that had not been true in me before, and will never cease to be true in me again." Thus to master book after book is to fill the mind with the great thoughts of God.[1]

Anstey's concern to encourage readers to read individual passages in light of the context of the letter was reiterated by William Larkin:

To the playful postmodern, biblical authority can commend itself if the church will present personal Bible study as a stimulating adventure which will probe beneath the surface with that "message" which postmoderns are waiting for. . . . The church should promote attractive personal Bible study by reintroducing a synthetic study of the text approach. The emphasis will be on direct encounter with the text in whole literary units and an experience of its personal impact.[2]

Achieving a general understanding of a book or letter is both an extremely simple yet extremely complex activity. The goal is to have a "telescopic survey of the subject [a book] deals with, or the ground it covers, to get a bird's-eye view of the whole extent of the book or letter in order to obtain a clear and a comprehensive general idea of its plan, structure, and content, and a vivid impression of its main tenor and general drift."[3]

A book study has four parts: reading the book or letter, studying the historical context, surveying the characteristics of the book or letter, and outlining it. The last step is to reflect on how these findings from the wider context enlighten the specific passage being studied.

READ THE BOOK

1. The crucial first step in a book study is to read the entire book or letter through at least once in *one sitting*. Even a long book like Acts can be read in less than two hours by the average reader. Ignore all titles and chapter, verse, and paragraph divisions, or find a Bible that has no verse divisions.[4]
2. Read the book or letter *continuously*, without a break or any interruptions. This means you will need to find a quiet place to read and ignore the telephone or doorbell ringing.

---

1. Martin Anstey, *How to Understand the Bible* (New York: Revell, 1916), 53–54.
2. William J. Larkin, "Approaches to and Images of Biblical Authority for the Postmodern Mind," *Bulletin for Biblical Research* 8 (1998): 137. See also Daniel M. Doriani, *Getting the Message: A Plan for Interpreting and Applying the Bible* (Phillipsburg, NJ: P&R, 1996), ch. 3.
3. Anstey, *How to Understand the Bible*, 54.
4. E.g., *NIV Books of the Bible*, 4 vol. set.

Discern the Wider Context | 29

3. Read the book or letter *repeatedly*, over and over again, until you have mastered the book or letter. Each time use a different Bible version so as to receive a different slant on the book or letter. Note where translations differ. Try to begin with a recent translation that is in readable contemporary English.

4. Read the book or letter *independently*, without consulting other people's interpretations, until you have formed your own conclusions as to its aim, content, and message from direct contact with the book or letter itself. During this time, if you have a study Bible, do not read its introduction, footnotes, or even its headings. Some people are unaware that headings, footnotes, and marginal references are added by editors and were not written by the original author. We want to treat the Bible as our primary source. If indeed one of the consequences of the new covenant is the permanent indwelling of the Holy Spirit in those who love God, then God should help us understand the revelation. The Spirit of God comprehends the thoughts of the Father (1 Cor. 2:10–12). Naturally, often the Spirit helps us comprehend the thoughts of God by speaking to us through other believers, but the opinions of others, if put in primary authority, can often limit our vision as to what is truly in the text. Reading the Bible independently can help us have original, dynamic thoughts that are founded on the Bible.

5. Read the Bible *prayerfully*, as a letter from God. To assist you in your reading, always ask the Divine Author who inspired the words of the text to help you understand. The Spirit of God is the one "Who is present both in the written Word and also in the heart of the devout reader, and Who interprets its meaning to the reader, and prepares the heart of the reader to receive it."[5]

Thus, your first step in studying the wider context of a book or letter is to read the entire book or letter continuously, repeatedly, independently, and prayerfully.

As you read the book or letter each time, keep a notebook, paper, and pencil next to you to write down your initial strong feelings, questions, insights, thoughts, applications, and explanations, in other words, everything that comes to mind as you read. The reason for this practice is to keep your mind on the reading and to remember all important initial feelings and insights. For example, you may even get ideas for future sermons. You will use the record of your feelings in the final application step. Later on you can search out your questions and verify the accuracy of your initial insights and applications. Also, being aware of your strong feelings toward a topic can help you to be more objective toward that topic.

---

5. Anstey, *How to Understand the Bible*, 52.

STUDY THE HISTORICAL CONTEXT OF THE BOOK

To visit friends at their homes is to have new vistas into their personalities. It is like visiting a foreign country. If you are a social worker, pastor, or teacher, and if you counsel someone, you might want to visit his or her home to learn more about the family context. In this section, this is what we will do. We will see a biblical message and biblical persons in the historical "home" in which the authors lived, viewing them beside their contemporaries and within their customs. Our aim herein is to come to an understanding of the historical situation that called forth the writing of the book or letter. To do this we need to answer five questions as exhaustively as possible from the Bible itself: Who wrote the book or letter? To whom was the book or letter written? When was the book or letter written? From where was the book or letter written? Why was the book or letter written? We are meeting the writer and the audience and their relationship to each other. The same Holy Spirit who worked on them works on us as we read. God assists the interpreter as we study God's revelation, especially if we ask God for help. This is *not* the time to collate all the different views we can find. That comes later. We are discovering the basic knowledge now from which we can evaluate different views later.

Who Wrote the Book or Letter?

Does the Bible give any direct or indirect information about the author? Not only do you want to discover the name of the person but also what kind of person (s)he was, her/his feelings, age, frame of mind, and any special circumstances in her/his life. Was (s)he happy, sad, contemplative, afraid, indignant? Was (s)he going to be sawed to death at two in the morning? What is the author's ethnic background? Was (s)he Jewish or Gentile? Are any character traits particularly exhibited in this book or letter?

How can you obtain this kind of information? Always begin by examining the primary source, the book or letter you are studying. After you have already read it several times in the manner suggested, reread it again and ask yourself this one question: "Who wrote the book or letter?" Write down all references that help you answer. Do not look at any secondary references at this time. After your own original study is complete and you have exhausted the information in the book or letter you are studying and the information in the rest of the Bible, and in any primary ancient references, write a first draft of your own findings. Then you may check various commentaries to double-check your own data and to supplement it. But always remember that the writer of a commentary ninety percent of the time employs the same book as a source that you have—the Bible. Further, what is said to be a fact may often only be a theory or opinion of that commentator. Thus, look for books that are scholarly and theologically sensible. Often the publisher can give you an indication of the assumptions of the author(s). The goal of your work is not to summarize all perspectives on your New Testament letter at this point. Later you can add any helpful supplemental information (regarding which you will, of course, footnote all references used).

As an example, look at the second letter of Paul to the Corinthians. The text directly tells you that the letter was written by "Paul, an apostle of Christ Jesus by the will of God, and Timothy our brother" (2 Cor. 1:1 RSV). Paul repeated his name in 10:1, "But I myself Paul exhort you by the meekness and gentleness of Christ." Paul described himself as a Hebrew, Israelite, and descendant of Abraham (11:22), a preacher, commissioned by God (1:1; 2:12). The letter, thus, is primarily from Paul. It also has much personal information about Paul. He considered himself the spiritual father of the Corinthians (11:2) and deeply loved them (7:3). Paul and Timothy considered themselves bold (3:12) and honest (4:2). This letter also has much information on the frame of mind and special circumstances in which the authors found themselves. In 1:8–9 and 7:5, Paul and Timothy mentioned "the affliction" they experienced in Asia. So tremendous was this affliction that they "despaired of life itself," and they felt that they had received the "sentence of death." Throughout the letter you can also see that Paul was feeling hurt, angry, defensive, and insulted by the malicious, childish insults of those whom he had brought to salvation.[6]

To Whom Was the Book or Letter Written?

Who were meant to be the original readers of the letter? What were their names? Where were they located? What was their situation like? What kind of people were they? What were their religious, social, and economic backgrounds and needs? What were their spiritual strengths and weaknesses? Were they Jews or Gentiles or both? Christians or non-Christians? What relation did they have with the author? Contemporary readers benefit by being told exactly to whom the second letter to the Corinthians is written: "To God's church, the one living in Corinth, with all the saints, the ones living in the whole of Achaia" (1:1). By reading and rereading the second, as well as the first, letter to the Corinthians, you can discover that people of all social and economic classes could be found at Corinth, but particularly many who were not wise, powerful, or of high social status (1 Cor. 1:26–28; 11:20–22; 2 Cor. 8:14). Once you have searched out the information on the people of a city in the letter you are studying, you may amplify your knowledge by looking at other Bible books that record information on the people. Always, however, take into consideration the matter of priority of context and the corresponding changes time may bring to a city and its people. As a whole, it seems that the congregation at Corinth was spiritually immature (1 Cor. 3:1–4; 6:7; 15:34; 2 Cor. 10:3–6), previously quite immoral (1 Cor. 6:9–11), and still tempted by the prevailing sexual immorality and idol worship (1 Cor. 5; 6:12–20; 10:14; 2 Cor. 12:21). Both Jews and Gentiles, free and enslaved people, had been converted (Acts 18; 1 Cor. 7:17–24). In particular, the Corinthians seemed

---

6.   2 Cor. 1:15–19, 23–25; 3:1–3; 6:11–13; 7:2–4; 10:1–2; 11:7, 19–21; 12:11–13.

32 | Study of the Literary and Historical Contexts of the Text

very susceptible to welcoming leaders with new and different ideas: "For you gladly tolerate anyone who comes to you and preaches a different Jesus, not the one we preached; and you accept a spirit and a gospel completely different from the Spirit and the gospel you received from us!" (2 Cor. 11:4 GNT).

Use your own Bible knowledge and a Bible concordance to see if the Corinthian readers are referred to elsewhere in the Bible. If you look up the instances of the word "Corinth," you will find the Corinthians mentioned in Acts 18:1–19:1 and 2 Timothy 4:20 in addition to the letters to the Corinthians. By reading Acts 18, you can learn something about Paul's and Timothy's past relationship with the Corinthians. Therein you discover that Paul came to Corinth shortly after leaving Athens. He worked as a tentmaker with Aquila and Priscilla, speaking on the Sabbath in the local synagogue. Paul preached full-time only after Silas and Timothy arrived from Macedonia. Paul stayed at Corinth one and a half years. Then he left Corinth with Priscilla and Aquila for Ephesus, his center of operations for three years while traveling throughout Asia.

Where the readers are living can be developed quite extensively, but at this time we are using only the Bible as our resource.

When Was the Book or Letter Written?

Usually, ancient authors will not date either their compositions or the historical events about which they write in the manner we do. Events are often dated, as Luke did, by stating the rulers at the time: "In the fifteenth year of the reign of Tiberius Caesar, Pontius Pilate being governor of Judea, and Herod being tetrarch of Galilee, and his brother Philip tetrarch of the region of Ituraea and Trachonitis, and Lysanias tetrarch of Abilene, in the high-priesthood of Annas and Caiaphas, the word of God came to John the son of Zechariah in the wilderness" (Luke 3:1–2 RSV). Are any people or events mentioned in the Bible book that might affect dating? Look for explicit and implicit information.

The second letter to the Corinthians gives us some information concerning when it was written. According to 13:1, we can see that it was composed before Paul's third visit to Corinth, and according to 8:10, within one year after the writing of 1 Corinthians. It occurred after Paul and Timothy experienced afflictions in Asia (2 Cor. 1:8–10); after Paul's stay in Troas (2:12–13; Acts 20:6); after or during his trip to Macedonia (2 Cor. 1:16, 23; Acts 20:1); after he received five times the forty lashes minus one (2 Cor. 11:24–25), was beaten with rods three times (Acts 16:23), stoned once (Acts 14:19), shipwrecked three times, and imprisoned (2 Cor. 6:5; 11:25; Acts 16:22–23); after he left Damascus in a basket when King Aretas guarded the city (2 Cor. 11:32–33; Acts 9:25); after writing a letter of anguish and tears (2 Cor. 2:4); and before going to Judea with the collection (2 Cor. 1:16; 8:22–24). The collection for Judea is an important factor in dating New Testament letters.

Converting the clues into our chronological system, in regard to the second letter to the Corinthians, most scholars date 2 Corinthians AD 56 or 57.[7]

From Where Was the Book or Letter Written?

Where was the author(s) when (s)he wrote a letter? Have you ever had a telephone conversation that was impaired by the two contrasting backgrounds of the speakers? Possibly one was lolling in bed playing soft music while the other was standing anxiously in a crowd at an airport. Knowing the place where a book or letter was written sometimes helps the reader understand its emphasis and tone. Also, knowing the place of composition usually helps determine the time of composition.

In Paul's second letter to the Corinthians, he did not specify his place of residence. However, he did tell us he had completed his journey to Macedonia (2 Cor. 2:12; 7:5). He employed the present tense, "I am boasting to Macedonia" (9:2) and subjunctive, "Macedonians may come with me" to Achaia (9:4). Therefore, 2 Corinthians was written from one area of Macedonia. The book of Acts describes that visit in 20:1–2.

Why Was the Book or Letter Written?

What was the historical occasion that called forth the letter? In other words, because of what events did the author write this particular letter at this time to these specific people? The answer often rests with the situation or problems of the hearers and the needs of the writer. Paul specified the occasion for writing his second letter to the Corinthians in 13:10: "I write this while I am away from you, in order that when I come I may not have to be severe in my use of the authority which the Lord has given me for building up and not for tearing down" (RSV). In other words, Paul had wanted to give the Corinthians an opportunity to remedy their un-Christlike activities before he came so he could then rejoice with them in their obedience to Christ rather than discipline them.

A brief summary of the historical context should be included in the exegesis paper. The goal of this study is to be exhaustive, careful, and accurate, relying primarily on primary sources, especially the letter one is studying.

Significance of Historical Context

One can never know ahead of time which of the questions (who wrote the letter, why, to whom was it written, when was it written, from where was it written) will prove to be most central to the illumination of the book or letter in question. When the book or letter was written is the key to opening up and disclosing the

---

7. For further reading, see Aída Besançon Spencer, *2 Corinthians*, People's Bible Commentary (Oxford: Bible Reading Fellowship, 2001), 19; Spencer, *Paul's Literary Style: A Stylistic and Historical Comparison of II Corinthians 11:16–12:13, Romans 8:9–39, and Philippians 3:2–4:13* (Lanham, MD: University Press of America, 1998), 63.

34 | Study of the Literary and Historical Contexts of the Text

central message of the second book of the Kings. In 2 Kings 17:22–23, we are told, "The people of Israel walked in all the sins which Jeroboam did; they did not depart from them, until the LORD removed Israel out of his sight, as he had spoken by all his servants the prophets. So Israel was exiled from their own land to Assyria until this day" (RSV). This same concept is also stated in 13:23 and 17:34, 41. The book ends with the king of Judah, Jehoiachin, in Babylon. By this we can deduce the second book of the Kings was completed during the captivity of the Jews. Thus, the original aim of the book or letter was to explain to the Jews why Israel and Judah were in exile and how this judgment by God related to God's original promise to give them the land of Canaan.

Practice

Throughout this book, we will take as our continuing practice example Paul's letter to Philemon, since it is short. While reading Philemon, jot down any feelings, insights, and questions you may have as you discover its historical context—namely, who wrote the letter, to whom it was originally addressed, when it was written, where it was written, and on what occasion it was written. Only after you thoroughly study Philemon in this manner should you compare your findings to mine.

I began by taking some scrap paper and writing the five headings at the top (who, to whom, when, from where, why) and noting any references in the letter that gave information on each question. For the first draft, using only Philemon in translation, this is what I learned:

Historical Context of Philemon: First Version

Who wrote the letter?

The letter was sent from Paul and Timothy (Philem. 1). However, verses 4–21, 23–24 use only the first person singular ("I, me, my"), including the sentence "I, Paul, am writing this with my own hand" (v. 19 NRSV), suggesting that only Paul wrote the letter. Timothy's name was included for some other reason. Paul was a prisoner at the time, not for criminal activities but because of his testimony for Christ Jesus (v. 1). He was also an "old man" (NRSV), "ambassador" (TEV, REB), or "elder" (author's translation, v. 9).

What do we learn of Paul's character? He was a person of prayer. He thanked God for other believers and desired that their lives as Christians develop (vv. 4, 6). Although Paul could conceive of himself as commanding, he preferred to appeal to people's voluntary will (vv. 8–9, 21). Paul not only prayed that his readers would share their faith effectively (v. 6), but he himself shared his faith effectively. He shared his faith with Onesimus, who became a follower of Christ (vv. 10, 16). Now Paul considered himself to be Onesimus's "father" (v. 10). Paul did not treat people impersonally, but rather became quite attached to them. He called Onesimus "my very heart" (v. 12 NIV). In the letter he demonstrated concern for his new convert.

To whom was the letter written?

The letter is addressed to Philemon, Apphia, Archippus, and the church in their home (vv. 1–2). Philemon is called a "dear friend and co-worker" (v. 1 NRSV) and "partner" (v. 17 NRSV). Apphia is called "sister," and Archippus "our fellow soldier" (v. 2 NRSV). "Our" indicates Philemon was a friend and coworker of both Paul and Timothy. Paul also called him "my brother" (vv. 7, 20 NRSV). "You" in English could be singular or plural, but the NRSV footnote indicates in verses 4–21 "*you* is singular." Therefore, those verses would appear to give information only on Philemon, the first person addressed in the heading. Philemon had demonstrated love for all the saints and faith toward the Lord (vv. 5, 7). His love had reached Paul too, giving him joy and encouragement (v. 7).

Paul and Philemon had a relationship of mutual love (vv. 7, 9). This relationship resulted in certain expectations. Paul expected Philemon to serve him in prison (v. 13). Paul believed Philemon owed Paul his whole self (v. 19). Nevertheless, Paul did not command him but asked for the voluntary completion of his duty (v. 14).

When and from where was the letter written?

Paul was in prison at the time of the writing. In a twenty-five-verse letter, he mentioned this fact five times (vv. 1, 9, 10, 13, 23)! Nevertheless, Paul expected to be released (v. 22). Timothy, Epaphras, Mark, Aristarchus, Demas, and Luke were with him (vv. 1, 23–24).

Why was the letter written?

Several times Paul explicitly stated why he wrote this letter. He appealed to Philemon to welcome Onesimus, his former slave, now a Christian, as he would welcome Paul himself (vv. 9–10, 17). He made this appeal based on their relationship of Christian love, Philemon's exemplary past Christian behavior, and duty (v. 8), and offered to pay any debts Onesimus had incurred (v. 18). Paul wanted his heart refreshed (v. 20). He also wanted Philemon to prepare a guest room for him (v. 22).

Further Thoughts in the Midst of Doing the Draft of the Paper

Some of the questions I want to research further in the original Greek text are the following: When are the first person singular and plural used? Was Paul an "old man" or "ambassador"? What did he mean "write with own hand"? Is the preposition "to" repeated (vv. 1–2) to set up four distinct readers (Philemon, Apphia, Archippus, and the church)? When was Paul in prison? When did Paul use the imperative (command) mood? Are any of the people mentioned referred to elsewhere in the New Testament or in Eusebius's *Church History*? What does verse 6 mean since it appears unclear? Were the debts literal (v. 18)? Is Greek as forthright as English in terms of "duty" and "obedience" (vv. 8, 21)?

36 | Study of the Literary and Historical Contexts of the Text

As a professor, I use the following cover sheet to evaluate the students' historical context papers. By reviewing the cover sheets ahead of time, the students can check their work for completeness before finalizing their essays. Each student should ask the following: "Have I given information on the author's name, character, and background? Have I included the readers' names, location, social and economic background, spiritual strengths and weaknesses, and relationship to the author? Have I used events as well as people and any other explicit and implicit information to learn about dating the writing and the location of the writer? Have I answered why the author wrote the letter? Did I place everything under the correct heading?"

The letter does not tell us whether Paul was Jew or Gentile, but his being a Christian is quite prominent. How did he feel? Hopeful? Confident? Or was he simply phrasing his appeal letter in a positive manner? I have nothing on the location or social and economic background of Philemon. Philemon's owning a slave and having a home where a church could meet suggests a certain economic wellbeing. Philemon was a Christian, already growing in the faith, but he could still learn more about how to share his faith more effectively (v. 6) and the ramifications of his faith in Christ for social relationships (v. 17).[8]

HISTORICAL CONTEXT COVER SHEET

Historical context of _____   To: [student's name]

Date: _____   Box/email: _____

From: [professor's name]   Grade: _____

The following items are rated according to the following symbols:

N = No
S = Sometimes/Somewhat
Y = Yes
I = Inadequate
A = Adequate
G = Good
S = Superior

---

8. In the cover sheet for historical context, under "Who," I include "For Paul, keep to one letter" so that readers will uncover more information about Paul from the letter being studied instead of simply turning to one of Paul's speeches in Acts, as many do, thereby missing what is revealed in the letter being studied.

RESEARCH METHODOLOGY:

Conclusions proved (supporting NT data,
   explanations, sources) ....I A G S

Exhaustive/comprehensive...I A G S

Accurate...I A G S

Insightful ....I A G S

Original...I A G S

(Primary sources studied—book/letter, rest of NT, early church traditions. Any secondary sources supplemental to own work)

COMPLETENESS OF STUDY:

Who includes name(s) ....N S Y

   kind of person (background, traits, feelings) ....N S Y

To Whom includes name(s) ....N S Y

   location of reader(s) ....N S Y

   social and economic information ....N S Y

   spiritual state...N S Y

   relation to author ....N S Y

When includes pertinent events ....N S Y

   and people...N S Y

From Where includes explicit..N S Y

   and implicit information..N S Y

> **Why** includes historical occasion(s)
>
> (Why at this time to these people?)................................ N S Y
>
> Optional: Purpose of book/letter, major theme............ N S Y
>
> All five questions answered.. N S Y
>
> Keeps to these five questions (i.e., extraneous material
> excluded) .... N S Y
>
> ### WRITTEN PRESENTATION:
>
> Well-organized (headings clear).. N S Y
>
> Literary style clear and succinct .... N S Y
>
> Spelling and grammar correct... N S Y
>
> Legible... N S Y
>
> Primary sources cited by chapter and
> verse/paragraph in parentheses..................................... N S Y
>
> (If commentaries used)
>
> Bibliography cited .... N S Y
>
> Facts and ideas of others noted in footnotes .... N S Y
>
> Footnotes have a consistent and correct citation .... N S Y

Further Thoughts After Doing the First Draft of the Historical Context Study

Studying a book or letter of the Bible is like detecting. Good detectives have certain types of clues they check, never knowing from which will come the solution. So, as interpreters, we ask the questions of who, to whom, when, from where, and why, not yet knowing how they will interrelate and which will provide our most significant clues.

Now, turning to the Greek text, I learn that indeed Philemon is described as "our" (v. 1). He could be "our dear friend and co-worker" (v. 1 NRSV) or, if a hendiadys, "our beloved coworker" (CEB). In a hendiadys, *"and"* connects two nouns yet the author intends one noun to modify the other noun. "Our" modifies Philemon but not Apphia in the Greek text (v. 2).[9] The dative "to" is repeated for Philemon, Apphia, Archippus, and the church, suggesting four readers. "Our" is also used in verse 3. The first-person singular is indeed used for the writer, and second-person singular is used for the reader in verses 4–21, 23–24. "Your" house is singular (v. 2). The second-person plural concludes the letter (v. 25). Thus, Paul wrote Philemon mainly, but he had his cowitness, Timothy, as sender and witnesses among the readers, Apphia, Archippus, and the church (vv. 2, 22, 25).

Paul is called *presbytēs* (v. 9). A word study should be done for further information on this keyword. If *presbytēs* means "old man," Paul used his age as a basis of appeal. But if *presbytēs* means "elder" or "ambassador," he was using his position of authority as a basis of appeal. The concordance indicates *presbytēs* has three other references in the New Testament. In Luke 1:18 it clearly refers to age: Zechariah said he was too old to have children. In Titus 2:2–3 *presbytēs* could refer either to age or authority. Authority is certainly included in the elders teaching the younger women. This kind of authority is implied as the basis for Paul's appeal to Philemon (v. 9). Thus, Paul's age also entails authority.

Paul used the imperative mood several times ("welcome," v. 17; "charge," v. 18; "refresh," v. 20; "prepare," v. 22). These uses of the imperative are helpful in the "why" section of the historical context. The verb for "appeal" (*parakaleō*, vv. 9–10) is not in the imperatival form but in the present active indicative form, demonstrating that Paul expressed his ongoing expectations but was not yet commanding Philemon. Paul did literally write with his own hands (v. 19). Including the pronoun "I" (*egō*) before "Paul," followed by "I will repay," implies he was making a point of establishing his voucher or "I owe you." He had countersigned on Onesimus's debt.

In the Greek text, verses 4–6 are one sentence. Literally verse 6 reads: "So that the fellowship (or partnership or sharing) of your faith may become effective (or active) in knowledge of every good (thing), the one (referring back to 'good') in us (or you) in Christ." I can see now why I found this passage puzzling. Is verse 6 part of all Paul thanked God for? Or was it what Paul would like for Onesimus? Does *koinōnia* refer to spiritual or economic matters? Is "us" or "you" the better reading? This might be a verse I could study further.

"Charge" (NIV) in verse 18 refers to *ellogeō*, which means "charge to one's account," suggesting a literal meaning. But this translation could benefit from a word study. "Duty" in verse 8 can also be translated "the appropriate thing" (*anēkon*). "Obedience" is a common translation for *hypakoē* (v. 21).

---

9. The KJV is helpful to discern singular and plural pronouns if Greek is not known. It indicates that "our" is not used for Apphia ("the sister," v. 2). The singular is translated as "thee" or "thy" (vv. 4–8, 10–21, 23), but the plural is translated as "you" or "your" (vv. 22, 25).

40 | Study of the Literary and Historical Contexts of the Text

To learn more about the people mentioned in the letter, I used a Bible concordance, beginning with the less common persons. I found Aristarchus is also mentioned in Acts 19:29; 20:4; 27:2; Colossians 4:10; Demas in Colossians 4:14; 2 Timothy 4:10; Luke in Colossians 4:14; 2 Timothy 4:11; Mark in Acts 12:12, 25; 15:37, 39; Colossians 4:10; 2 Timothy 4:11; 1 Peter 5:13; Epaphras in Colossians 1:7; 4:11–13; Archippus in Colossians 4:17. Philemon and Apphia occur only in the letter to Philemon. From these references we learn that everyone mentioned at the end of Paul's letter to Philemon is also mentioned in Paul's letter to the Colossians. Paul was also in prison when he wrote that letter (Col. 4:18). Thus, the letter to Philemon was written at a time when Paul was in prison and accompanied by Aristarchus (also a "fellow prisoner" in Col. 4:10), Mark, Epaphras (a Gentile from Colossae), Luke, and Demas (Col. 4:10–12, 14). Archippus, though, was at Colossae (Col. 4:17). Therefore, Archippus must have been in Colossae to receive Paul's letter to Philemon (v. 2). Both Aristarchus and Luke accompanied Paul to Rome in his imprisonment there (Acts 27:2), suggesting that Paul wrote Philemon during his two-year stay there (Acts 28:16, 30). In contrast, from Paul's imprisonment in Caesarea, he asked to go to Rome, not Colossae (Acts 25:10–12). By the time Paul wrote 2 Timothy, the situation had changed. Demas had deserted Paul, but Luke still remained with him (2 Tim. 4:10–11). Instead of asking for a guest room (Philem. 22), Paul talked about impending death (2 Tim. 4:6–8). Mark was no longer with Paul (2 Tim. 4:11). In Eusebius's *Church History,* a Roman presbyter named Philemon is mentioned (7.5.7), but he lived during the time of Bishop Dionysius, who lived during the mid-200s, long after Paul's death.

At this point, I decided to read all of Colossians and a few commentaries to see if I omitted any important information.[10] The concordance did not list any references to Colossae in the Bible. From doing these steps, I discovered I should next check Onesimus's name in a concordance and in Eusebius's *Church History.*[11] Onesimus, I found, is mentioned in Colossians as being from Colossae ("one of you" NIV), a "faithful and dear brother" (Col. 4:9 NIV), coming with Tychicus to Colossae to report what had been happening in Rome. Eusebius also mentioned an Onesimus whom Ignatius referred to as the pastor at Ephesus (3.36).

Checking in *Apostolic Fathers* for the epistles of Ignatius, I discovered that Ignatius, while in Smyrna on his way to be martyred in Rome (AD

---

10. Cf. Theodor Zahn, *Introduction to the New Testament,* trans. John Moore Trout et al., 3 vols., 2nd ed. (New York: Scribner, 1917), 1:260; Alfred Plummer, *A Critical and Exegetical Commentary on the Second Epistle of St. Paul to the Corinthians* (Edinburgh: Clark, 1915); Everett F. Harrison, *Introduction to the New Testament* (Grand Rapids: Eerdmans, 1964).

11. Donald Guthrie, *New Testament Introduction,* 3rd ed. (Downers Grove, IL: InterVarsity Press, 1974), 639. Onesimus's future presence in Colossae is "explicit information," according to Markus Barth and Helmut Blanke, *The Letter to Philemon,* Eerdmans Critical Commentary (Grand Rapids: Eerdmans, 2000), 141–42.

Discern the Wider Context | 41

108), indeed "received in the name of God your whole congregation in the person of Onesimus, a man of inexpressible love and your bishop, I beseech you by Jesus to love him, and all to resemble him. For blessed is he who granted you to be worthy to obtain such a bishop" (*Ignatius to Ephesians* 1.3). If indeed Ignatius referred to the same Onesimus, we have proof not only that Philemon forgave Onesimus, but he also freed him. From being a slave, Onesimus became a leader of the church. J. B. Lightfoot suggested Philemon and Apphia were husband and wife and Archippus was their son.[12]

Thus, after looking outside Philemon in the New Testament at some early church references and a few commentaries, checking some phrases in the Greek, and double-checking the New Testament references, I can propose the following final draft. *I have indicated additions in italics only for educational purposes.*

Historical Context of Philemon: Final Version

Who wrote the letter?

The letter was sent from Paul and Timothy (v. 1). However, verses 4–21, 23–24 use only the first person ("I, my"), including the sentence "I, Paul, am writing this with my own hand" (v. 19 NRSV), therefore suggesting only Paul wrote the letter. Timothy's name was included for some other reason, *possibly to serve as a cowitness of affection for the readers and of agreement with Paul's appeal.* Paul was a prisoner at the time, not for criminal activities but because of his testimony for Christ Jesus (v. 1). He was also an "old man" (NRSV), "ambassador" (RSV), or "elder" (v. 9).

What do we learn of Paul's character? Paul was a person of prayer. He thanked God for other believers and desired that their lives as Christians develop (vv. 4, 6). Although Paul could conceive of himself as commanding, he preferred to appeal to people's voluntary will (vv. 8–9, 21). Paul not only prayed that his readers would share their faith effectively (v. 6), but he himself shared his faith effectively. He shared his faith with Onesimus, who became a follower of Christ (vv. 10, 16). Now Paul considered himself to be Onesimus's "father" (v. 10). Paul did not treat people impersonally, but rather became

---

12. J. B. Lightfoot, *Saint Paul's Epistles to the Colossians and to Philemon* (Grand Rapids: Zondervan, 1959), 303. See also Richard R. Melick Jr., *Philippians, Colossians, Philemon*, New American Commentary 32 (Nashville: Broadman, 1991), 350. S. C. Winter thinks the bishop Onesimus could be the same person, but Philemon, Apphia, and Archippus were church, not household, members. S. C. Winter, "Philemon," in *Searching the Scriptures: A Feminist Commentary*, ed. Elisabeth Schüssler Fiorenza, 2 vols. (New York: Crossroad, 1993–94), 2:309–11.

quite attached to them. He called Onesimus "my very heart" (v. 12 NIV). In the letter he demonstrated concern for his new convert *to the point of being willing to pay his debts* (v. 19).

To whom was the letter written?

The letter is addressed to Philemon, Apphia, Archippus, and the church in their home (vv. 1–2). Philemon is called a "dear friend and co-worker" (v. 1 NRSV, or *"beloved co-worker,"* NLT) and "partner" (v. 17 NRSV). Apphia is called "sister," and Archippus "our fellow soldier" (v. 2 NRSV). *Some commentators think Philemon and Apphia were husband and wife and Archippus was their son.*[13] "Our" indicates Philemon was a friend and coworker of both Paul and Timothy. Paul also called him "my brother" (vv. 7, 20 NRSV). "You" in English could be singular or plural. *"You" is plural in verses 3, 22, and 25, but* "you" is singular *in verses 2, 4–21, 23.* Therefore, verses 4–21 would appear to give information only on Philemon, the first person addressed in the heading. Philemon had demonstrated love for all the saints and faith toward the Lord (vv. 5, 7). His love had reached Paul too, giving him joy and encouragement (v. 7). *Having owned a slave and being able to host a church suggests Philemon was wealthy. He was a Christian growing in the faith who still had more to learn about energizing his faith and acting on the ramifications of his faith for social relationships (vv. 6, 17). Since Archippus was in Colossae and Onesimus would be there, we know the readers were in Colossae (Col. 4:9, 17).*

Paul and Philemon had a relationship of mutual love (vv. 7, 9). This relationship resulted in certain expectations. Paul expected Philemon to serve him in prison (v. 13). Paul believed Philemon owed Paul his whole self (v. 19). Nevertheless, Paul did not command him but asked for the voluntary completion of his duty (v. 14).

When and from where was the letter written?

Paul was in prison at the time of the writing. In a twenty-five-verse letter, he mentioned this fact five times (vv. 1, 9, 10, 13, 23)! Nevertheless, Paul expected to be released (v. 22). Timothy, Epaphras, Mark, Aristarchus, Demas, and Luke were with him (vv. 1, 23–24). *They were also with Paul when he wrote the letter to the Colossians (Col. 4:10, 12, 14). Thus, Philemon was written about the same time as Colossians. Both letters were written during Paul's two-year imprisonment in Rome, most likely near the end, since he expected to be released soon (Acts 28:16, 30). Aristarchus and Luke had accompanied Paul to Rome (Acts 27:2).*

---

13. E.g., Lightfoot, *Saint Paul's Epistle to the Colossians and to Philemon*, 303.

Why was the letter written?

Several times Paul explicitly stated why he wrote this letter. He appealed to Philemon to welcome Onesimus, his former slave, now a Christian, as he would welcome Paul himself (vv. 9–10, 17). He made this appeal based on their relationship of Christian love, Philemon's exemplary past Christian behavior, and duty (v. 8), and offered to pay any debts Onesimus had incurred (v. 18). Paul wanted his heart refreshed (v. 20). He also wanted Philemon to prepare a guest room for him (v. 22).

Possibly this very Onesimus became pastor and overseer at Ephesus at the turn of the century (Eusebius, Church History 3.36; Ignatius to Ephesians 1.3), showing that Philemon did indeed forgive and also free Onesimus, an example of the transforming social power of Christ's grace (Philem. 25.)

Bibliography

The Apostolic Fathers. Translated by Kirsopp Lake. 2 vols. Loeb Classical Library. New York: Harvard University Press, 1912–1913.

Eusebius. *The History of the Church from Christ to Constantine*. Translated by G. A. Williamson. Rev. ed. New York: Penguin, 1989.

Guthrie, Donald. *New Testament Introduction*. 3rd ed. Downers Grove, IL: InterVarsity Press, 1974.

Lightfoot, J. B. *Saint Paul's Epistles to the Colossians and to Philemon*. Grand Rapids: Zondervan, 1959.

THEMATIC SUMMARY OF THE BOOK

In a thematic summary, one tries to understand the central characteristics of a book, its central message and content. Truly to understand an idea is to be able to perceive its profound center. Thus, a way in which to verify one's own understanding of a letter's themes is to be succinct in describing them. That is why the written conclusions of a thematic summary should not exceed one page (double- or single-spaced). A thematic study has four parts: the purpose of the author in writing a letter, the general message for all ages, the scope of the letter, and the keyword or key phrase. This is *not* a study of the characters mentioned in a book or letter; it is a summary of its key themes. Possibly, as Anstey suggested, "Each book in the Bible was written for some definite, specific purpose, and was intended to guard the Church in all ages against some definite, specific error."[14]

---

14. Anstey, *How to Understand the Bible*, 54.

Purpose

What is the purpose of the author in writing the book or letter? State in one clear sentence what the author meant to say to the people to whom (s)he was writing. Some hints or direct information concerning the original readers of the letter should have been obtained when you researched the previous section on the historical context: "To Whom Was the Book or Letter Written?" In seeking the purpose, we search to find the object of the book or letter, the primary aim the writer wanted to communicate that unites the book or letter. This is the combining of the theme of the book or letter with the needs of the originally addressed readers. It is not necessarily the only aim. The purpose is the author's main exhortation to the readers in which (s)he considered their needs and problems.

Since the Bible is written to affect our actions (e.g., 2 Tim. 3:7, 17), the revelation is meant to be obeyed rather than just abstractly considered; therefore, this purpose must be phrased in such a way as to imply action. Thus, rather than say the purpose of a particular book is "to show God's mercy," phrase it as "be merciful as God is merciful." Likewise, the name of the readers and of the writer should be included in this purpose sentence. Be specific. Choose only one central goal or purpose that is unique to that book or letter. Important subordinate ideas may be made into subordinate clauses.

Sometimes the purpose of a book or letter will be stated by its author, as in John 20:31: "These are written so that you may believe that Jesus is the Christ, the Son of God, and that by believing you may have life in his name." At other times a recurring verse or word will help indicate the purpose of a book or letter, as in Genesis: "I will establish my covenant between me and you and your descendants after you" (17:7). Thus, the broad purpose of the book of Genesis is to explain with whom God established the covenant, why God did so, and to show the resultant blessings of the covenant.

The occasion on which a letter was written (see "Why Was the Book or Letter Written?" above) sometimes will be different from the main message of a letter. If they are different, spend some time thinking about it, and reread the book or letter until you see how they interrelate. For instance, in the second letter to Timothy, Paul asked that Timothy come soon, before winter (4:9, 13, 21). This would be the occasion for the letter. Paul wanted Timothy to visit him in prison before traveling was impaired by the winter season. But the main message Paul wanted to communicate to Timothy was this: "Share in suffering with me for the gospel which you learned, unlike the others who abandoned me."[15] How does the occasion for writing and the purpose or main message of this letter relate? The action of coming to visit Paul in prison and the stigma and danger thereby entailed was part of Timothy's agreeing to share in Paul's hardship for the sake of the good news. Therefore, when you find that the occasion for a book or letter differs from its main message, write

---

15. See 2 Tim. 1:8, 12, 15–18; 2:3, 9, 11–13; 3:1, 11–12; 4:5–6.

that down. Then think about the differences to see if there is a higher unity or whether one is more significant than the other.

When we discover the purpose of a book, it can come as quite a surprise. To love one another has often been suggested to be the central message of the first letter of John. Rather than love, however, the key concept of 1 John is discernment. The purpose of 1 John might be phrased this way: "John writes to assure church members that those who follow his words and love one another are true believers, in opposition to the charges of certain unbelieving adversaries who once entered and now have left the church. First John is written to give criteria for discerning true believers, one of which is love for one another."

General Message of a Book or Letter

In essence the general message of a book or letter is simply the rephrasing of its purpose in a way to include similar readers of any time period. Possibly you may paraphrase the type of audience or the situation of the writer. The original readers of the book or letter are not cited. Sometimes students confuse purpose and general message and will write a general message for the purpose of a book. To understand the difference between these two concepts is to comprehend the main aim of exegesis. We must first understand the message of a book or letter when it was written before we can apply it to today.

For example, the apostle John's stated purpose for his gospel is already phrased as a general message: "that you may believe that Jesus is the Christ, the Son of God, and that believing you may have life in his name" (20:31 RSV). The general message of the book of Genesis is that God is faithful and blesses the covenant partner and descendants. If the purpose of Paul's second letter to Timothy is to "share in suffering with me for the gospel which you learned, unlike the others who abandoned me," then the general message might be: "Share in suffering with Christians standing for the truth without abandoning them." The general message of 1 John answers the question, How can we be sure we abide in God? We abide in God if we follow the mandates of the apostle John and if we love one another.

Thus, in a general message, we phrase the main thematic aim of a book or letter in such a way that the application is self-evident for today. Other than that, the sentence remains the same.

Scope of a Book or Letter

If the purpose of a book or letter is its object, the scope is its subject, that is, what is contained in a book. The scope of a book or letter is a brief survey of the subject matter it covers. In a historical book, the scope tells us where the story begins and ends. If more than one book covers similar historical events, as in the Gospels, the main events unique to each book will be highlighted. In a doctrinal letter, the scope gives the structure of the book or letter and its main ideas. Rather than use outline form, the scope is clearest when written out in essay form, in several paragraphs. The scope should include a description of the main headings of the outline. If in doubt where to place any additional data you find, place it under scope. The scope is usually one to three paragraphs in length.

The scope includes names of important people, countries, and places mentioned in the book or letter, the amount of time covered, the main events, the type of writing (whether it is historical narrative or a letter; poetry or law in the Old Testament), noteworthy or unusual content, the main themes, and significant relationships to other books in the Bible. The scope also mentions distinctive characteristics of the author's style and key illustrations. In effect, you will have a brief summary of the content of a book or letter of the Bible.

To write the scope about a historical narrative such as Genesis is less difficult than a doctrinal letter. The scope of Genesis might look like this:

> The book of Genesis tells us about the beginning of the world, of humans, and of the covenant line. It covers human history relating to their Creator: Adam and Eve leaving Eden because of their disobedience, the increase of sin on earth until the need for a total destruction, the first covenant with Noah, and the covenant continued with Abraham and Sarah, Isaac and Rebekah, Jacob and Rachel and Leah. God's call to Abraham to go to Canaan is recorded. The book ends with Jacob, the twelve sons in Egypt, and Joseph's death. Despite the book's attention to the covenant line, God takes care of those outside the covenant—for instance, Cain; Hagar and her son, Ishmael; and Esau.

The scope of a book or letter is always lengthier than either the purpose or general message. (The purpose, in contrast, is only one sentence in length.)

The scope of 2 Timothy might read like this:

> When Paul had been abandoned in prison in Rome by everyone in Asia except the household of Onesiphorus, he wrote Timothy to come and help him. To encourage Timothy not to be ashamed of Paul's suffering in prison, unlike the others, Paul exhorted him to endure suffering Persecution of Christians was to be expected. He also told him to charge his congregation in Ephesus to avoid senseless controversies, business Timothy needed to complete before leaving. Even though Paul expected to die soon, he gratefully remembered Timothy and his grandmother, Lois, and mother, Eunice. Paul used imagery from the army, farming, and household.

Keyword or Phrase

The discovery of a keyword or key phrase of a book or letter in the Bible is the concluding, climactic sign of comprehending the heart of a book. This keyword is best taken verbatim from the book or letter of the Bible you are reading and usually from the purpose sentence. The keyword will provide a clue to interpreting the book or letter. Thus, it will indicate the unique purpose of a book. At times the book or letter might also include a key verse that is significant. Readers may at times find that settling on one word to summarize the message of a book or letter is difficult. In that case, set the potential keywords in order of priority. If you do a synopsis study for every book and letter of the Bible, you need only remember sixty-six keywords or phrases to recall the central purpose for each book or letter in the Bible.

As an example, I had suggested the purpose for Paul's second letter to Timothy was to "share in suffering with me for the gospel which you learned, unlike the others who abandoned me." Thus, an excellent key phrase would be "share in suffering." Incidentally, this phrase is one word in the Greek New Testament, *synkakopatheō*, which means to "share in suffering or hardship with someone, undergo one's share of suffering."

The key verse for the book of Genesis is "I establish my covenant with you and your descendants after you" (9:9 RSV). A primary keyword for 1 John is "discernment" or, of secondary importance, "abide," since the aim of 1 John is to help us *discern* a true believer in God.

General Comments on Doing a Thematic Summary

In every section, always write down in parentheses the scriptural references that support your conclusions. In this manner, months later your mind can be quickly refreshed as to the basis of your reasoning. Original study is best. What is correct is what you can defend from the Bible text itself. Second in authority are good early church traditions, for which Eusebius's *Church History* is an excellent resource.

Look for each part of a thematic summary separately. Read to discover the tentative purpose, scope, and keyword. Rephrase the purpose into a tentative general message. Then, when you have all four parts of a thematic summary (purpose, general message, scope, keyword), reread the book or letter to see if they fit well together. Are they each accurate and complete? A cover sheet is helpful to make sure every aspect of the study is included.

When you have done this, you will have an excellent basis for further study. The book or letter will have come alive for you. Its fascination will possess you, and you will touch its heart thought. This method will immerse you in the book or letter so you will look at its material, then from it back at the world through the book or letter's main point. In that way you will be thinking scripturally. This method should lead you away from eisegetical thoughts (your thoughts) to exegetical thoughts (the book or letter's thoughts). And the

48 | Study of the Literary and Historical Contexts of the Text

process is not too difficult or too simple for anyone in the Holy Spirit's care to appreciate or use. Here are some things my students have concluded:

> I really loved how Dr. Spencer encourages us to look at the gospel as a whole, keeping in mind the main purpose and themes as we interpret the text. It was also very helpful to see her bring out important interpretation techniques we learned in our New Testament interpretation course.
>
> The thematic study of every New Testament book I did for New Testament Survey was one of the most helpful things I ever did. It got me out of the habit of running to the experts (commentaries, etc.) all the time, and gave me confidence in my own ability to dig and come up with answers with my own Spirit-guided mind. Thanks for helping my seminary experience to be a fruitful one. (Dave)
>
> By reading and rereading Luke, outlining the book for ourselves and researching the historical background . . . the dividends were unbelievable! I have never gotten more from a book study in my entire life. (Grace)
>
> The most beneficial part of this class has been spending time on the historical and thematic studies. I spent dozens of hours doing it, reading Luke probably twenty times. I feel I really got a feel for the gospel. Excellent exercise. (Chris)

Other students wrote:

> The thematic study and outline were really helpful tools for getting a sense of what makes Luke [or another book] distinctive.
>
> Historical and thematic studies are a good method to get a rapid and personal handle on a book. (J.)
>
> Thank you very much for this class. I learned a lot from you in New Testament exegesis, especially from the wider context study and sentence flow. These tools will help me a great deal in understanding the central idea of a book and how parts of the text are connected with each and to the chapter/book. (Lance)

OUTLINE THE BOOK OR LETTER

Outlining is a process that is done now as it was done in ancient times. For instance, Aristotle wrote, "If someone smeared a canvas with the loveliest colors at random, it would not give as much pleasure as an outline in black and white" (*Poetics* 7). About stories, he observed, "Stories, whether they are traditional or whether you make them up yourself, should first be sketched in outline and then expanded by putting in episodes" (*Poetics* 18). We write an outline to understand better the author's development of thought.

The outline of a letter is the plan of the author, the way (s)he structures the writing in order to carry out a purpose. An analytical outline develops a purpose. It is not simply topical. In fact, one of the most effective means for you to verify a purpose you have selected is by attempting to outline its development in a letter or book. If the outline seems to develop some other purpose, then you do not have the main purpose of the book or letter. You will then need to adapt the purpose to match the outline.

For our goals, the simpler the outline the better. Any outline over one page is too complex for an overview (unless you are outlining a very long book, such as Luke or Acts). In this way, the structure of the book or letter will be readily apparent at a glance. As in all sections, after you write your outline, reread the book or letter to verify it. For reference purposes, write down the chapters and verses included in every heading. If you have had little experience in writing outlines, you might consider reviewing a book such as *Writing with a Purpose*,[16] which has a helpful chapter titled "Shaping and Testing an Outline."

In an analytical outline, every heading is a full sentence with a subject and verb. All the headings should develop aspects of the purpose sentence in sequential order. The same verse cannot be included in a parallel heading. Therefore, copy over the purpose sentence at the start of the outline to remind you what you are developing. Use either the first and second *or* third person. Normally two or three levels are sufficient for this general understanding of the letter (I, A, 1). Every heading develops its larger heading. Use language from the purpose sentence whenever possible for clarity. For easy reading, 12 point font for legibility. Test the outline by asking, "Is my purpose sentence clearly stated? Is it the same as in the thematic study? Do the main headings prove and develop the purpose? Do the subheadings prove each heading? Do I show the sequence in which the author develops the purpose? Is the outline complete? Are similar categories grouped together? Does each heading have at least two subheads?" The format is important for understanding the author's thoughts. The cover sheet that summarizes all the aspects of a thematic study and outline of a book or letter and several sample thematic studies and outlines follow. I have kept them short for educational purposes, but usually the scope is much longer (yet not more than one page).

---

16.   Joseph F. Trimmer, *Writing with a Purpose*, 13th ed. (Boston: Houghton Mifflin, 2001).

THEMATIC SUMMARY AND OUTLINE COVER SHEET

Assignment: Thematic Summary and Outline of _____

To: [student's name]

Date: _____   Box/email: _____

From: [professor's name]   Grade: _____

I. The following items are rated according to the following symbols:
N = No   S = Sometimes/Somewhat   Y = Yes

A. Synopsis Study

Purpose (for then)

One sentence .... N S Y

A clear sentence .... N S Y

One idea predominates .... N S Y

Main theme of book/letter that addresses
    needs of readers .... N S Y

Specific or unique to book/letter .... N S Y

Author and audience are mentioned .... N S Y

Response from readers is clear .... N S Y

Purpose for now = "general message"

Same purpose .... N S Y

Similar audience as in purpose .... N S Y

Application clear .... N S Y

Content = Scope

Summary is adequate .... N S Y

Unique characteristics of book/letter are mentioned ... N S Y

Important unique names and events are mentioned .... N S Y

General structure of book/letter is mentioned .... N S Y

Author's perspective is highlighted .... N S Y

Paragraph form is employed .... N S Y

Keyword/phrase/verse

Relates to purpose .... N S Y

Helps interpret book .... N S Y

Keywords are set in priority (where applicable) .... N S Y

Grade: _____

B. Outline

Purpose (written above) outline .... N S Y

Same purpose .... N S Y

Full sentences used .... N S Y

Headings parallel to one another .... N S Y

Categories grouped together .... N S Y

Headings develop and prove purpose .... N S Y

Structure of book/letter clear .... N S Y

Bible chapters and verses indicated in
parentheses for each heading .... N S Y

Grade: _____

II. General comments:
I = Inadequate   A = Adequate   G = Good   E = Excellent

Exhaustive work... I A G E

Insightful.. I A G E

Thoughtful... I A G E

Accurate... I A G E

Conclusions proved.. I A G E

Satisfactory length .... I A G E

Organization of paper.. I A G E

Written presentation:

Literary style.. I A G E

Spelling and grammar.. I A G E

Legible.. I A G E

III. Comments

Discern the Wider Context | 53

Thematic Summary of 2 Timothy

Purpose for then: Paul wanted Timothy to share in suffering with him for the gospel—which Timothy had learned—unlike others who abandoned Paul.

Purpose for now (general message): Share in suffering with Christians standing for the truth without abandoning them.

Scope (summary): When Paul had been abandoned in prison in Rome by everyone in Asia except Onesiphorus's household, he wrote Timothy to come to help him. To encourage him from being ashamed of his suffering in prison, like the others, he exhorted him to endure suffering. Persecution of Christians was to be expected. Paul also told Timothy to charge his congregation at Ephesus to avoid senseless controversies, business Timothy needed to complete before leaving. Even though Paul expected to die soon, Paul gratefully remembered Timothy and his grandmother, Lois, and his mother, Eunice. Paul used imagery from the army, farming, and household.

Keyword (or phrase): "share in suffering" (*synkakopatheō*)

Outline of 2 Timothy
Paul wants Timothy to share in suffering with him for the gospel, which he learned, unlike others who abandoned him.

I. Letterhead: Paul reminds Timothy of the "promise of life, the one in Christ Jesus" (1:1–2).
II. Timothy should not be ashamed of suffering for the gospel or of Paul's suffering (1:3–2:13).
    A. Timothy should not be ashamed because of his faith and heritage (1:3–7).
    B. Timothy should not be ashamed because of the gospel and Paul's own example and teaching (1:8–14).
    C. Timothy should follow the example of Onesiphorus's household, who were not ashamed of Paul's chains, and should not imitate the others in Asia who turned away from him (1:15–18).
    D. Therefore, Timothy also should share in suffering (2:1–13).

III. Timothy needs to remind the people of these things while himself avoiding ungodly talking; he should become a vessel for good works (2:14–26).
   A. Timothy should treat truth with integrity and avoid ungodly talking (2:14–18).
   B. Despite ungodly talking, God's firm foundation stands (2:19).
   C. Timothy should become a vessel prepared for good works, pursuing virtues, avoiding controversies, gently guiding the opposition because they may repent (2:20–26).
IV. Timothy needs to continue in his ministry of evangelism and sound teaching despite opposition (3:1–4:8).
   A. Timothy needs to keep avoiding those who are not genuinely pious (3:1–5).
   B. Some of these people who oppose the truth will take women as prisoners, although eventually their folly will become evident (3:6–9).
   C. Instead, Timothy needs to follow Paul's model, including his persecutions, because the godly in Christ will be persecuted while evil people will be deceived (3:10–13).
   D. In contrast, Timothy needs to remain in the Scriptures that prepare him for every good work (3:14–17).
   E. Paul exhorts Timothy, in light of Jesus's judgment, to proclaim the Word at all times because a time is coming when people will turn from healthy teaching to myths and because Paul will be leaving soon (4:1–6).
   F. Paul and all who love the Lord will receive a just crown (4:7–8).
V. Paul wants Timothy to come soon because he is left alone by all except Luke, he needs supplies, and he has been opposed by Alexander and abandoned by all except the Lord (4:9–18).
VI. Paul sends final greetings (4:19–22): Paul greets Priscilla and Aquila and Onesiphorus's household; Paul explains where Erastus and Trophimus are; Paul reiterates: come soon; Christians in Rome greet Timothy; and Paul blesses Timothy and the church.

Outline of the Gospel of Mark

Purpose: Mark wrote Peter's testimony to the Roman Christians: Everyone needs to repent because even though Jesus the Messiah, God's Son, came to earth, he was met by hardened hearts that disbelieved and feared.

I. The good news is established (1:1–20).
II. Jesus's fame spreads (1:21–45).

Discern the Wider Context | 55

III. The scribes begin to criticize Jesus (2:1–3:6).
IV. While the multitudes follow Jesus, fear begins to encroach on others (3:7–6:29).
V. Even the disciples have hardened hearts (6:30–8:26).
VI. The disciples do not understand the Messiah must suffer (8:27–10:52).
VII. The religious leaders contrast with the crowds who welcome Jesus (11:1–14:2).
VIII. Even the disciples and crowds betray Jesus (14:3–16:8).

Practice

Read Philemon in the manner suggested. (See "General Comments on Doing a Thematic Summary, p. 47.") Draw out of your reading a one-page written summary of the author's purpose for writing, his general message, the scope of the letter, and the keyword. Afterward, outline the letter to ascertain whether it is structured to develop your indicated purpose. If you are reading this chapter in combination with another person or in a class situation, after you each complete your thematic study and outline of Philemon, compare the results of your purpose sentences and attempt to agree on one purpose. In this way, you may benefit from another person's perception and possibly enlightening dialogue. Then compare your joint results with mine for further dialogue.

Thematic Summary of Philemon

Purpose: Paul appealed to Philemon to welcome Onesimus as a beloved brother on the basis of the love and faith Philemon extended to others.

General message: Paul appealed to Christians, who have legal rights, to forgive on the basis of love and faith those transformed Christians who could be punished.

Scope: In his own hand, Paul, a prisoner, wrote Philemon a brief letter to encourage him to forgive the now-transformed slave, Onesimus. Timothy was included in the letter's heading. Paul also wrote the household of Apphia and Archippus and the church. Paul described Philemon as beloved, a ministry partner, causing refreshment to the hearts of the saints (vv. 1, 5, 7), because he wanted Philemon to use these same characteristics toward Onesimus (vv. 9, 12, 16, 17, 20). The letter is personal and full of pathos. Coworkers with Paul greeted the household.

Paul appreciated Philemon's love and faith, encouraged Philemon to welcome Onesimus as a beloved brother in Christ on the

56 | Study of the Literary and Historical Contexts of the Text

basis of love, and exhorted Philemon to welcome Onesimus as he would welcome Paul on the basis of their partnership in the faith. He concluded the letter confident of Philemon's decision.

Key phrase: "Welcome him as you would welcome me" (v. 17 NRSV).

Outline of Philemon

Purpose: Paul appealed to Philemon to welcome Onesimus as a beloved brother on the basis of the love and faith Philemon extended to others.

I.   Paul and Timothy wrote to Philemon, Apphia, Archippus, and the house church (vv. 1–3).
II. Paul was thankful for the love and faith of Philemon (vv. 4–7).
III. Paul encouraged Philemon on the basis of love to receive Onesimus as a beloved brother (vv. 8–16).
IV. Paul exhorted Philemon on the basis of partnership in the faith to receive Onesimus as he would receive Paul himself (vv. 17–20).
V.   Paul was confident Philemon would do what he asked and gave Philemon an opportunity to receive him soon (vv. 21–22).
VI. Paul's coworkers greeted them and prayed they would receive the Lord's grace (vv. 23–25).

Suggestions for Doing a Thematic Summary and Outline

I always begin by looking for the overall purpose of the letter, followed by its outline. By just reading the English text, this was my tentative purpose: "Although Paul could command Philemon, Apphia, Archippus, and the church in their house, 'yet for love's sake' he preferred to appeal to them to receive Onesimus as they would receive Paul himself." The key phrase was "yet for love's sake." Then I worked on the outline. Philemon 1–3 has the opening greetings. I began to jot down the main idea of each paragraph. I noticed, however, that verses 4–7 are three sentences in the NRSV text but one sentence in the Greek New Testament (4th and 5th editions). In light of my uncertainty about the relationship of verse 6 to the earlier verses and the brevity of the letter, I decided to translate all of Philemon and note the main verbs and subordinate clauses. I discovered that verses 4–6 are indeed one long sentence. The main verb is "I thank," which is modified by the participle "making remembrance." Paul remembered in his prayers two broad categories: what he heard (v. 5) and what he wanted to happen (v. 6). Thus, in my outline, I included verses 4–7 as one unit oriented around thankfulness. Philemon 9 and 10 both have the main verb "appeal" (*parakaleō*). Philemon 8–14 is one extended sentence that culminates in Paul's final appeal (vv. 15–16).

Therefore, I grouped verses 8–16 as a second section. Verse 17 begins with "therefore" and an imperative "welcome." The conjunction and imperative suggest a change of approach. Now Paul wrote a series of shorter imperatival sentences, all on similar themes of welcoming Onesimus, comprising the next section of the outline (vv. 17–20). Verse 21 moves to Paul's projection of Philemon's response, and verse 23 begins the closing greetings of the letter.

I learned that if, at the first stage, we write the outline from the translated text, at the end we can fine-tune the outline by looking at the Greek text, (that is, if we know Greek). After creating the outline, I reworded the purpose sentence, because now I noticed that love is not the only basis for the welcoming but also their partnership in faith. I added the modifier "beloved brother" because Onesimus's transformed spiritual state is an important theme in the letter. I also added Philemon's treatment of others, since Paul mentioned this at the beginning and alluded to it throughout. I eliminated my original subordinate clause "although Paul could command Philemon, Apphia, Archippus, and the church in their house" because it is not a central theme and the letter is mainly written to an individual. After I prepared the outline, I proofed all the Bible references.

I learned in the outline how beautifully structured this letter is, the interrelationships between the parts, and the expectations Paul had for Christians encouraging one another to mature in Christ. The letter allows freedom yet imposes pressure. "Prepare a guest room for me" is not a passing request but the very heart of the letter. Philemon also should "prepare a guest room" for Onesimus, his former slave, if indeed he was to welcome him as he would welcome Paul. Therefore, I decided to use verse 17, instead of verse 9, as my key phrase.

Then I wrote up the general message, trying to summarize Onesimus's and Philemon's situations. Since a slave owner could have punished a runaway slave, I included "legal rights" in my contemporary paraphrase. I also decided at a later time to learn more about the rights of a first-century master over a slave. I rephrased "welcome" as "forgive" because they are synonyms, but I kept the same two bases: love and faith.

To summarize the content, I reread the notes on the historical context and included some key information. I mentioned some aspects of Paul's style of writing and a few names, and I summarized the main points from the outline. I cited verses to substantiate the different lists of themes. Thus, months later, if I wanted to recall what struck me in my first reading of Philemon, it would all be there for me to see. When I did my exegesis of a specific sentence, I would be able to fit it within the larger context of the letter and the overall purpose.

HOW THE WIDER CONTEXT RELATES TO THE TEXT

The danger of an exegesis book such as this is that Bible students will amass such a plethora of material on a text (the verse or verses being studied) that the amount may make the subject matter appear uncontrollable. Nevertheless, in contrast, other approaches to studying the Bible may cover each manner of studying a book or letter as totally unrelated, thus never giving depth to the understanding of a verse. Therefore, to focus all the methodologies herein suggested is crucial. During, but especially at the end of this study, we need to ask, "What light has this step shed on my particular text? How does any new information help me comprehend further the meaning of my passage?" At the end of this section on wider context, ask yourself, "What light or understanding does any part of this wider context have on my text? What is the relationship of my text to the overall purpose of the book or letter of the Bible I am reading?" In the exegesis paper, write a brief summary of the historical context and how it affects and enlightens the meaning of the passage you are studying. This tentative paragraph can be developed later in the exegesis paper. The passage you are studying must be related to the overall purpose of the letter or book, the larger headings of your outline, and the immediate heading in the outline.

HOW TO AVOID COMMON ERRORS

1. Make sure you clarify not only the author's name but also the author's and the readers' personal and spiritual characteristics.

2. Cite proof for information from the Bible itself and from any helpful primary ancient sources, such as Eusebius's *Church History* and *Apostolic Fathers*.

3. Focus on the five headings of historical context and draw out all the information under these headings.

4. This is not an exercise on what commentators think but on your own discovery from the Bible.

5. Developing the purpose sentence takes thought in order to be succinct.

6. Make sure the scope is exhaustive, including a summary of the headings from your outline.

7. Write an analytical outline with each heading as a full sentence for maximum clarity. The format is important.

PART 2

PREPARATION FOR THE STUDY OF THE TEXT

CHAPTER 2

CHOOSE THE TEXT AND ITS IMMEDIATE CONTEXT

THE INITIAL STEPS IN EXEGESIS

I. Choose the text and its immediate context.
II. Observe overview of the exegesis paper.
III. Communicate your findings.

All steps can be done by both Greek and translation readers.

PRIORITY OF CONTEXT

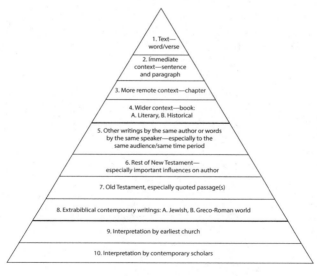

Figure 2.1. Priority of context (pyramid)

CHOOSE THE TEXT

After completing level 4 (the wider context) of the priority of context, we are ready to begin levels 2 and 3, starting with the choosing of a text[1] (in other words, a short passage,[2] extracted as a pericope,[3] to be examined in depth) or simply a single unit of thought, which will be in less danger of misinterpretation by the way it is chosen. Because of Greek grammar's developed case endings, Greek writers can use longer sentences and remain clear grammatically. The larger the text, the more cursory the study. A text is often one or two Greek sentences, which may be equal to one to three English verses. For instance, Romans 12:1–2 is one sentence in most Greek editions but two sentences in most English translations; and Philemon 4–6 is one sentence in most Greek versions and two sentences in most English translations.

The immediate context comprises the sentences around the text that are most important in determining the meaning. In Romans 12 your text might be verses 1–8. Of course, the entire letter is crucial, but you are looking for priorities of context within the original letter. Figure 2.2 shows another way to chart the different levels of the context:

Even English readers can find the Greek sentences by checking an interlinear version such as Paul McReynolds's *Word Study Greek-English New Testament.*[4]

How did I choose my text in Philemon? Philemon 1–3 is a traditional ancient letterhead with the authors' names, readers' names, and the greeting. With the use of the first-person singular, Paul began the letter (see, e.g., v. 19). The final greeting is verse 25. In my outline, I discovered four basic themes (vv. 4–7, 8–16, 17–20, and 21–22). I could have picked a text from any of those four groups of verses. In verses 4–7, Paul remembered in his prayers what he heard about Philemon's love and faith. (See "Literary Context" in chapter 8, "Sample Exegesis Paper: Philemon 4–6.") Verse 5 summarizes the two key elements of the letter, love and faith, which describe the two important principles in this letter on which I can focus in my study. But my text will include verses 4 and 6 since they are part of that same sentence. There is some

---

1. The word *text* is from the Latin *textere,* "to weave," and refers to the words, especially the words and sentences as originally written or printed.

2. A passage is a portion of something spoken or written, usually small or of moderate length, taken by itself, relating to some particular matter; a journey of words upon which we embark.

3. A pericope is a selected extract from a book or paper, passage, section, paragraph in writing, as if the passage is set out (from Gk. *koptō,* "to cut," plus *peri,* "around") from the paper and placed before us for examination.

4. Paul R. McReynolds, ed., *Word Study Greek-English New Testament* (Wheaton, IL: Tyndale House, 1999). McReynolds uses the third corrected edition of the Greek New Testament and the NRSV. Independently, Craig L. Blomberg and Jennifer Foutz Markley have a chart of similar concentric layers of literary context in *A Handbook of New Testament Exegesis* (Grand Rapids: Baker Academic, 2010), 93–102.

flexibility in choosing a text, but the main thing to avoid is choosing a text that misrepresents the whole meaning, such as choosing half of Philippians 2:12–13:

> Verse 12: Therefore, my beloved, just as you have always obeyed me, not only in my presence, but much more now in my absence, work on your own salvation with fear and trembling,

or

> Verse 13: for it is God who is at work in you, enabling you both to will and to work for his good pleasure. (NRSV)[5]

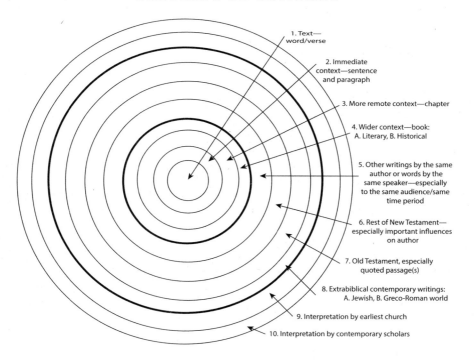

Figure 2.2. Priority of context (circle)

---

5. Bible Gateway (www.biblegateway.com) offers a simple way to add Bible verses to one's papers by copying and pasting needed verses, but you must indicate the English translation used in your paper and, if possible, delete the verse numbers within the quotation.

64 | Preparation for the Study of the Text

The mystery we hold is that humans, and certainly Christians, have a responsibility to act while God is simultaneously active in our lives. Choosing half the sentence would leave out the full truth.

How do we choose a text? Begin by keeping in mind your first readers or listeners. Will it be your professor? Will it be readers of a particular journal or magazine? Will it be the parishioners of a church? Will it be a college group? Les Stobbe wrote an insightful study of the gospel of Luke, pointing out that Luke had a target reader clearly in mind, namely, Theophilus. Luke selected and organized his materials for maximizing its impact on Theophilus and kept his clear purpose constantly in mind as he wrote.[6]

As you think about your professor (in case (s)he is the first reader), I recommend you avoid the professor's specialty or a topic over which you disagree. It would be most difficult for you to present a new idea. But do write something that interests the professor. My husband's interest is cults, and students who find a *new* cult he has never heard of are almost sure to get an A (if they do their searches in primary references)! After years of speaking to college students about the role of women in ministry, many years ago I decided to try to have my findings on 1 Timothy 2:11–15 published. Since my ministry is with college and graduate students, I wrote an introduction for my article to appeal to college students by expressing my feelings about the topic. The editor of the *Journal of the Evangelical Theological Society* (*JETS*) was interested in the topic but graciously recommended I rewrite the introduction for an academic audience. We might all have feelings, but it is rare that these are expressed at the beginning of a scholarly article.[7]

How might you find the text? With the Philemon study, I picked the text I thought encapsulated the main themes of the letter. The text might also come from your own concerns. However, if you plan on preaching the text you have chosen, you have to remember your concerns may or may not be the same as those of your congregation. The text might come from your own devotional study, but you need to find the appropriate audience. Luke 9:58–62 was a passage that leaped out to me as I read the gospel one year. Suddenly a passage I had never understood became personally meaningful. Jesus was warning his potential disciples that he has no country and warning them that they, too, would end up in this state. I feel at times as well that I have no country. Jesus's words appeal to people who are intercultural. I was born in

---

6.   Les Stobbe, "Earning the Right to Be Published," *Africanus Journal* 10, no. 2 (November 2018): 5. See also pp. 4–11.

7.   The rewritten article was published as "Eve at Ephesus: Should Women Be Ordained as Pastors according to the First Letter of Timothy 2:11–15?," *Journal of the Evangelical Theological Society* 17 (Fall 1974): 215–22. This article was then revised for a chapter in my book *Beyond the Curse: Women Called to Ministry* (Nashville: Thomas Nelson, 1985). The same material was then developed and included in a commentary on 1 Timothy in the New Covenant Commentary series (Eugene, OR: Cascade, 2013). So, you see, we can build on our previous studies and develop them and use them in different contexts.

a Hispanic country, Dominican Republic, but I was reared after ten years of age in New Jersey. Even in the Dominican Republic, I was a stranger, since my mother was from Puerto Rico and my father was from the Netherlands. Yet neither did I completely fit in the United States. I wrote up my thoughts first as a sermon to provincial North Americans of European descent for an ordination service. The newly ordained minister afterward came to me baffled and said, "I didn't understand it." Many years later I gave the sermon again in Santo Domingo at an international church, and I was swamped with appreciation. My mother wanted me to mail a copy to all of our relatives. One elder said, "Where have you been?" And some parents said to me, almost in tears, "Our boys reared here in Santo Domingo so much needed to hear that!" My sermon struck its recipients as either completely baffling or as a life raft.[8]

Sometimes your text might be assigned as part of a series. Your goal, then, is to determine why your text is where it is in light of the purpose of the section and the whole book or letter.[9] Next, plan how to communicate your findings in the most appropriate style to your readers or listeners.

Here I summarize the first step in the exegetical process:

I.   Define the text (a single unit of thought that will not be misinterpreted by the way it is chosen). Determine its beginning and ending. How?
   A.   Follow your outline. Do not take thoughts at random from different headings.
   B.   Use the Greek text to find tentative sentences. Do not break any sentence. Consider all of it so you do not misrepresent its point.
   C.   Check the United Bible Society (UBS) notes on different ways texts have been punctuated.[10]
   D.   Eventually your sentence flow will help you to understand further where to begin and end the sentences.
II.   Choose the immediate context (the next minimum place the thought can be cut). Read "Literary Context" in chapter 8, "Sample Exegesis Paper: Philemon 4–6."[11]

---

8. See Aída Besançon Spencer, "God the Stranger: An Intercultural Hispanic American Perspective," in *The Global God: Multicultural Evangelical Views of God*, ed. Aída Besançon Spencer and William David Spencer (Grand Rapids: Baker, 1998): 89–103.

9. See Daniel M. Doriani, *Getting the Message: A Plan for Interpreting and Applying the Bible* (Phillipsburg, NJ: P&R, 1996), ch. 3.

10. Barbara Aland et al., eds., *The Greek New Testament*, 5th rev. ed. (Stuttgart, Germany: Deutsche Bibelgesellschaft, 2014). The free online NA28th ed. has no critical apparatus: https://www.die-bibel.de/en/bible/NA28/MAT.1.

11. For further reading, see Gordon D. Fee, *New Testament Exegesis: A Handbook for Students and Pastors*, 3rd ed. (Louisville: Westminster John Knox, 2002), 9–11; Richard J. Erickson, *A Beginner's Guide to New Testament Exegesis: Taking the Fear Out of Critical Method* (Downers Grove, IL: InterVarsity Press, 2005), 62–68; Michael J. Gorman, *Elements of Biblical Exegesis: A Basic Guide for Students and Ministers*, 3rd ed. (Grand Rapids: Baker Academic, 2020), ch. 4; A. Berkeley Mickelsen and Alvera

66 | Preparation for the Study of the Text

> **Consider the Text as a Part of a Larger Study**
>
> An exegetical study of a New Testament text has eight essential steps or aspects of research:
>
> 1. Defining the text and immediate context
> 2. Discovering the true text
> 3. Understanding the grammar of the text (or syntax)
> 4. Understanding the meaning of words or phrases (or semantics)
> 5. Understanding the style
> 6. Studying the Greek, Roman, and/or Jewish ancient cultural backgrounds
> 7. Making the application to life
> 8. Finding other interpretations of the text

A knowledge of Greek is necessary for steps 2, 3, and 5 but not for steps 1, 4, 6, 7, and 8. The primary goal of an exegetical study is to understand the significance or meaning of your text for its original readers. The concluding goal is to explain that significance to contemporary readers or listeners. An interpreter (Lat. *interpres*) is an agent between (*inter*) two parties, such as a broker or negotiator. Are we agents between the biblical text and the people? When we communicate the meaning of a text, we become a broker between the text and the people. When we really believe the Bible is authoritative, we interpret it exegetically *and* we also obey its message. When we teach and learn methods for interpreting the Bible, we are doing what we can to understand God's revelation, to obtain God's meaning for a text, rather than simply giving a text the meaning we want it to have or think it should have.

For instance, when King Josiah heard that a book of the law had been found (probably the book of Deuteronomy), and after hearing it read, he sent a delegation to the prophetess Huldah to inquire of the Lord for him. She was to be an agent between God, God's text, the ruling leaders, and especially the king. Huldah had to explain, or interpret, Deuteronomy and apply it to their time (2 Kings 22:1–20). Here is an overview of all the steps in an exegetical study:

OVERVIEW: ELEMENTS IN AN EXEGESIS PAPER

I. Exegesis: What did the author intend the original readers to understand?

A. Context (literary and historical) of the text.

M. Mickelsen, *Understanding Scripture: How to Read and Study the Bible,* rev. ed. (Peabody, MA: Hendrickson, 1992), ch. 7; A. Berkeley Mickelsen, *Interpreting the Bible* (Grand Rapids: Eerdmans, 1963), ch. 5.

1. Wider context of the book or letter. Seek a general understanding of the book or letter.
   a. Write all initial thoughts, feelings, and questions.
   b. Study the historical context.
   c. Survey the thematic content of the book or letter.
   d. Outline the book or letter.
   e. Study how the wider context relates to the text.
2. Immediate context.
   a. Define text.
   b. Choose the immediate context, the thought unit around the text.
   c. Priority of context: immediate sentence, paragraph, book, other books or letters written by the same author in the same time period and/or in the same testament, and other biblical passages.
B. Study of the text: preparation for study of the text.
   1. Discover the true text.
   2. Seek a satisfactory translation.
C. Study of the text: in-depth.
   1. Introductory questions and insights.
   2. Understand the grammar of the text.
      a. Analyze the grammar of each word, phrase, and clause.
      b. Analyze the structure of the sentences and paragraphs.
   3. Understand the meaning of the words and phrases.
   4. Understand the style.
      a. Recognize kinds of writing.
      b. Decipher figures of speech and unusual word order.
   5. Compare text to its historical-cultural context: study further contextual resources (background and foreground).
      a. Bible.
      b. Extrabiblical Jewish and Greco-Roman culture and history.
      c. Post–New Testament (optional).
II. Make the application(s) to life.
   A. Derive principles and summarize the type of people or situation to which the text is addressed.
   B. Compare the passage with other biblical passages bearing on the same subject (as time and space allow).
   C. Make the direct application(s).

Each step in the study of the text is like a clue to help us solve a mystery. What did the text mean to its original readers? You can never be sure which clue will be the significant one. It is as if someone came to you for counseling. You listen and ask different questions, but you never know which question will reveal the true problem the person is experiencing.

68 | Preparation for the Study of the Text

At the end of (or even amid) the exegesis study, take these steps:

1. Reread the text and all the research you have done.
2. Pray and think: What is the main meaning of the text? How does each step contribute to this meaning? Which of the different aspects or steps should I emphasize to explain best the meaning of the text? At the end, skim all of the book or letter and ask yourself, "How does my text relate to the rest of the letter?"
3. Rewrite all of the sections into a single integrated whole, including all information that helps explain the meaning of the text. Possibly use headings.
4. Write everything in your own words unless you want to quote someone directly. But remember to footnote any ideas or content obtained from other people or sources.

Ask yourself, "Have I exhaustively and comprehensively studied my passage? Have I proved my conclusions from the context of the text itself and from primary references? Or have I simply relied on quoting others or making my own unfounded declarations?" Quoting a contemporary person is not proof. An authoritative tone is not proof.

In fact, an authoritative tone can be quite disarming. A student told me at the beginning of a class that the whole interpretative process was a waste of time. She had been commanded authoritatively by some scholars to promote and by others to discourage women's leadership in the church. She added that these were scholars who claimed to take the Bible as their reliable authority, and they knew Greek and Hebrew and had become practiced in interpreting the Bible. Did not this truth make it futile for her to study the Bible herself, a mere ingenue in scholarship?

After some thought, I suggested she consider the devil's forty-day temptation of Jesus in the wilderness, recorded by Matthew and Luke. The devil and Jesus both used scriptural texts as part of their authority for their respective commands. The devil challenged Jesus with Psalm 91:11–12, and Jesus answered with Deuteronomy 6:16:

Then the devil led [Jesus] to Jerusalem and placed him on the pinnacle of the temple and said to him, "If you are the Son of God, throw yourself down from here, for it is written,

'He will command his angels concerning you, to protect you,'

and

'On their hands they will bear you up, so that you will not dash your foot against a stone.'"

Jesus answered him, "It is said, 'Do not put the Lord your God to the test.'" (Luke 4:9–12 NRSV)

Is Psalm 91:11–12 no longer authoritative for us because it was used by the Evil One? Would God's angels not protect Jesus if he threw himself down from the pinnacle of the temple in Jerusalem? Of course they would. However, the devil was misusing Psalm 91:11–12 to put God to the test. I am sure Jesus would not want his disciples *not* to study the Bible because we do not always agree on the interpretation of specific passages! We Christians are responsible as individuals and in our churches and institutions to evaluate by scriptural standards what we are taught and what we teach and what we are doing. If we have no basis for evaluation, we will be baffled and our convictions will sway back and forth, pulled by competing impressive-sounding words. We do not simply want to be swayed by impressive speakers; we want to stand firm because we know why we believe what we are doing.

And our convictions after our study should be communicated to others. Humility is, of course, essential since God's truth is external to us and we are all reaching together to ascertain it. But we need to come to some conclusion, even if tentatively held. God can redirect us if we are wrong.

COMMUNICATE YOUR FINDINGS

When we write our paper, as with any technical essay, we should clearly present our goals and proofs up front and then summarize our findings at the end. In a fictional story, as in a mystery novel, we may hint at our main point but surprise the reader at the conclusion. In an exegesis paper or a sermon, the main purpose of the writing, which is the main meaning of the text, is presented early, after an introduction, in a thesis statement. The introduction might mention why this passage interests you or how your interpretation compares to interpretations that have been given by others (after you complete your secondary study). A sermon may attempt to relate the Bible text to the concerns of today. The thesis might be built on a new insight into the meaning you discovered. You will also want to present the scope of your paper, how you will develop it, and how you will prove the thesis. For instance, in the Philemon 4–6 study (see chapter 8), the *thesis* has two parts summarizing the two parts of the text: "We learn that a prayer of thanksgiving can indeed include a request in bold confidence" and that "faith needs to flow outward in 'sharing' with the Lord and with other believers." The *scope* or overview plan of the essay is this: "We will answer these questions by looking at the historical and literary contexts; verifying the text; studying the sentence's grammar, semantics (especially *mneia, energēs, koinōnia*), and literary aspects; and concluding with an application." What we will do and how we will do it are the thesis and the scope of our essay.

In a short academic word study I wrote, the thesis was: "Often translated 'stubbornness' (NASB, JPSV) or 'stubbornly' (RSV), *šərîrût* connotes a form of

70 | Preparation for the Study of the Text

self-reliance." The scope was: "The immediate contexts of the ten occurrences of *šərîrût*, the etymology, synonymous and contrasting terms, and the Greek translations in the LXX, lend support to *šərîrût* as a form of 'self-reliance.'"[12]

It is best to reread one's paper and take notes so you can summarize your findings at the end. "What did I prove?" and "How did I prove it?" are the questions that are the basis of your summary. The significance of the text may suggest some conclusions. The summary should include (1) the audience to whom the text is addressed and (2) the major theological principle or principles in the text. No new topics are raised in a summary. Save any new questions for a future study. The study of God's Word can keep you busy for eternity! Review your introduction and check to see that you have answered all of the questions you raised. Did you do what you said you would do? If not, change your purpose or thesis in the introduction to match the conclusion. Drop any questions you did not answer. Did you discuss areas you said you would? Is your writing purposeful and succinct? Are all aspects of the exegetical process interrelated in one overriding purpose?

In the dialogue of Phaedrus and Socrates, Socrates said that rhetoric must have an introduction first, at the beginning of the discourse; and the narrative must come second, with the testimony after it; followed by, third, the proofs; and, fourth, the probabilities and confirmation or refutations; and conclude or recapitulate (a summary of the points of the speech at the end of it, so as to remind the hearers of what has been said) (*Phaedrus* 267). As in ancient times, well-written technical essays should always have an introduction with a thesis and the scope of the paper, the body of the paper developing the thesis and giving proofs, and the final entry: the conclusion.

You need time to think prayerfully about your text. I have found that usually the two most important aspects of the exegetical process are (1) the wider context study and (2) the translation of the text and its immediate context. I will check to make sure I am using the best Greek text, parse every word of the text, look for unusual style features, pick keywords to study, and decide what in the ancient background might be helpful. As I work, I will begin to get a sense of what the text means. When I have about two-thirds of the research done and I am clear what my main idea is, I will write a tentative outline of my paper with my tentative purpose and then begin to write a first draft. I keep in mind the length I have available, often given to me by a publisher. I planned the sample paper here to be done in a week and to be twelve pages long (double-spaced). If I wait too long to write, I get too much information and likely will become overwhelmed by all of my notes. Then I leave space where I might have to do more research. I also note where data I already have might be leading me to adjacent topics.

---

12. Aída Besançon Spencer, "Critical Notes: *Šərîrût* as Self-Reliance," *Journal of Biblical Literature* 100 (June 1981): 247–48.

I prefer writing my first draft in longhand on scrap paper. My thinking aligns well with the speed of my writing by hand. Then I type my penciled comments into a Word document. Typing is a technical skill that keeps me distracted from my thoughts. My husband prefers typing his first draft. Some may prefer to dictate their first draft and then have it typed (or use software that transcribes speech). Others may think through the whole argument before writing. The process of writing is very individual. Find your own best style. It is the final product that counts: a thoughtful, succinct, and well-phrased study. The following offers a general format for writing a final version of the paper, moving from the broad to the narrower topic.

OVERVIEW: PRESENTATION OF AN EXEGESIS PAPER

I. Exegesis (what did the author intend the original readers to understand?): study of the text:
    A. Choose introductory question(s) that will be answered.
    B. Wider context of the book or letter (explain how the wider context relates to the text).
        1. Summarize the *historical context*, highlighting aspects that enlighten the text.
        2. Explain the *purpose* of the book or letter.
        3. Summarize the main outline of the book or letter in a paragraph (or longer if this is a key part of your study).
    C. Immediate context: explain how the immediate context relates to the text.
    D. Present the true text and why it is the true text.
    E. Present your own finished translation (or a literal version copied from others if you don't know Greek).
    F. Explain the grammar of the text.
        1. Analyze the structure of the sentences and paragraphs (*syntax*).
        2. Analyze the grammar of important *words*, *phrases*, and *clauses*.
    G. Explain the meaning of important words and phrases (*semantic analysis*).
    H. Explain the meaning of the text by a *stylistic analysis*.
        1. Recognize any effect from *kinds of writing*.
        2. Define and explain *figures of speech*.
    I. Study further contextual resources: background and foreground.
        1. Study important biblical background.
        2. Find helpful extrabiblical references (Jewish, Greco-Roman culture, history) that highlight the text.

II. Make the application(s) to life.
  A. Derive principles and summarize the type of people or situation to which the text is addressed.
  B. Make the direct application(s).

Figure 2.3 Paper Quest

The writing process might be compared to a global positioning system (GPS):

Search for: Introduction
- Where are you going? Where are you going to end? = meaning of your text
- How will you get there? = scope of paper

After you've traveled once, readjust the map to the actual destination

Road Traveled: Body of the paper

- Historical context = Who are you going with?
- Literary context = How does the destination relate to its area?
- Text criticism = Do you have the correct address?
- Grammar study = How do the terms relate to each other? For example, does an overpass or a sharp turn connect the highways?
- Word study = What do the terms mean? For example, is it a street, an avenue, a boulevard, a circle, a crescent, or a route?
- Style study = What is the difference if we use the terms *the Big Apple* or *New York City*?
- Jewish and Greco-Roman study = What are the key landmarks along the way?
- Where have you arrived? = Conclusion

Figure 2.4 illustrates the exegetical process.

How to Write an Exegesis Paper[13]

Goal: Explain the meaning and significance of the text and prove your interpretation.

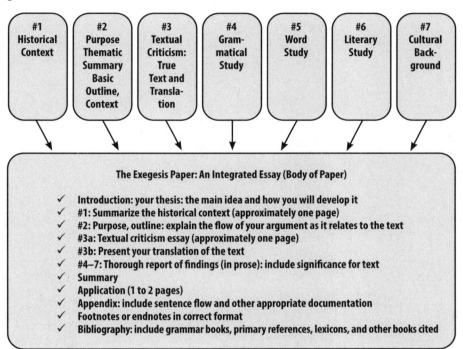

Figure 2.4. How to write an exegesis paper

---

13. This chart was originally designed by Marcella Charles. Used by permission.

EXEGESIS PAPER COVER SHEET

The following cover sheet can be used for review by the student and later for grading.

Exegesis of _____   To: [student's name]

Assignment: _____   Box/email: _____

Date: _____   Grade: _____

From: [professor's name]

I.   The following items are rated according to the following symbols:

I = inadequate   A = adequate   G = good   S = superior

RESEARCH METHODOLOGY:

Comprehensive/exhaustive...I A G S

Accurate ....I A G S

Insightful (optional) ....I A G S

Conclusions proved (supporting NT data, explanations, ancient sources) ....I A G S

Original (primary sources studied: letter, NT, first-century references, secondary work is supplemental to own work)...I A G S

COMPLETENESS OF EXEGESIS:

Textual Understanding

Text critical ....I A G S

Grammatical..I A G S

Lexical...I A G S

Stylistic ....I A G S

Contextual awareness

Literary..I A G S

Historical..I A G S

Background awareness (use of appropriate parallel texts)

Biblical (priority given to context) ....I A G S

Extrabiblical (Jewish and Greco-Roman culture) ....I A G S

Appropriate practical application ....I A G S

Bibliographical awareness (when applicable) ....I A G S

WRITTEN PRESENTATION:

Well-organized paper...I A G S

Literary style: clear and succinct ....I A G S

Spelling and grammar correct...........................I A G S

Print is readable (size 12 font,
double-spaced, single-sided)...........................I A G S

II. The following items need attention if checked:

☐ The exegesis paper needs to be a unified essay on the meaning of the text rather than a series of research notes.

☐ The paper needs balance. It gives too much space to less significant items and too little space to major items.

☐ The exegesis paper is too long or too short.

Preparation for the Study of the Text

☐ The pages should be numbered consecutively throughout.

☐ Cite dictionary/encyclopedia articles by author and title of the article (not by the editor).

☐ Cite primary sources by chapter and paragraph number (not by page number).

☐ Cite Greek words out of context in their lexical entry form.

☐ Accent Greek words in Greek font.

☐ Excessive use of the first and/or second person for a formal paper.

☐ Excessive use of passive verbs and "it is" without a clear antecedent.

☐ Use a consistent and/or correct format in footnotes and bibliography citations.

III. Comments:

HOW TO AVOID COMMON ERRORS

1. Pick a size text that can be discussed comprehensively in the page or time length available.

2. Do not cite the entire thematic, outline, and historical studies in your exegetical paper, but adapt them. Show how the text fits in the overall outline and historical context.

3. Make sure you have an introduction and a conclusion. Present the topics in the paper in the same sequence as they appear in the introduction.

4. Include your thesis and overview of the essay in the introduction.

5. Use spell-check for simple grammatical and spelling errors. If English is not your primary language, enlist an editor to improve your grammar. If necessary, in a footnote, give credit to the editor.

6. Proofread all quotations after you have printed the pages. I have found I can catch some errors on my monitor, but I always catch more errors after I print the pages. Keep your sources until you proof your pages and complete your bibliography (or photocopy or scan the pertinent pages, if necessary).

7. Answer all questions in the introduction. If you do not answer a question you originally planned to answer, delete that question from the introduction.

8. Use transitions between sections even if you use headings.

9. Double-check your work in light of the cover sheet.

APPENDIX: HOW TO INTERPRET A NARRATIVE PASSAGE

The following outline presents distinctives (and similarities) for interpreting a passage in the Gospels and Acts. Use the following procedural order when studying a passage.

How to Interpret a Narrative Passage
Teaching tends to be repetitive. You should interpret a person's teachings first in the passage being studied before relating the content to that person's teachings in another book.

I. See how the passage fits into the *overall purpose* of the narrative book.

[author's goals]

[historical context of book]

Narrative has two levels: (a) historical presentation of conversations and events, and (b) author's arrangement. What is normative in the narrative is God's perspective.

78 | Preparation for the Study of the Text

II. See how the passage fits into its *immediate context* of teachings or events.

Who is the audience in the immediate context?

[sentence flow]
[historical context of passage]

[person's teachings]

III. Understand *words*, primarily, as used by the speaker and then by the author of the book or letter [word study].
IV. Understand metaphorical language first as images and then as concepts.
V. Add appropriate information.
   A. Find references, if any, to this same event in another gospel. Verify if the historical description and time frame are the same. Add helpful details from another gospel if it has an account of the same event. Explain how apparent differences might be reconciled.
   B. See how an event in Acts fits into the rest of the New Testament. Add appropriate information from the letters in the study of Acts.
VI. Compare and contrast word(s) or concept(s) with extrabiblical references as helpful. See how the events in the New Testament may be enlightened by the Jewish and Greco-Roman worlds.
VII. Check Eusebius's *Church History* for helpful early church traditions.

CHAPTER 3

DISCOVER THE TRUE TEXT

A. Find at least one variation unit (variant reading) to study. Look at both the United Bible Society (UBS) and Nestle-Aland New Testaments.

B. List the manuscript (MS) symbol, age, and text type for each variant. See "One Variation Unit: Blank" sheet later in this chapter. Find by checking introduction and appendix lists in UBS and appendix in Nestle-Aland, along with their inserts. See also the appendix at the end of this chapter ("Important Witnesses for the New Testament: Papyri, Uncials, Versions").

C. Choose the more likely original variant based on the following.
    1. Earliest manuscripts (any early papyrus?).
    2. Good-quality text type (Alexandrian?).
    3. Good-quality manuscripts (e.g., ℵ, B).
    4. Variety of text types (Alexandrian, Western, Caesarian, early Byzantine).
    5. Manuscripts not genealogically related (e.g., F is genealogically related to G).

D. Summarize the reasons for the variant you chose on the "Summary Evaluation of Variation Unit" sheet and the reasons other variants were not chosen, including how these variants may have arisen. Note how intrinsic probabilities may supplement external evidence for the chosen variant.[1]

E. Write from a paragraph to a page summarizing your conclusions and why in essay form in the exegesis paper. Read "Textual Variation" in chapter 8, "Sample Exegesis Paper: Philemon 4–6."[2]

---

1. When you become more proficient, you may omit step D by only using processing under step C.

2. For further help, see Bruce M. Metzger and Bart D. Ehrman, *The Text of the New Testament: Its Transmission, Corruption, and Restoration,* 4th ed. (New York: Oxford University Press, 2005); Kurt

80 | Preparation for the Study of the Text

This step can be done by Greek readers, but the information is helpful for non-Greek readers as well.

INTRODUCTION

Every once in a while, a student wants to preach on a passage I cannot find in my own Bible. For example, "For there are three that bear record in heaven, the Father, the Word, and the Holy Ghost: and these three are one" (1 John 5:7 KJV). The NRSV has simply: "There are three that testify" (5:7).[3] Those three are the Spirit and the water and the blood (1 John 5:8). Yet the KJV translation is a wonderful testimony to the Trinity! (However, it is not the only witness to the Trinity; e.g., Matt. 28:19.) Why is this rendering of 1 John 5:7 only in the KJV? Unlike most other ancient manuscripts, every year scholars are finding more and more New Testament manuscripts. Martin Anstey said in 1916 that there were then 3,000 copies of the Greek New Testament manuscripts,[4] but in 2005 Bruce Metzger wrote that there were 5,735 manuscripts.[5] Between 1916 and 2005 the number of handwritten New Testament manuscripts almost doubled. And more manuscripts continue to be discovered. Further, this number does not include all the ancient translations and quotations from the early church fathers. When the Bible was translated in the time of Britain's King James I (1611), scholars relied on quotations from a few Latin church fathers (e.g., Cyprian [d. 258], Priscillian [d. 385]) and a few late Greek manuscripts (221 [10 c], 2473 [1634], 2318 [18 c]) to render 1 John 5:7. However, the earliest Greek manuscripts (א [4 c], A [5 c], B [4 c]) do not include the KJV extended verse 7.[6] No matter how much we like some words, these may not be the words used by the author (in this case John) if they are not in the best

---

Aland and Barbara Aland, *The Text of the New Testament: An Introduction to the Critical Editions and to the Theory and Practice of Modern Textual Criticism*, rev. ed. (Grand Rapids: Eerdmans, 1989); Philip Wesley Comfort, *The Quest for the Original Text of the New Testament* (Grand Rapids: Baker, 1992); Philip Wesley Comfort, *Early Manuscripts and Modern Translations of the New Testament* (Grand Rapids: Baker, 1990); Richard J. Erickson, *A Beginner's Guide to New Testament Exegesis: Taking the Fear Out of Critical Method* (Downers Grove, IL: InterVarsity Press, 2005), ch. 2; John D. Harvey, *Interpreting the Pauline Letters: An Exegetical Handbook*, Handbook for New Testament Exegesis (Grand Rapids: Kregel, 2012), 101–7; Craig L. Blomberg with Jennifer Foutz Markley, *A Handbook of New Testament Exegesis* (Grand Rapids: Baker Academic, 2010), ch. 1; Gordon D. Fee, *New Testament Exegesis: A Handbook for Students and Pastors*, 3rd ed. (Louisville: Westminster John Knox, 2002), 2:2; William W. Klein, Craig L. Blomberg, and Robert L. Hubbard Jr., *Introduction to Biblical Interpretation*, 3rd ed. (Grand Rapids: Zondervan, 2017), 184–90.

3. Also CEB, CEV, ESV, HCSB, NIV, NLT, AND REB agree, but they each include a footnote, such as "Other mss (Vg and a few late Gk mss) read *testify in heaven: the Father, the Word, and the Holy Spirit, and these three are One. And there are three who bear witness on earth*" (1 John 5:7–8 HCSB).

4. Martin Anstey, *How to Understand the Bible* (New York: Revell, 1916), 29.

5. Metzger and Ehrman, *Text of the New Testament*, 50.

6. See further Metzger and Ehrman, *Text of the New Testament*, 146–47.

attested manuscripts. Therefore, we would be interpreting, teaching, and preaching a late tradition if we use them as our basis instead of the reliable and authoritative Bible.

F. G. Kenyon summarized, "There were more early vellum manuscripts of the Bible than of any other ancient book, and the interval between the date of composition and the earliest extant manuscripts was less in the case of the books of the New Testament than in that of any work of classical literature."[7] Daniel Wallace specifies, "We have more than 1,000 times as many copies of the NT as we do of almost any Greco-Roman author."[8] Many ancient manuscripts would last 100 to 150 years. Tertullian in the second century wrote that some of the original letters by Paul could be examined in Corinth, Philippi, Thessalonica, Ephesus, and Rome. In AD 300 Ephesus also had the original gospel of John.[9] Reading the Bible as God's revelation was so important to early Christians that they popularized the codex form (instead of scrolls).[10] Readers could quickly turn in the codex, like our books today, to specific pages.[11]

If reading the Bible as it was written by the original authors is important to us today, we need to make sure we verify the text.

PROCEDURE FOR CHOOSING THE TRUE TEXT

1. A quick glance may help.

Many Bibles have footnotes indicating, "Other ancient authorities. . . ." Those references are usually *not* the earliest texts. Texts marked by double brackets ([[. . .]]) "enclose passages which are regarded as later additions to the text, but which are of evident antiquity and importance."[12] These additions

---

7. F. G. Kenyon, *The Text of the Greek Bible*, 3rd ed. (London: Duckworth, 1975), 5–6.

8. Daniel B. Wallace, "Challenges in New Testament Textual Criticism for the Twenty-First Century," *Journal of the Evangelical Theological Society* 52, no. 1 (March 2009): 88.

9. Craig A. Evans, "How Long Were Late Antiquity Books in Use? Possible Implications for New Testament Textual Criticism," *Bulletin for Biblical Research* 25, no. 1 (2015): 28–32.

10. "For the first five hundred years of the Christian era, approximately ninety percent of all Christian books were written on a codex while only fourteen percent of all non-Christian books were written on a codex." Daniel B. Wallace, "Medieval Manuscripts and Modern Evangelicals: Lessons from the Past, Guidance for the Future," *Journal of the Evangelical Theological Society* 60, no. 1 (March 2017): 8.

11. Comfort, *Quest for the Original Text*, 49; E. Randolph Richards, "The Codex and the Early Collection of Paul's Letters," *Bulletin for Biblical Research* 8 (1998): 154, 164. According to Kurt Aland and Barbara Aland, "The codex form was used by Christian writers from the very beginning. . . . Only four of the ninety-six known papyri (p^{12}, $p^{13,}p^{18}$, p^{22}) are from scrolls" (*Text of the New Testament*, 102).

12. Barbara Aland, Kurt Aland, Johannes Karavidopoulos, Carlo M. Martini, and Bruce Metzger, eds., *The Greek New Testament*, 5th rev. ed. (New York: United Bible Societies, 2014), 58 Introduction, 891. See also Fee, *New Testament Exegesis*, 62–65; Blomberg and Markley, *Handbook of New Testament Exegesis*, 14–17.

82 | Preparation for the Study of the Text

are never the earliest texts. Why are they retained in our Bibles? They are well known and important to some Christians. They may be early traditions, but they are never the best New Testament texts.

The key Greek manuscripts are fourth-century Greek Codex Sinaiticus (א) and Codex Vaticanus (B) and early papyri.[13] If these all support the Greek text and are evaluated as {A} ("certain") by the UBS committee, most likely the text is the original.[14]

If the variant is unimportant for the meaning and interpretation of a text, you may ignore it for a sermon or a lesson. Most variants fall into this category.[15]

2. A more detailed look is necessary if completing a scholarly study for an exegesis paper or if the text is not certain.

I require my exegesis students to study thoroughly one variation unit. The UBS lists only texts its editors deem most important, but their apparatus is more detailed and easier to use than that of the Nestle-Aland text,[16] which has more variants, but its apparatus is less detailed and more difficult to use (because of many abbreviations). This chapter includes a summary of the findings for one variation unit in Philemon 4–6 (our sample exegesis paper). The sample listing for the exegesis paper and the blank "One Variation Unit" follow. I have found this format the most accessible to use.

Each variant is listed on the "One Variation Unit" sheet in the following sequence, from most important to less important for the evaluation process: Greek papyri,[17] Greek uncials or majuscules,[18] versions or translations, church fathers, minuscules,[19] and lectionaries. Since minuscules and

---

13. Metzger and Ehrman agree the concurrence of B and א is "very strong and shows that they cannot be far from the original text" (*Text of the New Testament*, 179).

14. See Aland et al., *The Greek New Testament*, 8–9 Introduction.

15. See Erickson, *Beginner's Guide*, 46–49. You may check for comparison purposes: Bruce M. Metzger, *A Textual Commentary on the Greek New Testament*, 2nd ed. (New York: American Bible Society, 2002).

16. Barbara Aland, Kurt Aland, Johannes Karavidopoulos, Carlo M. Martini, and Bruce Metzger, eds., *Novum Testamentum Graece*, 28th ed. (Stuttgart: Deutsche Bibelgesellschaft, 2012) (abbreviated as Nestle-Aland). To understand how to read the textual apparatus, a personal teacher is best, but some YouTube videos may be helpful, such as Florian Voss, "How to Use the Nestle-Aland," or David Hutchison, "Understanding the Symbols in Nestle-Aland 28."

17. A manuscript (MS, MSS) is a book written by hand. Papyri may be dated between AD 70 and 700. Papyrus is a plant twelve to fifteen feet in height, which at the time was cut and laid with two layers and then sold as a sheet or roll. The roll was wound around a stick (e.g., p^{52}, p^{75}) (Metzger and Ehrman, *Text of the New Testament*, 4, 7).

18. A majuscule, or uncial (AD 300–1100), was written in a more formal style of writing, similar to capital letters, indicated by zero followed by an Arabic number or by English or Greek capital letters. Often they were written on parchment, which was made from the skins of cattle, sheep, and goats, where the hair was removed, the skin washed, treated, dried, and lined with dots (e.g., א, B) (Metzger and Ehrman, *Text of the New Testament*, 9–10).

19. A minuscule (AD 900–1500) was written in smaller letters, similar to cursive, indicated by Arabic numbers, not preceded by zero (e.g., 81).

lectionaries are later, I have rarely found them to be important for the evaluation of a specific reading. The symbol and the date are easily listed for Greek papyri, uncials, and church fathers because these can be found in the UBS and/or Nestle-Aland introductions and appendices. Versions may be dated by the estimated date of the translation or the earliest date of a manuscript. I recommend students indicate both dates. The UBS will list only the dates of the original translation.

Outside of noting the date of the manuscripts, the text types (or types of texts) should also be noted. Text types will not be found in the UBS or Nestle-Aland Greek texts, but they can be found in a book introducing text criticism. To make the process simpler, I have summarized all the important papyri, uncials, and versions in the appendix to this chapter. The earliest manuscripts were copied from exemplars. Christian leaders tended to follow the principles of transmission of key schools.[20] (See figure 3.1.) Manuscripts can be placed in textual groups or affinities, wherein they agree (at least 70 percent) in all places of genetically significant variation. A "family" is a group of texts with a common origin, all descendants of one archetype.[21]

---

20. B. H. Streeter, *The Four Gospels: A Study of Origins*, rev. ed. (London: Macmillan, 1930), 24, chs. 2–5.
21. Metzger and Ehrman, *Text of the New Testament*, 87, 176, 234.

Map of Text Types

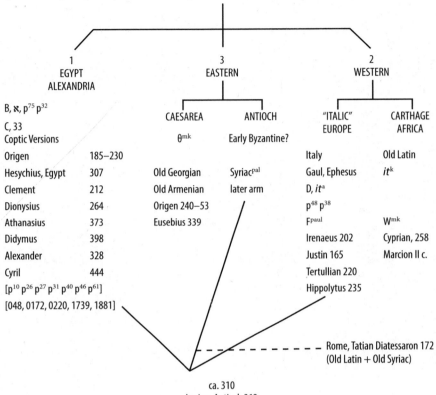

Figure 3.1. Map of text types

Most scholars agree that the Alexandrian school in Egypt had the best manuscripts. Alexandria was the center of the Christian world until the city was besieged by Muslim Arabs in AD 640.[22] Egypt had an excellent climate to preserve papyri. The gospel of John's earliest manuscript comes from Egypt

---

22. M. Bahy Hepny, "Alexandria," *Collier's Encyclopedia* (1987), 1:525.

(p^{52}). Papyrus[52] (excerpt of John 18) may be one of the two oldest extant New Testament manuscripts, dating from the late first century to c. AD 125. Papyrus[64] (excerpts from the gospel of Matthew) may have been written in the first century, after the destruction of the temple in Jerusalem (AD 70).[23] The goal of the Alexandrian school was to find the oldest manuscripts, not simply the most contemporary. Christians had their own college in Alexandria by AD 185, and many orthodox Christians taught there, including Clement, Origen (in his earliest years, AD 185–230), Dionysius, Athanasius, and Cyril.[24]

The second oldest text type is known as Western, which originally came from Carthage in Africa and Italy, Gaul, and Ephesus. Most scholars consider the Western text type to have the greatest number and most remarkable variations from what is usually taken to be the normal New Testament text. These scribes freely added and sometimes omitted words, sentences, and incidents. Bruce Metzger considered them to be the least reliable in terms of fidelity to the original text, although they may include early traditions. Codex Bezae (D) is an excellent example.[25] There was much travel between Ephesus and Rome. For instance, Irenaeus studied under Polycarp in Ephesus, and then he taught in Rome and Lyons.

The third text type is Caesarean, a text used by Origen when he moved to Caesarea in AD 240. This text is quoted by the church historian Eusebius, the bishop of Caesarea. There were two schools in the east, at Caesarea and at Antioch. The Caesarean text was formulated by someone who knew both the Western and Alexandrian readings and made a compromise between the two, generally following the Alexandrian text—for example, Codex Koridethi in the gospel of Mark (θ). The Armenian and Georgian versions used the Caesarean text type. Armenia was the first kingdom to declare itself a Christian nation (AD 287–314) under Tiridates III. Metzger called the Armenian version the "Queen of the Versions" because it is one of the most beautiful and accurate translations.[26]

The fourth text type is Byzantine (also known as Syrian, Ecclesiastical, Koine, Antiochian, or Common), which became the prevailing text throughout the Byzantine church when Emperor Constantine adopted it

---

23. Carston Peter Thiede, "Papyrus Magdalen Greek 17 (Gregory-Aland p[64]): A Reappraisal," *Tyndale Bulletin* 46, no. 1 (May 1995): 29–42. Both these papyri are Alexandrian text types. See also Comfort, *Early Manuscripts*, 55–59. Peter M. Head still dates p[64] at AD 200. See "The Date of the Magdalen Papyrus of Matthew (P. Magd. 17 = P64): A Response to C. P. Thiede," *Tyndale Bulletin* 46, no. 2 (November 1995): 251–85.

24. Metzger and Ehrman, *Text of the New Testament*, 277–78, 312–13. See also summary of text types in Blomberg and Markley, *Handbook of New Testament Exegesis*, 10; Erickson, *Beginner's Guide*, 43.

25. Metzger and Ehrman, *Text of the New Testament*, 71–73, 276–78, 307–9.

26. Metzger and Ehrman, *Text of the New Testament*, 117–18, 310–11; Bruce M. Metzger, *The Early Versions of the New Testament: Their Origin, Transmission, and Limitations* (Oxford: Clarendon, 1977), 153–54. The translation was done in the fourth century, but the earliest manuscript dates are from the fifth and sixth centuries.

86 | Preparation for the Study of the Text

at Constantinople (c. AD 380). John Chrysostom, as patriarch of Constantinople, promoted this text type. Lucian of Antioch in AD 310 revised the text of Antioch with the Alexandrian and Western text types. This text type aimed to smooth the text and make it easier to understand. After AD 600 there was a push by the church to make the Bible more standard. Most scholars consider the Byzantine text a later derivative text.[27] For example, Metzger and Ehrman pointed out, "No ante-Nicene father quotes a distinctively Syrian [Byzantine] reading."[28] If a variant is supported only by Byzantine texts, even though there are many, it is not the original text, which is the reason why Metzger reminded us, "Witnesses are to be weighed rather than counted."[29] Examples of Byzantine texts are Alexandrinus (A) in the Gospels (fifth century) or Codex Laudianus in the Gospels (E) or S (tenth century). Ulfilas (d. 380) used a predominately Byzantine text in his Gothic version.[30]

The Kurt Aland and Barbara Aland system gives five categories to text types: category 1 = early Alexandrian (e.g., א, B); categories 2–3 = Caesarean (e.g., C); category 4 = Western (e.g., D); category 5 = Byzantine (e.g., L).[31] Category 1 is closest to the original text, and category 5 is furthest away.

One Variation Unit: Philemon 6

Text in which variation unit is found: Philemon 6

                                               Student: [your name]

Greek ed. used: UBS 5th, Nestle-Aland 28th   Box/email: _____

---

27. Metzger and Ehrman, *Text of the New Testament,* 279–80. Harry A. Sturz, *The Byzantine Text-Type and New Testament Textual Criticism* (Nashville: Nelson, 1984). He shows some Byzantine elements are present in a few early papyri, such as p^{45}, p^{46}, and p^{66}. He claims the Byzantine text is simple, lucid, full, unpretentious, and plain in style.
28. Metzger and Ehrman, *Text of the New Testament,* 180–81.
29. Metzger and Ehrman, *Text of the New Testament,* 302.
30. Metzger and Ehrman, *Text of the New Testament,* 115–16. The translation was done in the fourth century, but the earliest MS dates from the fifth or sixth century.
31. Aland and Aland, *Text of the New Testament,* 335–36.

Witnesses	Variant 1: ἐν ἡμῖν			Variant 2: ἐν ὑμῖν			Variant 3: omit phrase		
	Symbol	Date	Text type	Symbol	Date	Text type	Symbol	Date	Text type
Greek papyri, uncials	A	5 c	Alex	p^{61}	AD 700	Alex + Byz			
	C	5 C	Byz + Alex	ℵ	4 C	Alex			
	D	6 C	West	F	9 C	West			
				G	9 C	West			
	K	9 C	Byz	P	9 C	Alex			
	L	9 C	Alex	0278	9 C				
	Ψ	8–10 C	Alex + Byz						
	048	5 C	Alex + Byz	075	10 C	Caes			
	0150	9 C	Caes						
Versions	it^d	5/6 C	West	it^{ar}	9 C	West	vg	6 C	West + Alex
	it^o	15 C	West	it^b	8–9 C	West	eth	(4–7) 15 C	Byz
	vg	541–46 (4 C)	West + Alex	it^f	9 C	West			
	syr^h	6 C	Byz	it^g	9 C	West			
	geo	897	Caes	vg	6 C	West + Alex			
Church fathers				syr^p	5 C	West			
	Chrysostom	d407	Byz	syr^h	6 C	West			
	Theodore	d428		cop^{sa}	(3–4) 6–7 C	Alex			
	Ambrosiaster	4 C		cop^{bo}	5 C	Alex			
	Jerome	d419		arm	(5 C) 887	Caes			
	Pelagius	4–5 C		slav	9 C	Byz			
Greek minuscules and lectionaries	81	1044	Alex	Chrysostom	407	Byz	629	14 C	Caes
	424	12 C							
	436	11 C		33	9 C	Alex			
	630	12–13 C		104	1087				
	1241	12 C	Byz	256	11 C				
Text types are Alexandrian, Western, Caesarean, and Byzantine. If unknown, leave blank	1319	12 C		263, 365	13 C				
	1852	13 C		459	1092				
	2200	14 C		1505	12 C				
				1573	12 C				
	Lect	10 C		1739	10 C	Alex			
				1881	14 C				
				l 590	11 C				
				l 680, 895	13 C				
				l 593, 1159	14–15 C				

Highlight the earliest and best-quality manuscripts and the variety of text types for each variant.

88 | Preparation for the Study of the Text

One Variation Unit: Blank

Text in which variation unit is found: _____ Student: [your name]

Greek ed. used: _____ Box/email: _____

Witnesses	Variant 1: _____			Variant 2: _____			Variant 3: _____		
	Symbol	Date	Text type	Symbol	Date	Text type	Symbol	Date	Text type
Place in the following sequence:									
Greek papyri, uncials									
Versions									
Church fathers									
Greek minuscules and lectionaries									
Text types are Alexandrian, Western, Caesarean, and Byzantine. If unknown, leave blank.									

Highlight the earliest and best-quality manuscripts and the variety of text types for each variant.

The "Summary Evaluation of Variation Unit" is used to summarize one's findings before writing them up in the exegesis paper. "External" evidence is the key evidence, relying on the earliest manuscripts, better quality text types, a variety of text types, and manuscripts that are not copies of one another (have no genealogical relationship). Normally scholars agree when looking only at external evidence. When might there be a difference of opinion? In rare cases, such as where one variant is supported only by early Alexandrian text types, while another variant has one early Alexandrian text and an early Western text. This reading would have a significant variety of text types, while the first variant would have a good-quality text type.

Then we can look at the versions. What do the early versions have? Often, changes made to later versions are done in order to be more acceptable to contemporary ecclesiastical pressures. Sometimes the church fathers may comment on readings, which is always helpful. Philip Wesley Comfort proposed that "the original text looked like א and B in most books. . . . The Alexandrian scribes faithfully transmitted the original text (with minor editorial revisions)."[32] He suggested specific early papyri that he considered to be ancestors of these fourth-century uncials for each New Testament book in his book *The Quest for the Original Text of the New Testament.*

I recommend choosing the best variant reading based on external evidence, and then making scholarly hypotheses for how the other variants may have occurred, based on transcriptional and intrinsic probabilities (which is internal evidence). Scribes might simplify or might make copying errors. (See the following "Basic Criteria for Evaluating Variant Readings" outline.) For example, a scribe might accidentally omit or repeat a letter or word. Such internal evidence, based on guesswork, is subjective while external evidence is more objective. However, internal evidence might be helpful if the external evidence is inconclusive. If only internal evidence is used, the interpreter, in effect, becomes the basis for authority. Some students incline toward subjective probabilities because doing so is easy, but they forget it is also dangerous. Anyone with a good imagination can come up with a probability and, as a result, undermine the true text. Context can help us interpret a text, but it does not help us guess what was the original text. Can we presume to predict every word of a person who lived two thousand years ago? What is to keep our desire to justify any sinful action or our comfortable lifestyle or any present limited understanding of God from being the criteria for choosing a certain variant reading? A reading may sound pietistic but not reflect God's revelatory word. Looking at internal evidence is worthwhile as long as it is supplementary to external evidence.[33]

---

32. Comfort, *Quest for the Original Text,* 104.
33. Fee agreed that the criterion of intrinsic probability is "the most subjective of all the criteria and therefore must be used with caution" (*New Testament Exegesis,* 67).

90 | Preparation for the Study of the Text

Even not knowing Greek, students can choose the best variant. However, they will not know what they have chosen! Discovering the true text is the preliminary step before doing an interpretation of the meaning of the passage.

Basic Criteria for Evaluating Variant Readings[34]

I. External evidence.
    A. The date of the witness and the type of text it embodies.
    B. The variety of text types and the geographical distribution of the witnesses who agree in supporting a variant.
    C. The genealogical relationship of texts and families of witnesses.
II. Internal evidence.
    A. Transcriptional probabilities (unintentional and intentional).
        1. In general the more difficult reading to the scribe is to be preferred.
        2. In general the shorter reading is to be preferred, except in these cases:
            a. Parablepsis (a looking to the side) arising from homoeoteleuton (a similar ending of lines) may have occurred.
            b. A scribe may have omitted material that (s)he deemed to be superfluous, harsh, or contrary to pious belief. Haplography (accidental omission of one or two or more similar letters, syllabi, words, phrases, etc.) is possible.
        3. In general the passage that is not parallel with its same event or narrative is preferred. However, of course, the original reading may be harmonious with its parallel.
        4. Scribes would sometimes replace an unfamiliar word with a familiar synonym, adjust a less refined grammatical form or less elegant lexical expression to a more elegant expression or a contemporary atticizing preference, or add pronouns and conjunctions to make a smooth text.
        5. Scribes may have accidentally repeated letters or words (dittography). This error is the opposite of haplography.
    B. Intrinsic probabilities.
        1. The reading chosen should be similar to the style and vocabulary of the author throughout the book or letter.
        2. The reading should fit in the drift of the immediate context.
        3. The reading should be harmonious with the teaching of the author elsewhere and in the Gospels.

---

34. This outline is an adaption of Metzger and Ehrman, *Text of the New Testament*, 302–5. See also Blomberg and Markley, *Handbook of New Testament Exegesis*, 19–24.

Summary Evaluation of Variation Unit: Philemon 6

Passage: Philemon 6   Name: Box/email: _____

Greek text(s) and other references: UBS 5th edition, supplemented by Nestle-Aland 28th edition.

Variant chosen: #2—ἐν ἡμῖν.

I.   External evidence.
     A.   Earliest support: fourth century—ℵ, syrᴾ—fifth century.
     B.   Text type(s) Alexandrian, Western, Caesarean, Byzantine.
     C.   Geographic distribution and genealogical distinctiveness (variety): yes.
     D.   Quality of supporting witnesses: ℵ only complete New Testament and early uncial; all Coptic versions.

II. Transcriptional probabilities.

If original, how one would explain variants not chosen:

Variant #1: conscious effort to be more inclusive or accidental error because of closeness in sound.

Variant #3: simplify sentence.

Summarize why external evidence for variants *not* chosen is inferior:

Variant 3 has very late support. Variant 1 has good support (fifth century) and variety of text types, but the Alexandrian texts are later.

III. Intrinsic probabilities (optional). Is variant chosen reinforced by the following?
     A.   Comparison with author's vocabulary: _____.
     B.   Comparison with context: "Among you" fits context well since Paul addressed Philemon's faith.
     C.   Comparison with teaching of author elsewhere and rest of New Testament: _____.

Overall evaluation: Variants 1 and 2 are both good, but variant 2 is better.

Preparation for the Study of the Text

Summary Evaluation of Variation Unit: Blank

Passage: _____   Student: [your name]

Greek text(s) and other references: _____   Box/email: _____

Variant chosen as original text: _____

I.   External evidence

    A. Earliest support: _____
    B. Text type(s): _____
    C. Geographic distribution and genealogical distinctiveness (variety): _____
    D. Quality of supporting witnesses: _____

II. Transcriptional probabilities

If the variant you have chosen is original, how might you explain how the other variants not chosen came about?

Variant #: _____

Variant #: _____

Variant #: _____

Summarize why external evidence for variants *not* chosen is inferior: _____

III. Intrinsic probabilities (optional). Is variant chosen reinforced by the following?

    A. Comparison with author's vocabulary: _____
    B. Comparison with context: _____
    C. Comparison with teaching of author elsewhere and rest of New Testament: _____

Overall evaluation: _____

HOW TO AVOID COMMON ERRORS

1.   Some manuscripts have a one-letter symbol but a different date for the Gospels and Paul's letters. For example, D is a Western text type.

The Gospels and Acts in Codex Bezae (also known as Codex Cantabrigiensis) are dated to the fifth century, while D^p (or D^2) for Paul's letters is dated to the sixth century (Codex Claromontanus).[35]

2. Nestle-Aland will sometimes list one-half of the evidence for a variation unit, the evidence for one to two variant(s), but not all of them. To find the evidence for the variant chosen for the text, the interpreter must find the "Consistently Cited Witnesses" for that letter in the introduction[36] and then do two steps:
    a. Delete any witnesses cited in the "Consistently Cited Witnesses" used for the variant(s) cited in the apparatus.
    b. Delete any witnesses that do not have the verse being studied.

To find what verses are in particular manuscripts, one must look in the appendix under "Codices Graeci et Latini in Hac Editione Adhibiti" in the far-right column (cont.). For example, Philemon 6 has a variant that adds the word *ergou* after *pantes*. It is supported by F and G. The omission of *ergou,* according to the "Consistently Cited Witnesses" paragraph for Philemon, includes p^{61}, p^{87}, ℵ, A, C, D, I, K, L, P, ψ, 048, and 0278, as well as some minuscules. According to appendix I.A, "Codices Graeci," Philemon 6 is not included in p^{87}, C, or I. Therefore, by subtraction, the omission of *ergou* is supported by p^{61}, ℵ, A, D, K, L, P, ψ, 048, and 0278. Since G is a copy of F, the two manuscripts serve in the same family. Omission of *ergou* is supported by the earliest manuscripts (fourth-century ℵ, fifth-century A and 048), good-quality Alexandrian text types (ℵ, A, P, ψ, 048), and a full variety of text types (Western [D]; Byzantine [L]; and Caesarean [p^{61}, K]). One way to simplify this process is by photocopying the consistently cited witnesses when studying a particular book of the Bible. If you will be studying several variation units in one book, making your own list of consistently cited manuscripts with the age and text type for each manuscript will speed the analysis of individual passages. A shorter way to do the same exercise is to use the evidence cited for a previous variation unit, but it may not be completely accurate. These extra steps are never needed when using the UBS text, since it lists in the apparatus at the bottom of the page all of the evidence for all of the variants in the variation unit.

3. Do not treat the Nestle-Aland "*textus*" as the original text. *Textus* is simply the variant reading that was chosen in this particular edition by the Nestle-Aland committee.
4. Choose by external, not internal, evidence.
5. Do not be afraid to choose the best text.

---

35. Metzger and Ehrman, *Text of the New Testament,* 70–74.
36. Aland, et al., *Novum Testamentum Graece,* Introduction III.2.

94 | Preparation for the Study of the Text

6. Spell "minuscule" correctly (not "miniscule").
7. Remember to note date and text types of manuscripts in parentheses in your exegesis paper, as demonstrated in the sample exegesis paper in chapter 8 and also in the number 2 common error listed here.

APPENDIX: IMPORTANT WITNESSES FOR THE NEW TESTAMENT: PAPYRI, UNCIALS, VERSIONS

Papyri through the First Four Centuries

Manuscript	Age	Text Type	Aland's Category	Content
P^1	III	Alexandrian	1	Matt. 1:1–9, 12, 14–20
P^4	II–III	Alexandrian, similar to p^{64}	1	Pt. Luke
P^5	III	Alexandrian	1	Pt. John
P^6	IV	Alexandrian	2	Pt. John
P^8	IV	Alexandrian	2	Pt. Acts
P^9	III		1	1 John 4:11–12, 14–17
P^{10}	IV	Alexandrian	1	Rom. 1:1–7
P^{12}	III		1	Heb. 1:1
P^{13}	III–IV	Alexandrian	1	Pt. Heb.
P^{15}	III	Alexandrian	1	1 Cor. 7:18–8:4
P^{16}	III–IV	Alexandrian	1	Phil. 3:10–17; 4:2–8
P^{17}	IV	Alexandrian and Byzantine	2	Heb. 9:12–19
P^{18}	III–IV	Alexandrian	1	Rev. 1:4–7
P^{19}	IV–V		2	Matt. 10:32–11:5
P^{20}	c. 275	Alexandrian	1	James 2:19–3:9
P^{21}	IV	Alexandrian and Western	3	Matt. 12:24–26, 32–33
P^{22}	III	Alexandrian?	1	Pt. John
P^{23}	250–300	Alexandrian	1	James 1:10–12, 15–18
P^{24}	III–IV	Alexandrian	1	Rev. 5:5–8; 6:5–8
P^{25}	IV			Pt. Matt.
P^{27}	III	Alexandrian	1	Pt. Rom.
P^{28}	III	Alexandrian	1	John 6:8–12, 17–22
P^{29}	III	Western	1	Acts 26:7–8, 20
P^{30}	III	Alexandrian	1	Pt. 1, 2 Thess.
P^{32}	c. 175–200	Alexandrian	1	Titus 1:11–15; 2:3–8
P^{35}	IV?	Alexandrian	1	Matt. 25:12–15, 20–23
P^{37}	III	Caesarean	1	Matt. 26:19–52
P^{38}	c. 300	Western	4	Acts 18:27–19:6, 12–16
P^{39}	III	Alexandrian	1	John 8:14–22
P^{40}	III	Alexandrian	1	Pt. Rom.
P^{45}	150–250	Caesarean	1	Pt. Matt., Mark, Luke, John, Acts
P^{46}	85–200	Alexandrian	1	Pt. Paul's writings (p)[37]
P^{47}	III	Alexandrian	1	Pt. Rev.

---

37. Abbreviations: e = Gospels; a = Acts; p = Paul's letters and Hebrews; c = Catholic letters; r = Revelation; pt. = part (of a New Testament book). If "part" is indicated, check Nestle-Aland appendix for specific content.

Manuscript	Age	Text Type	Aland's Category	Content
P[48]	c. 220	Western	4	Acts 23:11–17:25–29
P[49]	III	Alexandrian	1	Eph. 4:16–29; 4:32–5:13
P[50]	IV–V	Alexandrian	3	Acts 8:26–32; 10:26–31
P[52]	c. late I–125	Alexandrian	1	John 18:31–33, 37–38
P[53]	c. 260	Alexandrian	1	Pt. Matt; Acts
P[57]	IV–V	Alexandrian	2	Acts 4:36–5:2, 8–10
P[62]	IV	Alexandrian	2	Matt. 11:25–30
P[64/67]	c. late I (75)–200	Alexandrian	1	Pt. Matt.
P[65]	III	Alexandrian	1	1 Thess. 1:3–2:1, 6–13
P[66]	c. 125–200	Alexandrian and Western	1	Pt. John
P[69]	III	Western	4	Pt. Luke 22
P[70]	III		1	Pt. Matt.
P[71]	IV	Alexandrian	2	Matt. 19:10–11, 17–18
P[72]	c. 275	Alexandrian	1	Pt. 1, 2 Peter, Jude
P[75]	150–225	Alexandrian	1	Pt. Luke, John
P[77]	II–III	Alexandrian	1	Matt. 23:30–39[38]
P[78]	III–IV		1	Jude 4–5, 7–8
P[80]	III		1	John 3:34
P[81]	IV	Alexandrian	2	1 Peter 2:20–3:1, 4–12
P[82]	IV–V	Alexandrian	2	Luke 7:32–34, 37–38
P[85]	IV–V	Alexandrian	2	Rev. 9:19–10:1, 5–9
P[86]	III	Alexandrian	2	Matt. 5:13–16, 22–25
P[87]	II–III	Alexandrian	1	Philem. 13–15, 24–25
P[88]	IV	Alexandrian	3	Mark 2:1–26
P[89]	IV			Heb. 6:7–9, 15–17
P[90]	150–175	Alexandrian and Western		John 18:36–19:1–7
P[91]	III	Alexandrian		Acts 2:20–37, 46–3:2
P[92]	III–IV	Alexandrian		Pt. Eph.; 2 Thess.
P[95]	III			John 5:26–29, 36–38
P[98]	II?			Rev. 1:13–20
P[100]	III–IV			James 3:13–4:4, 8–5:1
P[101]	III			Matt. 3:10–12; 3:16–4:3
P[102]	III–IV			Matt. 4:11–12; 4:22–23
P[103]	II–III			Matt. 13:55–56; 14:3–5
P[104]	II			Matt. 21:34–37, 43–45?
P[106]	III			John 1:29–35, 40–46
P[107]	III			John 17:1–2, 11
P[108]	III			John 17:23–24; 18:1–5
P[109]	III			John 21:18–20, 23–25
P[110]	IV			Matt. 10:13–15, 25–27
P[111]	III	Alexandrian	1	Luke 17:11–13, 22–23
P[113]	III			Rom. 2:12–13, 29
P[114]	III			Heb. 1:7–12
P[115]	III–IV	Alexandrian and Byzantine		Pt. Rev.

---

38. See the discussion in Peter M. Head, "Some Recently Published New Testament Papyri from Oxyrhynchus: An Overview and Preliminary Assessment," *Tyndale Bulletin* 51, no. 1 (2000): 1–16.

Manuscript	Age	Text Type	Aland's Category	Content
p117	IV–V			2 Cor. 7:6–8, 9–11
p118	III			Pt. Rom.
p119	III			John 1:21–28, 38–44
p120	IV			Pt. John 1
p121	III			John 19:17–18, 25–26
p122	IV–V?			Pt. John 21
p123	IV			Pt. 1 Cor.
p125	III–IV			1 Peter 1:23–2:5, 7–12
p126	IV			Heb. 13:12–13, 19–20
p133	III			1 Tim. 3:13–4:8
p137	150–200			Mark 1:7–9, 16–18
p138	200–300			Luke 13:13–17, 25–30
p139	IV–V			Philem. 6–8, 18–20
p141	200–300			Pt. Luke

Uncials through the first nine centuries

Manuscript	Age	Text Type	Aland's Category	Content
ℵ 01 Sinaiticus	IV ℵ² 6–7 C, ℵ³ 12 C	Alexandrian	1	All
A 02 Alexandrinus	V	Byzantine in Gospels; Alexandrian rest	3	All (missing pt. Matt, John, 2 Cor.)
B 03 Vaticanus	IV, B² 6–7 C	Alexandrian	1	eap (missing 1 Tim.–Philem.; pt. Heb.)
C 04 Ephraemi	V, C² 6 C, C³ 9 C	Alexandrian and Byzantine	2	Pt. eapr
D 05 Bezae/Cantabrigiensis	V, D¹ 6–7 C, D² 9 C, D³ 12 C	Western	4	ea
Dp (D²) 06 Claromontanus	VI	Western	2	p (missing Phil, 1, 2 Thess)
E 07 Basiliensis	VIII	Byzantine	5	e
Eᵃ (E²) 08 Laudianus	VI	Western and Byzantine	2	a
Ep (E³) Sangermanensis	IX–X	Western, copy of Dp		p
Fᵉ 09 Boreelianus	IX	Byzantine	5	e
Fp (F²) 010 Augiensis	IX	Western	2	p
G 011 Wolfii A/ Harleianus/Seidelianus I	IX	Byzantine	5	e
Gp (G³) 012 Boernerianous	IX	Western, similar to Fp	3	p
Hᶜ 013 Wolfii B/Seidelianus II	IX	Byzantine	5	e
Hᵃ (H²) 014 Mutinensis	IX	Byzantine	5	a
Hp (H³) 015 Coislinianus	VI	Alexandrian	3	p
I 016 Washingtonensis/ Freemanus	V	Alexandrian	2	p (missing Rom.)
Kᶜ 017 Cyprius	IX	Byzantine	5	e
Kᵃp (K²) 018 Mosquensis	IX	Byzantine		apc
Lᵉ 019 Regius	VIII	Alexandrian	2	e
Lᵃp (L²) 020 Angelicus	IX	Byzantine	5	apc
M 021 Campianus	IX	Byzantine	5	e
N 022 Purpureus Petropoolitanus	VI	Byzantine	5	Pt. e
O 023 Sinopensis	VI	Caesarean/Byzantine	5	Matt. 13–24
Pᵉ 024 Guelferbytanus A	VI	Byzantine in Acts	5	ep
Pᵃpr (P²) 025 Porphyrianus	IX	Alexandrian; Byzantine in Acts and Revelation	3/5	pacr

Manuscript	Age	Text Type	Aland's Category	Content
Q 026 Guelferbytanus B	V	Part Byzantine	5	Luke, John
R 027 Nitriensis	VI	Western/Byzantine	5	Luke
T 029 Borgianus	V	Alexandrian	2	Pt. Luke, John
U 030 Nanianus	IX	Byzantine	5	e
V 031 Mosquensis	IX	Byzantine	5	e
W 032 Freerianus	IV–V (VII–John 1:1–5:11)	Alexandrian (Luke 1:1–8:12; John), Byzantine (Matt.; Luke 8:13–24:53); Western in Mark 1:1–5:30; Caesarean in Mark 5:31–16:20	3	e
Y 034 Macedoniensis	IX	Byzantine	5	e
Z 035 Dublinensis	VI	Alexandrian	3	Pt. Matt.
Δ 037 Sangallensis	IX	Byzantine; Alexandrian in Mark	3	e
Θ 038 Koridethi	IX	Byzantine; Caesarean in Mark	2	e
Λ 039 Tischendorfianus	IX	Byzantine	5	e
Ξ 040 Zacynthius	VI	Alexandrian	3	Pt. Luke
Π 041 Petropolitanus	IX	Byzantine	5	e
Σ 042 Rossanensis	VI	Byzantine	5	Matt., Mark
Φ 043 Beratinus	VI	Byzantine	5	Matt., Mark
Ψ 044 Athous Laurae	VIII–IX	Byzantine in Matt., Luke, John; Alexandrian + Western in Mark	3/2	eapc
Ω 045 Athous Dionysiou	IX	Byzantine	5	e

The following uncials include only the first four centuries

Manuscript	Age	Text Type	Aland's Category	Content
057	IV–V		1	Pt. Acts
058	IV		3?	Pt. Matt.
059	IV–V		3	Pt. Mark
0160	IV–V		3	Pt. Matt.
0162	III		1	John 2:11–22
0169	IV		3	Rev. 3:19–4:3
0171	300	Western	4	Pt. Matt.; Luke
0176	IV–V		3	Gal. 3:16–25
0181	IV–V		2	Luke 9:59–10:14
0185	IV		2	Pt. 1 Cor.
0188	IV		3	Mark 11:11–17
0189	II–III	Alexandrian	1	Acts 5:3–21
0206	IV		3	1 Peter 5:5–13
0207	IV		3	Rev. 9:2–15
0212 Tatian's *Diatesseron*	III	Western		Pt. e
0214	IV–V		3	Mark 8:33–37
0219	IV–V		3	Pt. Rom.
0220	III	Alexandrian	1	Rom. 4:23–5:3, 8–13
0221	IV		3	Pt. Rom.
0228	IV		3	Pt. Heb.
0230	IV		–	Eph. 6:11–12

Preparation for the Study of the Text

Manuscript	Age	Text Type	Aland's Category	Content
0231	IV		3	Pt. Matt.
0242	IV		3	Pt. Matt.
0270	IV–V		2	Pt. 1 Cor.

Early versions

Manuscript	Age	Text Type		Content
Arm Armenian	IX–X (5 C)	Caesarean		All
cop^{sa} Coptic Sahidic	III–VII (3–4 C)	Alexandrian		All
cop^{bo} Bohairic	IV–IX (4 C)	Alexandrian		All
cop^{fay} Fayyumic	IV–VII	Alexandrian		eapc
cop^{ach} cop^{ach2} Achmimic	IV–V (3 C)	Alexandrian		epc
Eth Ethiopic	X–XV (4–7 C)	Byzantine and Alexandrian		All
Geo Georgian	IX–X (5 C)	Caesarean		All
Goth Gothic	V–VI (4 C)	Byzantine		ep
Slav Slavonic	X–XIII (9 C)	Byzantine		All
syr^s, syr^c Old Syriac	IV–V (2–3 C)	Western		e
syr^p Peshitta	V–VI(5 C)	Byzantine in Gospels; Western in Acts		eapc
syr^{pal} Palestinian	XI–XII (5–6 C)	Caesarean		eap
syr^h syr^{ph} Harclean, Philoxenian	VI–XII (6 C)	Western		All
Vulgate in Latin	V–VII (382)	Western and Alexandrian		All
Italic or Old Latin	IV–XIII (2–3 C)	Western		All
it^a Vercellensis	IV	Western European		e
it^k Bobbiensis	400	Western African		Pt. Matt.; Luke

References used: Metzger and Ehrman, *Text of the New Testament,* is the primary reference. Dr. Bruce Metzger was my professor for paleography and textual criticism. He is known for his high view of the Bible and his careful work. While Dr. Metzger was alive, Dr. Bart Ehrman revised Metzger's text with his consultation and agreement. My chart was supplemented by Aland and Aland, *Text of the New Testament.* Aland and Aland have a thorough listing of manuscripts up to the time of the publication of their book. Comfort, *Early Manuscripts and Modern Translations of the New Testament,* was a helpful digest of data from a high view of the Bible. The appendix of the 28th edition of *Novum Testamentum Graece* has a thorough listing of all manuscripts. The committee included Barbara Aland and Kurt Aland and Dr. Metzger. Metzger, *Early Versions of the New Testament,* has a thorough discussion. For an update on recent papyri, I consulted "List of New Testament Papyri," https://en.wikipedia.org/wiki/List_of_New_ Testament_papyri, accessed April 10, 2023. New papyri are continually being discovered. My list is dated to the 2023 findings. The Center for the Study of New Testament Manuscripts (https://manuscripts.csntm. org/) may also help. Do not hesitate to add papyri to your own list as they are being discovered.

PART 3

IN-DEPTH STUDY OF THE TEXT

CHAPTER 4

SEEK A TRANSLATION AND UNDERSTAND THE GRAMMAR OF THE TEXT

UNDERSTAND THE GRAMMAR OF THE TEXT

I. Study the internal structure of words.
   A. *Parse* and list possible meanings for every word in your text. Do your own parsing, using only grammar books and lexicons. Remember to mention basic parts of speech, such as subject, verb, direct object, indirect object, adverb, preposition, conjunction, and so on. After your own work is complete, double-check any difficult parsing.
   B. Determine how grammatical categories might help *explain* the meaning of a text. Ask, "What difference does the parsing make?" The more grammar one knows, the more this area of inquiry can be developed. Decide what aspect of morphology may help most. But, conversely, do not attempt to apply what you do not know. Always relate back to the specific context of the text.
   C. Engage in some sample activities:
      1. Choose the types of participles, infinitives, cases, and conditional sentences you may have.
         a. Participles can be adjectival or adverbial.
         b. Infinitives can be substantive or verbal.
         c. Datives can be proper, locative, or instrumental.
         d. Genitives can function like adjectives (adnominal), adverbs, or ablatives.
      2. Divide the text into sentences and clauses. (See II. Study the external structure of words.)
      3. Analyze Greek tense, use of articles, and so on.

102 | In-Depth Study of the Text

    D. Optional: Fill out a grammatical information sheet if your professor wants to double-check your work. Note your text at the top. Jot down information verse by verse. Every word must be included. List the article with the word modified.
1. "Text form" is the Greek word as it appears in the New Testament.
2. "Lexical form" is the form of each Greek word in the lexicon.
3. "Description" is the full parsing, including the basic part of speech.
4. "Use/meaning" is the definition plus any significance of the grammar.
II. *Study* the external structure of words.

This chapter can be done principally by Greek readers, but some aspects can be done by translation readers.

INTRODUCTION

For me, the two most helpful aspects of the exegetical process are studying the wider context of the New Testament book and doing a translation. Studying the wider context sets our thoughts in the most appropriate context. Translation is another way to enter another culture. Sometimes even speaking another language can evoke aspects of our character that are dormant. For example, I found that my Dutch father was more relational when he spoke in Spanish as opposed to English. Why did Jesus sometimes speak in Aramaic? One reason may be that he thereby spoke more intimately, as when he prayed, "*Abba*, Father," in Gethsemane (Mark 14:36) and cried at the cross, "*Eloi, Eloi, lama sabachthani*" (Mark 15:34). Normally, when reading Greek, we may want speed and therefore jot down only the words we do *not* know, using a helpful reader's lexicon that provides less frequent vocabulary,[1] but for exegesis, being careful and slow is advised for accuracy.

Overuse of analytical lexicons that give all the parsing and vocabulary acts like a sleeping pill. Sleeping pills are fine for emergencies, but if overused, they deprive us of our own ability to sleep. Analytical lexicons, whether software or printed, should be saved for the end of the process to double-check parsing, as Bill Mounce recommends: "When you cannot discover the word's parsing or are not sure."[2] When it comes to careful exegesis, though, every word should be parsed, also indicating the basic part of speech, how the word is functioning in

---

1. E.g., Michael H. Burer and Jeffrey E. Miller, *A New Reader's Lexicon of the Greek New Testament* (Grand Rapids: Kregel, 2008); Sakae Kubo, *A Reader's Greek-English Lexicon of the New Testament* (Grand Rapids: Zondervan, 1975).
2. William D. Mounce, *The Analytical Lexicon to the Greek New Testament* (Grand Rapids: Zondervan, 1993), ix.

the sentence as a noun, adjective, verb, adverb, or pronoun. If the parsing will be checked by another person, you may follow the example in the appendix of this chapter of Grammatical Information Sheet: Blank.

Here are some reminders of the meaning of parts of speech.

BASIC GRAMMATICAL CATEGORIES

Subjects: Identify the people, places, things, ideas, qualities, or conditions that act, are acted upon, or are described in a sentence. A subject can be a noun, pronoun, phrase, or clause.[3]

Verbs: These words express action that is performed by or to the subject or the state of being of the subject.

Objects: Nouns or pronouns (and in Greek a phrase or clause)[4] that complete the ideas expressed by subjects and verbs.
  A. **Direct objects:** The word(s) denotes the thing(s)/person(s) that receives the action of the verb and answers the question what or to whom.
  B. **Indirect objects:** The word(s) denotes the thing(s)/person(s) indirectly affected by the action of the verb and answers the questions to whom or to what or for whom or for what.

Modifiers: These describe or limit subjects, verbs, objects, complements, or other modifiers (e.g., adjectives, adverbs, prepositional phrases).
  A. **Adjectives:** These words modify a noun or pronoun. In Greek an adjective in form (also frequently genitives) can function as a noun or adverb.
  B. **Adverbs:** Such words modify verbs, adjectives, adverbs, phrases, or clauses. In Greek an adverb in form can be used as an adjective or noun in function.

Grammar is a broad term, traditionally describing the study of the form of words (*morphology*) and the manner of their combination in phrases, clauses, and sentences to show their mutual relations (*syntax*). Syntax comprises the rules governing the combination of words in sentences or the orderly arrangement and interrelationships of words, their thought relations. Syntax is the external structure of words, while morphology refers to the internal structure

---

3. For these definitions, see Joseph F. Trimmer, *The New Writing with a Purpose*, 14th ed. (Boston: Houghton Mifflin, 2004), 476–78.
4. E.g., an infinitive phrase can serve as the subject or object of a sentence. Daniel B. Wallace, *Greek Grammar beyond the Basics: An Exegetical Syntax of the New Testament* (Grand Rapids: Zondervan, 1996), 590.

of words. Morphology also includes inflection, a change in the form of a word to express its relation to other words in a sentence. Morphology also includes derivation, the way new words are formed from existing words or roots.[5] We might use, as an analogy, a comparison between police and ministers or counselors. Police, like syntax, emphasize the orderly arrangement of people. Ministers and counselors, like morphology, want more the internal change of the individual. All are necessary for a better society.

Greek and Latin are "inflecting" languages, in which many changes within words express their relation to other words. English is a more "analytic" or isolating language than Greek, in which words tend to be more constant or uniform. Chinese and Vietnamese are also even more analytic or isolating languages.[6]

Once the text is parsed and translated, as interpreters we should ask questions of the text, for example, grammatical questions, such as "Why does Paul exhort 'through the mercies of God' in Romans 12:1?" In Philemon 4–6, how can Paul thank God and then expect that Philemon will become more active in sharing his faith? What is the relationship between sharing one's faith and having the knowledge of good? What kind of faith does Philemon have? Then consider the significance of what you have found. Never assume any part of a sentence can be ignored. The writer, inspired by God, thought each part was essential. No interpretation should be adopted unless it is grammatically possible, but syntax does not settle all questions of interpretation. Do not try to separate the syntactical links the author joined together. As Berkeley Mickelsen advised, "All such separations (for even the most noble of purposes) will only lead to eisegesis (reading in of one's own ideas). Eisegesis is the substitution of the authority of the interpreter for the authority of the original writer."[7]

Here are some basic reminders about some Greek parts of speech.

GREEK PARTS OF SPEECH

I.   Overview of Greek Verb(s)
    A.   Greek has tense and aspect.[8]

	Three Kinds of Action	Time of Action	State of Action: Past
1	Durative or linear (–) action in progress	Primary (present)	Secondary (augmented verb: imperfect)
2	Punctiliar (.)	Future	Aorist
3	Perfected (· –)	Pluperfect	Perfect

---

5.   John Lyons, *Introduction to Theoretical Linguistics* (Cambridge: Cambridge University Press, 1968), 54, 194–95.

6.   Lyons, *Theoretical Linguistics*, 187–89, 192.

7.   A. Berkeley Mickelsen, *Interpreting the Bible* (Grand Rapids: Eerdmans, 1963), 158.

8.   See A. T. Robertson, *A Grammar of the Greek New Testament in the Light of Historical Research* (Nashville: Broadman, 1934), 344. Both aspect and time have been consistent understandings of the Greek verb. See Chrys C. Caragounis, *The Development of Greek and the New Testament: Morphology, Syntax, Phonology, and Textual Transmission* (Grand Rapids: Baker Academic, 2006), 316–36.

B. Voice. Relates action to the subject.
1. Active. The subject is represented as acting or existing (most common).
2. Middle. The subject is acting in relation to himself/herself. It calls especial attention to the subject.
3. Passive. The subject is represented as the recipient of the action. Subject is acted upon.
C. Mood/mode. An attitude of mind in which the speaker conceives the matter stated. The manner of affirmation.
1. Indicative. A positive assertion, states a thing is true. Reality is perceived as actual. (Most common.)
2. Subjunctive. Doubtful statement, implying possibility, doubt, hesitation, proposal, will, hope. Reality is perceived as possible or potential. (Optative is more doubtful: wish, hope, prayer.)
3. Imperative. Commanding statement, ordering life to change. Action is possible only if one person's will prevails over another.
4. Infinitives and participles. Infinitive is a verbal noun. Participles are verbal adjectives.[9]
II. Prepositions. An adverb specialized to define a case usage. Study of root idea or ground meaning can assist effect in each context.
III. Articles aid in pointing out, like an index finger.[10]

The first half of the study of the external structure of words follows.

HOW TO STUDY THE EXTERNAL STRUCTURE OF WORDS: A SENTENCE FLOW (PART 1)

I. Divide Greek passage into sentences and clauses.
A. Divide text into sentences.
B. Classify each sentence by function: statement, question, exclamation, or command.
C. Classify and analyze the elements of each sentence.
1. Identify each clause (by finding all finite verbs).

---

9. "There are few languages that have equaled the Greek in the abundance and variety of its use of the participle, and certainly none has surpassed it." H. E. Dana and Julius R. Mantey, *A Manual Grammar of the Greek New Testament* (Toronto: Macmillan, 1955), 220.

10. "Nothing is more indigenous to the Greek language than its use of the article" (Dana and Mantey, *Manual Grammar*, 135). For further information on grammar, see Robertson, *Grammar of the Greek New Testament*, "syntax"; William W. Klein, Craig L. Blomberg, and Robert L. Hubbard Jr., *Introduction to Biblical Interpretation*, 3rd ed. (Grand Rapids: Zondervan, 2017) ch. 7, 344–60; Wallace, *Greek Grammar*.

In-Depth Study of the Text

2. Classify each clause as main (independent) or subordinate (dependent).
3. Classify each subordinate clause as adverbial, adjectival, nominal (noun), or parenthetical.
4. Classify each adverbial clause as conditional, temporal, local, comparative, causal, or final (purpose or result).

II. Visualize the flow of the argument by showing how the parts of the sentences relate to each other.

III. Analyze the relation of the sentences to each other, if time permits.

A variety of methods can be employed to study the external structure of words. Three samples are included in this chapter: sentence flow, diagram, and discourse analysis. I recommend the sentence flow format because it does not require as much grammatical knowledge as diagramming, is simpler than the discourse analysis, separates grammar from style analysis, and is easier to transfer to interpretation.

Steps in Doing a Sentence Flow

1. Begin by *dividing the text into sentences,* by choosing punctuation according to thought units and considering New Testament Greek punctuation. Do not simply copy English punctuation. Verse categorization is a late process. Robert Estienne (Stephanus) in his fourth edition of the *Greek New Testament* (1551) first divided the text into numbered verses while journeying from Paris to Lyons.[11] Early Greek manuscripts might leave spaces to indicate new thought units. Because of the nature of English, most sentences in English are much shorter than their Greek originals. The United Bible Society (UBS) text includes notes at the bottom of each page to show differences in punctuation. For instance, the Greek UBS text for Philemon 4–6 has two sentences, but I chose one sentence for the three verses because the Greek has only one finite main verb ("I am thanking," v. 4). "So that" introduces a subordinate adverbial clause dependent on verse 4. (See my "Sentence Flow of Philemon 4–6" below).

2. *Classify each sentence* by function: statement, question, exclamation, or command. A statement is a description of the world. For example, Philemon 4–6 is a statement. Most New Testament sentences are statements. A command wants the world to change, as in Philemon 17: "Welcome him as me" (v. 17) or "Charge this to me" (v. 18) or

---

11. Bruce M. Metzger and Bart D. Ehrman, *The Text of the New Testament: Its Transmission, Corruption, and Restoration,* 4th ed. (New York: Oxford University Press, 2005), 150.

"Prepare for me a guest room" (v. 22). These verbs are all imperatives in Greek, and their imperatival force comes out in the English translations. An imperative is a demand, exhortation, prohibition, entreaty, or permission.[12] Alternative Greek forms for the imperative are the future indicative (e.g., you shall welcome him) and the volitive subjunctive (e.g., you might welcome him).[13]

An exclamation is something spoken in strong emotion, communicating one's feelings about the world. It would be a sentence in which the speaker shouts or speaks suddenly and vehemently, as in surprise or with emotion. Several examples may be found in Romans: "Wretched person that I am!" (Rom. 7:24 NRSV) and "Thanks be to God through Jesus Christ our Lord!" (v. 25 NRSV).

A real question indicates that one wants an answer and is not sure about the description of the world, as when the tribune asked Paul's nephew: "What is it you want to tell me?" (Acts 23:19 NIV). The tribune did not know, and Paul's nephew wanted to tell him about the forthcoming plot to kill Paul while on a journey. But what is called a rhetorical question is a question that in fact is an exclamation or command or statement. For instance, "Therefore, what shall we say concerning these things?" (Rom. 8:31) is a statement in the form of a question while "If God is for us, who is against us?" (v. 31 RSV) is an exclamation in the form of a question. We are comparing form (a question) to function (statement, command, exclamation). "Are all apostles?" (1 Cor. 12:29 RSV), although in the form of an open-ended question, presupposes the answer no because *me* is used. It is really a statement in function: "All are not apostles, are they?" No one believer has all the spiritual gifts in 1 Corinthians 12:29–30. The point is this: Christ's body needs many different parts to work (1 Cor. 12:27).

3. *Classify and analyze the elements of each sentence.*[14]
   a. Identify each clause: A clause is a group of words with its own subject and a finite verb. The finite verb can be elliptical. In Greek all indicative, subjunctive, and imperative verbs are finite verbs,

---

12. Robertson, *Grammar of the Greek New Testament,* 941, 946.
13. Sometimes the infinitive and participle may function as imperatives. But if the principal verb is present, the participle does not function as an imperative. Sometimes the imperatival finite verb is implied but not expressed, as in 1 Peter 3:8–9 (Robertson, *Grammar of the Greek New Testament,* 943–46).
14. See also F. Blass, A. Debrunner, and Robert W. Funk, *A Greek Grammar of the New Testament and Other Early Christian Literature* (Chicago: Chicago University Press, 1961); Dana and Mantey, *Manual Grammar*; J. Gresham Machen, *New Testament Greek for Beginners* (Toronto: Macmillan, 1951); A. T. Robertson and W. H. Davis, *A New Short Grammar of the Greek Testament* (Grand Rapids: Baker, 1977).

108 | In-Depth Study of the Text

a complete thought, while normally infinitives and participles are not finite verbs. For instance, "I loose, I may loose, loose!" are finite verbs. These verbs can stand by themselves as complete thoughts. "To loose" or "loosing" are not finite verbs since they do not communicate complete thoughts.

Greek, though, has four exceptions: the genitive absolute,[15] accusative absolute, imperatival infinitive, and infinitive with its own subject. The genitive absolute tends to occur in the narrative books[16]—for example, in Matthew 9:33 ("And after the demon [genitive] had been cast out [participle in genitive].''). Accusative absolutes are rare, but they do occur in Luke's use of literary Koine Greek, as in Acts 26:3 ("You [accusative] are [participle with accusative ending] acquainted"). An old but rare use in the New Testament of the infinitive is when it serves as a command, as in Philippians 3:16 ("Let us hold [infinitive] to it"). This use occurs chiefly after an imperative.[17] More common are infinitives that function like finite verbs with the noun or pronoun in the accusative case serving as the subject or cause of the action,[18] as in Mark 14:30 ("that today this night before twice rooster [accusative] crows [infinitive]").

b. Classify each clause as main (independent) or subordinate (dependent). A main clause, like a finite verb, provides a complete thought. In Greek, since the subject is often contained in the verb, we can have a main clause with only one finite verb. Every main clause is a sentence, but a sentence can have more than one main clause. For example, Philemon 4–6 has three finite verbs: "I am thanking" (*eucharistō*), "you have" (*echeis*), and "might become" (*genētai*); therefore, it has three clauses. "I am giving my God thanks always" is a complete thought, while "which you have" and "so that the sharing of your faith might become active" are not complete thoughts and cannot stand by themselves. The first clause is the main clause, while the second and third clauses are subordinate clauses. Usually, if clauses are connected by *and* or *but*, they are each the same type of clause.

---

15. "Genitive absolute" is a noun or pronoun with a participle, both in the genitive case, which stand out of connection with the rest of the sentence. "Absolute" means loosed or separated. Then, when the noun in the genitive case becomes the subject of the subordinate clause, which usually begins with "when" or "after," the verb becomes finite.

16. Robertson, *Grammar of the Greek New Testament*, 513.

17. Robertson, *Grammar of the Greek New Testament*, 943–44.

18. "When the infinitive is used with the accusative, it indicates the agent who has to do with the action by the accusative, since the infinitive can have no subject in the technical case" (Robertson, *Grammar of the Greek New Testament*, 489–90, 1051–52).

A "phrase," in contrast, is a group of words without its own subject and predicate. In Greek the verb is the keyword for which to look. For example, sometimes participles, when translated into English, sound like finite verbs: "as I remember you," "because I hear about your faith," "I pray that you may be active," "we have in Christ" (NIV). This English translation for Philemon 4–6 has seven clauses, while the Greek has three clauses. But our grammatical analysis must be based on the Greek text, not its English rendering.[19]

Subordinate clauses can be further defined if the interpreter has the ability to do so. But at a minimum, clauses need to be recognized. Clauses are a more precise category than even sentences. We can extend sentences with semicolons, but every clause must have a finite verb.

4. *Classify each subordinate clause* as adverbial, adjectival, nominal, or parenthetical. If we can understand the meaning of an adverb, adjective, noun, and parenthesis, we can understand the meaning of adverbial clauses, adjectival clauses, nominal/substantive clauses, and parenthetical clauses. For example, in the sentence "I thank always my God," "I" is a pronoun and the subject, "thank" is a finite verb, "always" is an adverb describing how frequently Paul thanks God, "my" is an adjective modifying the noun "God," and "God" is a noun serving as the object of whom Paul is thanking.

Similarly, an adverbial clause, which is the most frequent type of subordinate clause, is a clause modifying a verb, adjective, or adverb in a sentence. The last clause in Philemon 4–6 is adverbial ("so that the sharing of your faith might become active in knowledge of every good, the one among you toward Christ" [v. 6]). It explains the result of giving thanks. An adjectival clause is a subordinate clause modifying a noun or pronoun in a sentence. Toward whom does Philemon have "faithful love"? It is toward Jesus and the saints ("which you have toward the Lord Jesus and toward all the saints," v. 5).

A nominal/substantive (noun) clause is sometimes confused with an adjectival clause. A noun clause is a subordinate clause serving as a subject, object, or complement in a sentence. In contrast, in an adjectival clause, we can always find the noun or pronoun being modified ("who" or "which"). For instance, if we adapt Philemon 4–6, we can create a noun clause: "I tell you that I am giving my God thanks." What am I telling? The object is "that I am giving my God thanks." Or "I am giving my God thanks is what I am telling you." Here, the

---

19. The Reina-Valera translation of the Greek into Spanish has six clauses: "doy gracias," "porque oigo," "la fe que tienes," "y pido," "fe sea eficaz," "el bien que esta" (Philem. 4–6).

110 | In-Depth Study of the Text

noun clause ("I am giving God thanks") is the subject of the sentence, answering the question of *what* or *who*.

The introduction to a quotation may be a main clause or an adverbial clause. For example, Jesus said, "Many will ask me in that day, 'Lord, Lord, did not in your name we prophesy" (Matt. 7:22). The question (the second clause) is a noun clause, indicating the content or object of what many ask. Paul wrote, "As it is written" (an adverbial clause) in Romans 8:36. The content of the Old Testament quotation that follows in that verse contains two main clauses ("that for your sake we are facing death all the day, we are regarded as sheep to be slaughtered").[20]

If a subordinate clause is not adverbial, adjectival, or nominal (a noun), it may be a parenthetical clause. A parenthetical clause is an explanation or a comment in the form of a clause within an already complete sentence. It is rare. An artificially created parenthetical clause might be: "I love to say it, I thank God always for you." "I love to say it" is an aside disconnected from the rest of the sentence.

The final analysis of the type of adverbial clause may be delayed until the visualizing of the flow of the argument. Adverbial clauses may be conditional, causal, final, local, temporal, or comparative. Certain key conjunctions may introduce each type of adverbial clause. In the appendix to this chapter is a chart ("The Structural Relation of Clauses") summarizing the different types of adverbial clauses and the common introductory conjunctions and some examples from the New Testament. A relative clause could function adjectivally or substantively or adverbially. For instance, Philemon 6 is an adverbial clause that gives the result of Paul's thanks and answers the question *with what result* or "so that" (*hopōs*). Conditional clauses tend to answer *if*; temporal clauses answer *when* or *while*; local clauses answer *where*; comparative clauses answer *like, such as,* and *just as*; causal clauses answer *because, since*; and final clauses, if purposive, answer *in order to, with the purpose that,* or, if resultative, *so that, with the result that.*

This may seem like a lot of work to excavate and comprehend. That is why you want to keep your text short! Philemon 4–6 is only one sentence! But our goal is to dwell on the Bible text with the intent to understand more deeply and more accurately what God has communicated so we may make appropri-

---

20. For examples of clause embedding, see Aída Besançon Spencer, "Does James 'Show Thee Christ'? A Comparison of the Content and Communication Styles of Jesus and James (Matthew 7:7–27 vs. James 1:2–27)," *Journal of Language, Culture, and Religion* 3, no. 1 (2022): 63–88; Spencer, *Paul's Literary Style: A Stylistic and Historical Comparison of II Corinthians 11:16–12:13, Romans 8:9–39, and Philippians 3:2–4:13* (Lanham, MD: University Press of America, 1984), 30–32, 110–14, 171–78, 154–64; Spencer, *A Commentary on James,* Kregel Exegetical Library (Grand Rapids: Kregel Academic, 2020).

ate applications for today. Isn't it worth our while to study what the great God of the universe is saying through the New Testament writers? I have found it most worthwhile and most enjoyable.

All this analysis leads to the two final stages of the process: visualizing the flow of the argument of the text and, when possible, also the immediate context, as well as analyzing the relation of the sentences to one another. Here are the steps to follow.

HOW TO STUDY THE EXTERNAL STRUCTURE OF WORDS: A SENTENCE FLOW (PART 2)

I.   Divide the Greek passage into sentences and clauses.
II. *Visualize the flow of the argument* by showing how the parts of the sentences relate to one another.
  A.   At the top left, *indicate any conjunction* that begins a sentence as a structural signal. Keep conjunctions between appropriate words, phrases, clauses, or sentences.
  B.   In each clause, place the *subject, verb, direct object, and indirect object on one line*, after any introductory conjunction.
  C.   *Subordinate*: Indicate modifiers by placing them under and to the right of each word being modified. Keep prepositions together with objects on the same line. Keep participial phrases together.
  D.   *Coordinate*: Place parallel words, phrases, and clauses under each other.
  E.   Optional: *Color-code* recurring words and phrases.
  F.   *Study* how the parts of each sentence relate and their effect on meaning and emphasis.
III. Analyze the relation of the sentences to one other, if time permits.

Example: Doing a Sentence Flow of Philemon 4–6

To do the first step in visualizing, begin by writing the sentence out in pencil on scrap paper. When this is complete, copy it over by arranging an electronic version of the Greek New Testament text. (Employing an electronic version of the New Testament text is more accurate than typing out each word in the Greek font.[21]) Looking at the Greek text, mark in color, underline, or bold all the finite verbs and conjunctions. At the top left, indicate any conjunction that begins a sentence or a clause. Then, for each clause, indicate the subject, verb, direct object, and indirect object on one line. Look for what is left. These

---

21.   I use Linguist's Software, whose founder, Dr. Philip Payne, provides the Greek and Hebrew font for the American Bible Society. Other software is also available. But be sure the edition of the Greek you use is the latest edition. Nestle-Aland's 28th edition may also be available online: https://www.die-bibel.de/bible/NA28/.

112 | In-Depth Study of the Text

should mainly be modifiers or parallel words. Indicate modifiers by placing them under and to the right of the word modified. Keep prepositions together with their objects on one line. Keep participles with their objects on one line together. Place parallel words, phrases, and clauses under each other.

For instance, in Philemon 4–6 (see in the appendix to this chapter "Sentence Flow of Philemon 4–6"), the core of the main clause is "I am giving thanks to God." "Always" (*pantote*) modifies when Paul did his thanking. It is not sometimes or never, but always. "My" (*mou*) modifies "God." Paul was not thanking other people's god or gods but his own God. The article is in reality a modifier. Paul was writing not about any god but "the" God, the one and only God. The article may be placed under the word it modifies or next to the word it modifies (since there are often many articles in a text and it may look more confusing to place them all under the word modified).[22] The participle "while making" modifies "I am giving thanks." When did Paul thank God? At the same time as he remembered Philemon. That will raise the question for the application: When people remember you, do they always thank God for you? The object of "making" is "remembrance" (*mneia*); therefore, place it on the same line as the participle "making" (*poioumenos*). Two sets of words modify "remembrance": "of you" and "at the time of my prayers." Therefore, place them under "remembrance," one under the other. Paul was remembering "you," which in Greek is singular. So although Paul wrote Philemon, Apphia, Archippus, and the church in their home, the letter is particularly addressed to Philemon. Yet in the final verse, Paul again used the plural "you." In the application, you might note that times of prayer can include thanking God for coworkers.

Paul then used another participle ("hearing," *akouōn*) that again modifies "I am giving thanks" (*eucharistō*), so place it under the earlier participle. "Your" (*sou*) modifies whose love Paul has heard about. Why did Paul thank God for Philemon? Because he heard of Philemon's love. "And" (*kai*) usually combines equal items. Here it connects "love" and "faith," thus place *kai* between the two words it combines: "love" and "faith." Later you can think about the relationship between faith and love. The adjectival clause modifies "faith," so place the clause in brackets under the word it modifies. All subordinate clauses may be encircled by brackets for clarity. Often subordinate clauses begin with a conjunction. In this case, it is the relative pronoun *hos, hē, ho*. "You have" (*echeis*) has no object, so it stands on one line by itself. The subject is contained in the verb. The prepositional phrase "to/toward" has as an object "Jesus"; thus, they are both on one line. Which Jesus is this? It is "the Lord," so place "the Lord" under "Jesus." Philemon's love was not just directed to Jesus, but also "to/toward the saints." The "and" (*kai*)[23] connects the two prepositional phrases, so place "and" between the two phrases; and "toward

---

22. But if the article is functioning as a pronoun, place it in the subject line.
23. This *kai* is functioning as a conjunction ("and"). When it is translated as an adverb ("also, even"), then it is placed as a modifier.

all the saints" is parallel to "to/toward the Lord Jesus." Philemon's love was not just toward some saints but "all" the saints, so place "all" under "saints" as a modifier. When you apply this text, you can mention that Onesimus, the former slave, was one of those "all the saints" and also was to be treated in a loving manner. A bracket closes the adjectival clause.

What should be the result for thanking God for others' faithful love? The adverbial clause then indicates this. Keep all subordinate clauses under the original main clause and slightly to the right, in the sequence in which the words appear. The adverbial clause also begins with a conjunction ("so that," *hopōs*); place it first in the clause. Underneath it on one line is the core meaning of the clause: "sharing" (subject), "might become," and "active." "Active" (*energēs*) is the object or complement of the verb. What kind of fellowship did Paul have in mind here? It is not a literal business co-op but a "faith" type of sharing. The potential types of genitive for "sharing" will be a question to search out later. The participial phrase "in knowledge" modifies "active" and thereby is placed under and to the right of "active." "Good" modifies the type of "knowledge," while "every" modifies which "good." Paul did not want Philemon to gain the knowledge of evil. To which good did Paul refer? He used an article as a pronoun for "the one," so this article stands by itself, modifying "knowledge of every good." Two parallel participial phrases modify "the one": "among you" (now plural) and "toward/into Christ." In the same way that Paul balanced faithful love toward the Lord Jesus and toward all the saints in verse 5, here he balanced knowledge between humans and Christ.

The visualizing of the thought relations between the words in this sentence by itself is suggestive of many theological thoughts and applications.

There are variations on how to develop a sentence flow. Should you revert all items to the most common word order—subject, verb, object, modifying phrases, and clauses? Or should you show the author's order? Or should you show some of the author's order but not all? Any is possible, but be consistent. Keep in mind the goal: to visualize the structure and the flow of the argument. This cannot be done until all the parsing is completed. My preference is always to place a clause on one line but show the sequence of clauses as well. When I turn to the style analysis, I can note the change of order compared to the original text.[24]

After the flow is complete, the most important step is now to study the flow and meditate prayerfully and thoughtfully on what you learned about the meaning and emphasis of the text. What is the relationship between a subject and its

---

24. Gordon D. Fee includes many examples of doing a sentence flow in *New Testament Exegesis: A Handbook for Students and Pastors*, 3rd ed. (Louisville: Westminster John Knox, 2002), 41–58. We independently developed the sentence flow format. See also Richard J. Erickson, *A Beginner's Guide to New Testament Exegesis: Taking the Fear Out of Critical Method* (Downers Grove, IL: InterVarsity Press, 2005), 74–93; John D. Harvey, *Interpreting the Pauline Letters: An Exegetical Handbook*, *Handbook for New Testament Exegesis* (Grand Rapids: Kregel, 2012), 132–36.

verb? The subject "God" makes all the difference in the world in this sentence: "If *God* is for us, who is against us?" (Rom. 8:31 RSV). What is the relationship between the verb and its predicate? "God predestined" is limited by its modifying prepositional phrase: "to be like the image of his Son" (Rom. 8:29). In Romans, Paul was not talking about God predestining some people to hell, to be always separated from his love, but discussing God predestining those he foreknew to be like the Son's image. What is the relationship between modifier and modified? Humans are to be similar in likeness to whom? God's wonderful Son. These thoughts are what should be in your paper or sermon. You should explain the meaning of the text to your listeners. For an example, please see my use of grammatical analysis in the sample paper on Philemon (ch. 8) under the heading "Grammatic, Semantic, and Stylistic Analysis." The charts in the appendix at the end of this chapter also help with morphology, types of cases, infinitives, and participles.[25] Any Greek grammar book can be of assistance.

ANALYZE THE RELATION OF THE SENTENCES TO ONE ANOTHER (PART 3)

A	B
Basic Cognitive Message[26]	**Develop a Proposition**
initial: ( ) the first sentence of a paragraph	additive (+) a proposition that has no organic relationship with its predecessor; not essential; an addition, "and"
explanatory (=) a restatement, definition, or expansion of the previous proposition, interpretation of a fact, "in other words," "that is"	adversative (-) a proposition that changes the direction of the argument; almost a negation, negative-positive, "but," "however," "yet," "on the other hand," "only," "still"
illustrative (X) an illustration or instance, "for example," "for instance," "for comparison"	alternative (0) a proposition that may be substituted for the previous one, "or," "in other words"
illative (:) the conclusion, inference, "therefore," "consequently," "so," "thus," "hence"	causal (!) any proposition that provides the cause or ground for a preceding conclusion, "for"

---

25. Craig L. Blomberg and Jennifer Foutz Markley have a helpful chart summarizing important tasks in grammatical analysis (*A Handbook of New Testament Exegesis* [Grand Rapids: Baker, 2010], 131). They refer to a study of cases, articles, tenses, participles, imperatives, clauses, modifiers, and pronouns.

26. First summarize each sentence stripped of all stylistic and affective aspects: normalize word orders, omit connective links, simplify, replace pronouns with antecedents, delete redundancies, replace figurative with literal, restore ellipses. See Spencer, *Paul's Literary Style*, 30–32, 110–14, 171–78.

The third major step in a sentence flow is to analyze the relation of the sentences to each other. This would entail a study of the text compared to its immediate context. To begin, simplify each sentence. Then study to see what sentences fit in each of the eight basic propositions: initial, explanatory, illustrative, illative, additive, adversative, alternative, and causal.[27] Philemon 4–6 is the first or initial sentence of the paragraph after Paul's introduction or letterhead (who writes, to whom he writes, and the greeting, vv. 1–3). Verse 7 explains further why Paul was thankful. Verses 8–10 give his conclusion: "therefore" Paul was now going to command Philemon to do some things to help Onesimus.

Often my students never get to this last stage in a sentence flow, but it is a way to relate the text to its immediate context. Whether this aspect of a sentence flow is used or not, still the text must be related to its immediate context at the end of the in-depth study. A discourse analysis that overlaps syntax and style study focuses on analyzing whole passages or discourses: "a method of determining the way in which words, phrases, clauses, sentences, paragraphs, and whole compositions are joined to achieve an author's purpose."[28] The appendix at the end of this chapter includes a sample discourse analysis and a link to make the analysis easier.

I have emphasized analysis using Greek grammar in this chapter. But what do you do if you do not know Greek? I once did a style study comparing 2 Corinthians 11:16–12:13 in Greek with the King James Version and Good News Translation. The KJV, NRSV, and NASB are formal ("literal") translations that try to preserve the form of the original Greek to convey meaning. The emphasis is the original text, while the GNT, NIV, and NEB are dynamic equivalent translations ("functional equivalence") that emphasize the meaning of the Greek text in the natural form of the receptor language—in this case, English. The equivalence in meaning or thought is stressed. A more literal translation forces the reader to interpret more, while the dynamic equivalent translation helps the reader by doing more interpreting. A paraphrase is a freely rendered restatement of another translation in different words, such as the original Living Bible.[29] After I did my style study, I did not learn as much about the meaning of the passage as I did about the basic format of each language or translation. I learned that the KJV more approximates the original Greek than the GNT in having fewer words yet longer sentences and more variety of sentence length. As a dynamic equivalent translation, the GNT uses more words and more syllables to explain the original, more active verbs than the original, and shorter

---

27. See further Spencer, *Paul's Literary Style*, 31–32, 174–77.
28. David Alan Black, with Katharine Barnwell and Stephen Levinsohn, eds., *Linguistics and New Testament Interpretation: Essays on Discourse Analysis* (Nashville: Broadman, 1992), 41. See also 194.
29. See John Beekman and John Callow, *Translating the Word of God with Scripture and Topical Indexes* (Grand Rapids: Zondervan, 1974), 259.

clauses and sentences than the original. However, surprisingly, the GNT has a greater verb density (more verbals, such as participles and infinitives), causing the language to be less clear! The results of this study are presented in the following chart.

COMPARING DIFFERENT TRANSLATIONS WITH THE GREEK: 2 CORINTHIANS 11:16–12:13

Stylistic operations	Greek	KJV	GNT
1. Number of words	505	692	823
2. Number of syllables	1068[30]	973	1025
3. Variety of sentence length	37.9	24	15 Greek has 2.5x more variety than GNT, 1.5x more variety than KJV
4. Average clause length = syllables ÷clauses*	$1068 \div 91 =$ 11.74		$1025 \div 112 = 9.15$ (78% Greek)
5. Average length of main clause=syllables ÷ main clauses**	22.259		15.53 (70% Greek)
6. Average length of a sentence = syllables ÷ sentences***[31]	34.45	25.605	22.78 (66% Greek)
7. Active vs. passive verbs	$70 \div 13 = 83$ (84% active verbs)		$108 \div 7 = 115$ (94% active verbs)
8. Verb density = verbals ÷ finite verbs (as verb density goes down, language becomes more structured and clearer to read)	$13 \div 83 = .157$		$31 \div 115 = .269$

Thus, doing a sentence flow of the English text will tell you more about the translation used than it will about the original Greek text. On the other hand, if others do a sentence flow of the Greek and add their own inter-linear literal translation, that would make the sentence flow helpful to all readers. Otherwise, the best way to start a study for English-only readers is to compare several translations, more literal ones and more dynamic equivalent ones and even paraphrases. See where they agree and where they differ. Where they differ indicates places where interpreters may differ,

---

30. Greek as an inflecting language uses fewer words in sentences than English but more syllables.
31. The most important measure in this study has three asterisks (***). The less important measures have two asterisks and one asterisk

but where they agree, all interpreters are much in agreement. Then ask questions of the text. Some may be answered in a variety of ways, such as by word studies. Asking some of these questions to those who know Koine Greek will encourage all to think and have a lively discussion on the Bible. When I have had this format in a class, surprisingly, most of the questions were asked by the English-only readers, but they could be answered by everyone.

HOW TO AVOID COMMON ERRORS

1. Make sure the essay is complete.
2. Cite your own translation of the text in the paper instead of copying a printed version. If you do not know Greek, you can cite a version. Always cite in parentheses the abbreviations of your chosen translation (e.g., NIV). If preaching, I normally read the passage from the pew or projected Bible version so the listeners can see the words cited as I read them. But during the sermon, I may cite my own translation.
3. Integrate the translation into your essay.
4. Note helpful details for interpretation from the text and the immediate context.
5. Focus on your text and its letter. Do not jump to other New Testament passages too quickly.
6. Explain your reasons for your conclusions. Do not use an opinionated and haughty tone.
7. Allow your conclusions to flow from your text. Do not allow preconceived theology and redemptive history to shape and frame the exegesis. Your job is to let the text speak for itself.
8. Include the sentence flow in the appendix, but explain its meaning in paragraph form in the paper.
9. Use quotation marks around English words being defined, but use italics, not quotation marks, for transliterations. Use transliterations or Greek font, not both, in one essay.
10. Make sure "it" has a clear antecedent. Do not overuse passive verbs and "it is." Use strong verbs in your writing and clear syntax. Be direct, not repetitious and wordy.
11. Use accents with the Greek font, even if you have to handwrite the accents.
12. Use full sentences with subjects and verbs. Prepositional or participial phrases or subordinate clauses are not sentences.
13. Use the first-person singular only when necessary in a *formal* essay.
14. Use inclusive language for humanity, such as *human(s)* or *people*.
15. Make sure the font is readable. Many computers now have size 11 as a default size. Ask your reader what size is wanted; usually it is size 12. In most cases, double-space the essay.

118 | In-Depth Study of the Text

16. Only present parsing if it makes a difference in the discussion.
17. Normally Greek words are presented in their lexical, not text, format.
18. Use standard abbreviations for the Bible as illustrated by an acceptable style manual. Do not use abbreviations from other books, such as concordances or lexicons, whose abbreviations may have been created by the author.
19. Cite the Greek text only when the argument depends on it, not for displaying your knowledge. Always include a translation (in parentheses) for easier reading.
20. Number every page.

APPENDICES: GRAMMATICAL HELPS

How to Study the External Structure of Words: A Sentence Flow (Parts 1, 2, 3)

I. Divide the Greek passage into sentences and clauses.
   A. Divide the text into sentences.
   B. Classify each sentence by function: statement, question, exclamation, or command.
   C. Classify and analyze the elements of each sentence.
      1. Identify each clause (by finding all finite verbs).
      2. Classify each clause as main (independent) or subordinate (dependent).
      3. Classify each subordinate clause as adverbial, adjectival, nominal, or parenthetical.
      4. Classify each adverbial clause as conditional, temporal, local, comparative, causal, or final (purpose or result).
II. Visualize the flow of the argument by showing how the parts of the sentences relate to each other.
   A. At the top left, indicate any conjunction that begins a sentence as a structural signal. Keep conjunctions between appropriate words, phrases, clauses, and sentences.
   B. In each clause, place its subject, verb, direct object, and indirect object on one line, after any introductory conjunction.
   C. Subordinate: Indicate modifiers by placing them under and to the right of the words they modify. Keep prepositions together with objects on the same line. Keep participial phrases together.
   D. Coordinate: Place parallel words, phrases, and clauses under each other.
   E. Optional: Color-code recurring words and phrases.
   F. Study how the parts of each sentence relate and their effect on meaning and emphasis.

Seek a Translation and Understand the Grammar of the Text | 119

III. Analyze the relation of the sentences to each other, if time permits.

A
Basic Cognitive Message[32]

initial: ( )
the first sentence of a paragraph

explanatory (=)
a restatement, definition, or expansion of the previous proposition, interpretation of a fact, "in other words," "that is"

illustrative (X)
an illustration or instance, "for example," "for instance," "for comparison"

illative (:)
the conclusion, inference, "therefore," "consequently," "so," "thus," "hence"

B
Develop a Proposition

additive (+)
a proposition that has no organic relationship with its predecessor; not essential; an addition, "and"

adversative (-)
a proposition that changes the direction of the argument; almost a negation, negative-positive, "but," "however," "yet," "on the other hand," "only," "still"

alternative (0)
a proposition that may be substituted for the previous one, "or," "in other words"

causal (!)
a ny proposition that provides the cause or ground for a preceding conclusion, "for"

Sentence Flow of Philemon 4–6

Initial statement. 1 sentence
Main clause:

[Εὐχαριστῶ	θεῷ	*I am giving my God*
πάντοτε	τῷ	*thanks always*
	μου	
ποιούμενος	μνείαν	*while making remembrance*
	σου	*of you at the time of my prayers*
	ἐπὶ προσευχῶν	
	τῶν	
	μου,	
ἀκούων	ἀγάπην	*because of hearing of your*
	τὴν	*love and faith (faithful love),*
	σου	
	καὶ,	
	πίστιν,	
	τὴν	

---

32. First summarize each sentence stripped of all stylistic and affective aspects: normalize word order, omit connective links, simplify, replace pronouns with antecedents, delete redundancies, replace the figurative with the literal, restore ellipses. See Spencer, *Paul's Literary Style*, 30–32, 110–14, 171–78.

120 | In-Depth Study of the Text

Adjectival clause: [ἣν — *which you have toward the Lord Jesus*

ἔχεις
πρὸς Ἰησοῦν
τὸν
κύριον
καὶ — *and toward all the saints*
εἰς ἁγίους
πάντας
τοὺς,

Adverbial clause:
result [ὅπως — *so that the sharing of your faith*
κοινωνία γένηται ἐνεργὴς
ἡ ἐν ἐπιγνώσει
πίστεώς ἀγαθοῦ — *might become active*
τῆς παντὸς — *in knowledge of every good (thing),*
σου τοῦ — *the one among you toward Christ.*
ἐν ὑμῖν
εἰς Χριστόν.]

Sentence Flow with Parsing and Lexical Forms: Philemon 4–6[33]

		(noun s. dat—direct object of verbs	
Initial statement 1s.pres.act.indic./subj. verb		*with strong idea of personal relation)*	
Main cl.:	Εὐχαριστέω	Θεός	
	[Εὐχαριστῶ	θεῷ	*I am giving my God*
	I give thanks	God	*thanks always*
	adv. πάντοτε	τῷ	
	always	*gen. s. pron.*	
		μου	
		my	
		noun acc. s.	
	ποιέω	μνεία, ἡ unusual order	*while making*
manner/temp	ποιούμενος	μνείαν	*remembrance of you*
pres. M/P part.	making for	remembrance, mention	*at the time of my*
n.m.s.verb	myself	*gen. s. pron.*	*prayers*
		σου	
		of you	

---

33. Verbs are abbreviated: pres.=present; s.=singular; act.=active; indic.=indicative; subj.=subjunctive; M/P=middle/passive; part.=participle; n.=nominative; m.=middle; aor.=aorist. Nouns and pronouns are abbreviated: dat.=dative; acc.=accusative; gen.=genitive; n.=nominative; pl.=plural; s.=singular; f.=feminine; rel. pron.=relative pronoun; adj.=adjective. The same information may be found in a subsequent chart: Grammatical Information Chart of Philemon 4–6.

Seek a Translation and Understand the Grammar of the Text | 121

prep.   προσευχή *noun gen. pl.*
ἐπὶ*   προσευχῶν
prayers
   τῶν
   gen. s.
   μου,
   my

              because of hearing of your

verb: pres. act. part. m.s.n.   *noun acc. s.*   *love and faith (faithful love),*
   ἀκούω   ἀγάπη
   ἀκούων love
hearing, receiving   ἀγάπην
news of
   τὴν

         σου *gen. s. pron.*
         of you

     conj.   καὶ,
         and
         πίστις
         πίστιν,
         faith
         τὴν   } *Pleonasm, Hendiadys*

Adjectival cl.: ὅς, ἥ, ὅ   [ἣν *pres. act. ind. 2s verb*   *which you have*
       f. acc. s.   ἔχω   *toward the Lord Jesus*
rel. pron.   ἔχεις
     which   you have

         prep.   Ἰησοῦς *noun acc. s.*
         πρὸς   Ἰησοῦν
         toward Jesus
           τὸν

              Κύριος
              κύριον
              Lord

           conj.
           καὶ   *and toward all the saints*
           and

              noun pl. acc.
              ἅγιος
         prep. εἰς   ἁγίους
         toward saints
              πᾶς *acc. pl.*
              πάντας
              all
                τοὺς,
                the

122 | In-Depth Study of the Text

Adverbial cl.: conj. aor. m. subj. verb 3s   *n.s. noun*

result   [ὅπως   γίνομαι   ἐνεργὴς   *so that the sharing*
       so that, in order that   *of your faith might*
       n.s. noun   *become active*
       κοινωνία   γένηται   ἐνεργὴς
       fellowship,   might become *effectual, effective, active,*
       partnership, sharing   *powerful*
                            ἡ
                           the

     gen. s. noun   *dat. s. noun*

     πίστις   ἐπίγνωσις   *in knowledge of every*
     πίστεώς   *prep.* ἐν ἐπιγνώσει   *good (thing),*
     faith   in knowledge
         τῆς
         the
         subj. gen.
         σου
         of you

                 ἀγαθός gen. s.
                 ἀγαθοῦ
                 good
                   πᾶς gen. s.
                   παντὸς
                   of every
              substantive article functioning as adj., ellipsis
                       gen. s. pron. pl. dat.
                             τοῦ   *the one among you*
                             the one   *toward Christ.*
                     ἐν ὑμῖν
                     in/among you
                     prep. noun acc. s.
                             Χριστός
                           εἰς Χριστόν.]
                           toward Christ

1 sentence = statement

Semantic Structural Analysis: Philemon 4–6 (Roy Ciampa)

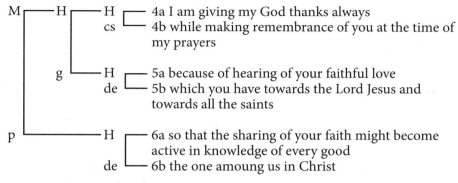

Symbol	Name	Definition
H cs	circumstance HEAD	The support unit (circumstance) provides information about the event or state that forms a background for the mainline information presented in the head unit.
H de	HEAD description	The semantic equivalent to a nonrestrictive relative clause that gives information about an item and comments on contextually old information. It functions as background to the HEAD unit. Example: "The boys, *who knew they were trespassing*, ran off quickly."
H g	HEAD grounds	A relation in which the grounds supply the basis for the HEAD.
M p	MEANS purpose	The MEANS answers the question "*What* action was undertaken to achieve the intended result?" There is a component of intention, but the result is not indicated as realized. Example: "He studied twenty hours a day [MEANS] in order to pass the exam [purpose]."

There is no standard order in which any of these relations are found. Any of them can be found with either of the items coming first or last.

The above analysis was created digitally using discourse analysis software available at http://sourceforge.net/projects/satool/files/. The software was created for students by a student, Joyce Lin, and includes a key of available symbols, of which the above chart is a subset. The key is based on chapter 8 of John Beekman, John C. Callow, and Michael F. Kopesec, *The Semantic Structure of Written Communication*, 5th ed. (Dallas: Summer Institute of Linguistics, 1981).

Grammatical Diagram: Philemon 4–6 (Edward Keazirian)

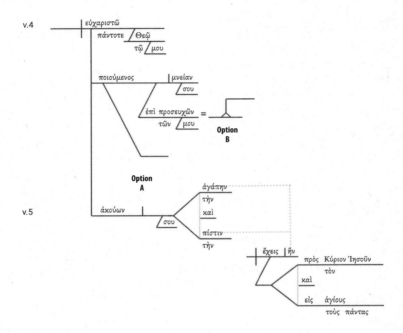

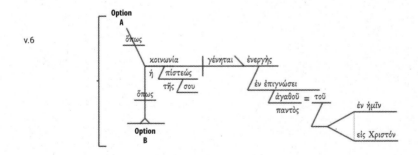

Pedagogical Notes

1. This grammatical diagram was constructed using *Biblearc*, a multipurpose Bible study tool developed and distributed by Bethlehem College and Seminary. The app is available for guests or subscribers at www.biblearc.com.

2. One of the advantages of diagramming can be seen here in verse 4. Regardless of which option you prefer for representing the structure of the passage, it is clearly and visually evident that the material written later in verse 6 is grammatically and logically dependent on the prior material in verse 4. Significant insights like this could easily be overlooked without this kind of visual clue to Paul's intended meaning and the logical flow of his letter.

Grammatical Notes

This passage has several possible configurations grammatically.

1. The ὅπως clause (v. 6) could express *purpose, content,* or *result.* As diagrammed here, *option A* expresses *purpose,* using an obtuse angle terrace (_) to represent a subordinate adverbial clause. Alternatively, *option B* expresses *content,* using a vertical standard (⌐) to represent a subordinate substantival clause. A third option, not diagrammed here but also possible, could express *result.* Graphically, it would use the same obtuse terrace as option A, but instead of connecting to ποιούμενος, the terrace would be connected to ἔχεις.
2. The adverb πάντοτε (v. 4) can alternatively be diagrammed as modifying ποιούμενος rather than modifying εὐχαριστῶ, as shown here.
3. Grammatically, the antecedent for the relative pronoun ἥν (v. 5) seems to be πίστιν. However, the personal pronoun σου precedes both ἀγάπην and πίστιν, adding emphasis and identifying both as qualities belonging to Philemon. Thus, alternatively, the relative pronoun ἥν, though singular, could include both as its antecedent.

The Structural Relation of Clauses[34]

Clause Definitions	Freq.	Neg.	Mood	Conj.	Kinds and Examples
1. Relative clause: a clause that brings two clauses together by agreement in gender, number, and sometimes case with the antecedent (expressed or unexpressed) in the principal clause. *The relative pronoun* expresses the relation between clauses. *Attraction* is usually an accompanying feature; the relative agrees with the antecedent in gender, number, and sometimes case due to attraction ("who, which, what").	Most freq.	Usually οὐ, occas. μή + indef. pron.	Usually indic., also subj.	ὅς ὅτι ὅπου ὡς ἕως ὅτε ὅπως ἵνα	*1. Adjectival:* the true relative is an adjectival pronoun that describes the antecedent. E.g., "Lazarus, *whom* Jesus raised from the dead" = Λάζαρος, ὃν ἤγειρεν ἐκ νεκρῶν Ἰησοῦς (John 12:1).
					2. Substantival (noun clause): the relative clause is used as a substantive and is itself the subject of the principal verb, introduced by ἵνα, ὅτι, or an infinitive (e.g., Matt. 10:38).
					3. Adverbial: e.g., "as we also forgave" = ὡς καὶ ἡμεῖς ἀφήκαμεν (Matt. 6:12); "with *what* judgment you judge" = ἐν ᾧ κρίματι κρίνετε (Matt. 7:2).

---

34. Abbreviations used: verb: aor. = aorist; impf. = imperfect; indic. = indicative; inf. = infinitive; pres. = present; purp. = purpose; opt. = optative; plpf. = pluperfect; subj. = subjunctive; noun or pronoun: indef. pron. = indefinite pronoun; other: freq. = frequent; occas. = occasionally

126 | In-Depth Study of the Text

Clause Definitions	Freq.	Neg.	Mood	Conj.	Kinds and Examples
2. *Conditional clause: a* subordinate clause that introduces a condition or supposition (protasis), which, if fulfilled, leads to certain results (apodosis, conclusion).[35] ("if")	Most freq.		Indic.	εἰ, ἐάν	1. A speaker represents a condition as real or determined; e.g., "If I by Beelzeboul cast out the demons, by whom do your sons cast them out?" = εἰ ἐγὼ ἐν Βεελζεβοὺλ ἐκβάλλω τὰ δαιμόνια, οἱ υἱοὶ ὑμῶν ἐν τίνι ἐκβάλλουσιν (Matt. 12:27).
					2. Condition contrary to fact, e.g., Luke 7:39.
					3. Condition doubtful or undetermined with prospect of determination, e.g., Heb. 6:3.
			Impf. aor. plpf. subj.	εἰ	4. Condition doubtful with remote prospect of determination, e.g., 1 Peter 3:14.
	Freq.			ἐάν, εἰ εἰ, ἐάν	
	Rare		Opt.		
3. *Concessive clause:* a clause that communicates realization despite the protasis ("even if").				καί, εἰ ἐάν εἰ καί	"Even if," "although," "if also," "though," "even though," "but if," and "if"
4. *Temporal clause:* a clause that defines a thought by means of its temporal relations. The function of the clause is to limit the action of the verb in the principal clause by the introduction of a relation of time ("when").			Indic. or subj.	ἐν ᾧ ἕως ἐπάν ἐφ᾽ ὅσον ἡνίκα ὅταν ὅτε ὡς	1. "*When*" or "while" (contemporaneous time—action parallel with the action of the principal verb): a. "in which time" / "while," e.g., "while I am coming" = ἐν ᾧ δὲ ἔρχομαι (John 5:7) b. "whenever," "for so long a time as," "so long as," "as," "when" 2. "*Until*" (subsequent action—action after action of principal verb):
				ἀφ᾽ οὗ ἄχρι ἕως μέχρι πρίν πρό τοῦ ἐν τῷ	a. "from which time" / "since," "from that time," "when" / "when once"; e.g., "three years since I have been coming" = τρία ἔτη ἀφ᾽ οὗ ἔρχομαι (Luke 13:7) b. "until," "so long as," "while" 3. The infinitive in a temporal clause:[36] a. "before" (antecedent time) b. "while" = ἐν τῷ + pres. inf. "when" = ἐν τῷ + aor. inf.
				μετά τὸ ἕως τοῦ	c. "after" = μετά τὸ d. "until" = ἕως τοῦ 4. The temporal participle[37]

---

35. The four different types of conditional clauses are described here and under types of conditions, below.
36. See also types of infinitives, below.
37. See also types of participles, below.

Seek a Translation and Understand the Grammar of the Text | 127

Clause Definitions	Freq.	Neg.	Mood	Conj.	Kinds and Examples
5. *Local clause:* a clause introduced by a relative adverb of place. The clause localizes the action of the main clause (*"where"*).			Usually indic.	ὅπου ἐν ᾧ οὗ ὅθεν	"Where" or "whence," with verbs of rest or motion; e.g., "in Bethany . . . , where John was" = ἐν Βηθανίᾳ . . . , ὅπου ἦν ὁ Ἰωάννης (John 1:28)
6. *Comparative clause:* a clause that introduces an analogous thought for the purpose of elucidating or emphasizing the thought expressed in the principal clause. Its function is description or emphasis. Conjunctions used are all relative in origin (*"as"*) or make comparisons (*"like," "such as," "just as"*).	Freq. in NT		Usually indic.	ὡς καθό καθώς καθάπερ καθότι ὅσος ἤ ὃν τρόπον	1. ὡς and its compounds (*"as"*); e.g., "in order that all will honor the Son as they honor the Father" = ἵνα πάντες τιμῶσιν τὸν υἱὸν καθὼς τιμῶσιν τὸν πατέρα (John 5:23) 2. Compounds of relative with κατά = "according as," "as," "according to," "precisely as," "just as," "even as also"; e.g., "precisely as it stands written" = καθὼς γέγραπται (Rom. 3:4)
7. *Causal clause: a* clause that states or implies the cause, ground, or reason for the assertion contained in another clause (*"because," "since"*).		Almost always οὐ	Only indic. in NT	ὅτι διότι καθότι ἐπεί ἐπειδή ἐπειδήπερ ὅθεν ἐφ᾿ ᾧ ἐφ᾿ ὅσον ἀνθ᾿ ὧν οὗ χάριν ὅν ὅστις διό	E.g., "because you remember me in all things" = ὅτι πάντα μου μέμνησθε (1 Cor. 11:2); "whom he receives" = ὃν παραδέχεται (Heb. 12:6)
8. *Final clauses* (aim and end): a. *Purpose clause* (contemplated result): a clause that expresses the aim or intention (deliberate, general direction, contemplated results) of the action denoted by the main verb (*"in order to," "with the purpose that"*). b. *Result clause* (achieved purpose): that which is consequent upon or issues from the action of the main verb (*"so that," "with the result that"*). c. *Consecutive clause:* a clause that communicates neither pure purpose nor pure result, hovering between the two extremes.	Most freq. for pure purp. Most freq. for result	μή	Subj. in aor. or pres.	ἵνα ὅπως ὡς μή μήποτε μήπως ἵνα μή ὅτι ὥστε ὅπως μή	"That," "so that," "in order that," "lest," "whether," "perchance," "that not"; e.g., "that you may come to know and keep on knowing" = ἵνα γνῶτε καὶ γινώσκητε (John 10:38) E.g., if I have all faith, so as to remove mountains" = ἐὰν ἔχω πᾶσαν τὴν πίστιν ὥστε ὄρη μεθιστάναι (1 Cor. 13:2)

128 | In-Depth Study of the Text

Summary of Key Types of Grammatical Forms: Cases, Infinitives, Conditions, Participles[38]

Dative case (four basic types)

I. *Dative proper:* designating the more remotely concerned person.
    A. *Dative of indirect object:* dative proper. Case of the indirect object. Nearest simple root idea: the one for whom/in whose interest an act is performed, "to"/"for"; e.g., "I say a word to the apostles" = λέγω λόγον τοῖς ἀποστόλοις.
    B. *Dative of advantage and disadvantage (dative of personal interest):* growing out of the dative of indirect object. A more specific expression of personal interest. The dative serves to designate the person whose interest is affected; e.g., "to bear witness to someone" = μαρτυρεῖν τινι.
        Dative of possession: personal interest particularized to the point of ownership.
        (*In the dative, the object possessed* is stressed; *in the genitive,* acquisition is recent and *emphasis is on the possessor.*)
        Clue words: εἶναι, γινέσθαι, ὑπάρχειν; e.g., "They had no child" = οὐκ ἦν αὐτοῖς τέκνον (Luke 1:7).
    C. *Ethical dative:* a strong emphasis on the personal idea; e.g., "beautiful to God" = ἀστεῖος τῷ θεῷ (Acts 7:20).
    D. *Dative of reference:* the force of interest in the dative diminished to the idea of mere reference. Occurs mainly with things; e.g., "*in the interest* of edification" = ἔδωκεν εἰς μοι οἰκοδομὴν (2 Cor. 13:10).
II. *Locative case/the instrumental:* associative dative, "in," "at," "on," "among," "by." It indicates a point within limits set by the word and context. Case of *position.*
    A. *Dative/locative of place:* Limits indicated are spatial. Nearest simple root idea: ἐν + locative; e.g., "The disciples came in the little boat" = οἱ . . . μαθηταὶ τῷ πλοιαρίῳ ἦλθον (John 21:8).
    B. *Temporal dative/locative of time:* Limits indicated by locative are temporal.
        1. The time *at which*—that is, a point of time. ἐν = point and duration of time, time when. Answers question of "when." Quite common in the New Testament; e.g., "on the third

---

38. These grammatical categories are drawn from Blass, Debrunner, and Funk, *A Greek Grammar;* Dana and Mantey, *Manual Grammar;* Machen, *New Testament Greek;* Robertson and Davis, *Short Grammar;* Wallace, *Greek Grammar.* Students should consult their own Greek grammatical textbook for fuller descriptions. I find most helpful for interpretation Robertson, *Grammar of the Greek New Testament,* under "syntax."

day" = τῇ τρίτῃ ἡμέρᾳ (Matt. 20:19); ἐν τῇ + infinitive = "while," "as"; ἐν τῷ = "when."

    2. Answers "how long." Used instead of the accusative to avoid a second accusative; e.g., "For many a time it had seized him" = πολλοῖς γὰρ χρόνοις συνηρπάκει αὐτὸν (Luke 8:29).

  C. *Locative in sphere/dative of respect/rule:* metaphorical use of dative. Limits suggested are logical, confining one idea within the bounds of another, thus indicating the sphere within which the former idea is to be applied. May occur with nouns, verbs, or adjectives. Used to indicate the respect in which anything exists or is true; e.g., "in pure conscience" (i.e., pure so far as the conscience is concerned) = ἐν καθαρᾷ συνειδήσει (1 Tim. 1:5).

III. *Instrumental case/instrumental—associative dative:* closely related to the idea of association and instrumentality, "with/by." A person is in a sense associated with the means by which (s)he accomplishes an objective, and in personal association, the second person supplies the means of fellowship. Root idea = means.

  A. *Instrumental of means:* the use lying closest to the root meaning. The most prevalent use of case in the New Testament. The intermediary means by which a result is produced. A method for expressing *impersonal means.* "By means of" (personal agent = ὑπό + ablative); e.g., "We act by means of great boldness" = πολλῇ παρρησίᾳ χρώμεθα (2 Cor. 3:12).

  B. *Instrumental/dative of cause:* an original factor producing a cause or reason. "On account of," "because," "according to"; e.g., "Because of fear of death, they were subjects of bondage" = φόβῳ θανάτου . . . ἔνοχοι ἦσαν δουλείας (Heb. 2:15).

  C. *Instrumental/dative of manner:* one of the most obvious uses of the instrumental. The method *by means of which* an act is performed or an end achieved. Frequently adverbs of the instrumental form; e.g., "publicly" = δημόσια. The associative dative is used more loosely to designate accompanying circumstances and manner; e.g., *"with* thankfulness" = χάριτι μετέχω (1 Cor. 10:30).

  D. *Instrumental of measure/instrumental of time:* Two points of time or space are separated by means of an intervening distance. In the New Testament, this kind of dative is chiefly used with reference to time. It also may be used to express a degree of difference. It is similar to the temporal dative; e.g., "For a long time he had worn no clothes" = χρόνῳ ἱκανῷ οὐκ ἐνεδύσατο ἱμάτιον (Luke 8:27).

  E. *Instrumental of association:* In personal association the second person supplies the means of fellowship. This kind of dative is used extensively in the New Testament. To have association, a second party must furnish the means of that association. Predominantly *personal*, though not necessarily so. Chiefly with verbs, some adjectives; e.g., "A certain young man followed with him" = νεανίσκος τις συνηκολούθει αὐτῷ (Mark 14:51).

IV. *Dative with verbs.*

    A. Very common with compound verbs and their derivatives, though most common as the *indirect object* of verbs (ἀντί-, ἐν, παρά-, περί-, πρόσ-, ὑπό-, σύν, ἐπί); e.g., "They are bringing little children to him" = προσέφερον αὐτῷ παιδία (Mark 10:13).

    B. *Direct object* of verbs with a strong idea of *personal relation* (ἀπειθέω, διακονέω, λατρεύω, προσκυνέω, ὑπακούω); e.g., "to please God" = θεῷ ἀρέσαι (Rom. 8:8).

    C. When infinitive is used for purpose; e.g., "We came to worship him" = ἤλθομεν προσκυνῆσαι αὐτῷ (Matt. 2:2).

Genitive case (three basic types)

The genitive case is the case of definition or description. It is *functionally adjectival* and usually limits a substantive or substantival construction. The qualifying force of the genitive case is more emphatic than that of an adjective. It is employed to qualify the meaning of a preceding noun and to show in what more definite sense the noun is to be taken. Its basic function is to *define*. It is the specifying case, expressive of *genus* or *kind. Its root meaning is attribution.*

I. *Adnominal/adjectival genitive:* The genitive is most commonly used to function as an *adjective*. Like an adjective, it can be either attributive or a predicate (dependent on εἶναι, γίνεσθαι, etc.).

    A. *Genitive of possession:* idea of ownership; to make one noun the attribute of another in the relation of privilege or prerogative. This is the most prevalent use of the genitive, especially with personal pronouns. Often the article alone occurs; e.g., "the slave of the high priest" = τὸν δοῦλον τοῦ ἀρχιερέως (Matt. 26:51); "one of the boats, which was Simon's" ("the one was Simon's") = ἐν τῶν πλοίων, ὃ ἦν Σίμωνος (Luke 5:3).

    Genitive of origin and relationship: A person is defined by the attribution of some familial or marital relationship. This case is closely akin to the genitive of possession—with a special application. It is employed to identify a person by his father, a mother by her son, a wife by her husband, slaves by a family, and so on; e.g., "Mary, the mother *of Jesus*" = Μαριὰμ τῇ μητρὶ Ἰησόυ (Acts 1:14).

B. *Genitive with nouns of action:* The noun defined by the genitive signifies action. The noun in the genitive indicates the thing to which the action is referred, either as the subject or the object of the verbal idea. Each example is decided by its own context.
   1. *Objective genitive:* The noun in the genitive *receives* the action, being thus related as *object* to the verbal idea contained in the noun modified; e.g., "zeal *for* God" = ζῆλος θεοῦ; "the blasphemy *of* [*or about, against*] the Spirit" = ἡ . . . τοῦ πνεύματος βλασφημία (Matt. 12:31); "have faith in God" = ἔχετε πίστιν θεοῦ (Mark 11:22).
   2. *Subjective genitive:* The noun in the genitive *produces* the action, being therefore related as *subject* to the verbal idea of the noun modified. The noun in the genitive is the originator or the cause; e.g., "the preaching of Jesus Christ" = τὸ κήρυγμα Ἰησοῦ Χριστοῦ (Rom. 16:25).
C. *Partitive genitive:* The genitive of the divided whole, while not yet extinct, is being driven out by the use of the prepositions. The noun is defined by indicating in the genitive the whole of which it is a part. This case approaches closely to the ablative idea. It sometimes occurs as the subject with "some" (τινές) understood; e.g., "the tenth of the city" = τὸ δέκατον τῆς πόλεως (Rev. 11:13).
D. *Genitive of quality/description:* an attributive that would ordinarily be provided by an adjective. Combinations with σῶμα are especially favored; e.g., "the body of sin" ("the body marked by [or characterized] by sin") = τὸ σῶμα τῆς ἁμαρτίας (Rom. 6:6).

   Genitive of description: the use of the genitive that lies closest to its root meaning; e.g., "We are not shrinking back" = ἡμεῖς δὲ οὐκ ἐσμὲν ὑποστολῆς (Heb. 10:39).

   Genitive of apposition/content: a type of *genitive of quality*; e.g., "the house of the tent" ("the house consisting in the tent") = οἰκία τοῦ σκήνους (2 Cor. 5:1); "the guarantee that consists in the Spirit" = τὸν ἀρραβῶνα τοῦ πνεύματος (2 Cor. 1:22). The genitive stands in exact apposition with the noun it modifies; e.g., "the cities of Sodom and Gomorrah" = πολεῖς σοδόμων καὶ γομόρρας (2 Peter 2:6).
E. *Genitive of the articular infinitive:* This use is sometimes employed without any preposition to express purpose (infinitive + article in genitive case). It is an old and common use; e.g., Jesus came to John "*in order to* be baptized by him" = τοῦ

βαπτισθῆναι ὑπ' αὐτοῦ (Matt. 3:13). The attraction of the relative pronoun to the genitive case of the antecedent is idiomatic; e.g., "all that he did" = πάντων ὧν ἐποίησεν (Acts 10:39).

II. *Adverbial genitive:* The genitive is sometimes used to define a verbal idea by attributing local or temporal relations, or by qualifying an adjective. The attributive function is still present, for it is a kind of action that is being emphasized.

A. *Genitive of time ("by," "in"):* focuses on time within which something takes place rather than a point of time (locative) or on a duration of time (accusative); communicates "this time rather than some other time"; e.g., "this one came to him within the night" = οὗτος ἦλθεν πρὸς αὐτὸν νυκτὸς (John 3:2).

B. *Genitive of place/local use of the genitive:* probably the earliest and most objective. "Here and not there." The common adverbs of place are all in the genitive: αὐτοῦ ("here"), οὗ, ὅπου ("where"), ποῦ ("where"), πανταχοῦ ("everywhere"), ὁμοῦ ("together"). Various prepositions may be used to clarify the local use of the genitive, such as ἀντί, ἐναντίον, ἕνεκα, ἐντάς, ἐπί, μετά, περί, and πλησίον. Adverbs of place take the genitive: ἔξω, ἐγγύς ("near"); e.g., "not only at Ephesus" = οὐ μόνον Ἐφέσου (Acts 19:26).

C. *Genitive of reference/genitive with adjectives:* The genitive is sometimes used with adjectives to refer their qualifying force to certain limits. This use is parallel to that with substantives; e.g., "my own benefit" = τὸ ἐμαυτοῦ σύμφορον (1 Cor. 10:33) .

D. *Genitive with verbs:* With verbs the genitive means "this and no other," whereas the accusative with verbs means "this and no more." The genitive is translated as a direct object.

  1. Verbs of emotion and sensation (e.g., "to bear with," "care for," "touch," "take hold of," "remember," "forget," "smell"), as well as verbs of perception, may take the genitive. With respect to ἀκούω, the person whose words are heard stands in the genitive; the thing/person one hears stands in the accusative; e.g., "remember Lot's wife" = μνημονεύετε τῆς γυναικὸς Λώτ (Luke 17:32).

  2. Verbs of sharing and filling, such as "bread to spare" = περισσεύονται ἄρτων (Luke 15:17).

  3. Verbs of ruling, striving, desiring, and reaching; e.g., "to strive after," "desire," "to reach," "obtain," "to fill," "be full of," "rule," "surpass," e.g., ἄρχω (Mark 10:42).

  4. Verbs of buying, selling, being worthy of serve as the genitive of price or value; e.g., "to buy," "sell," "agree on," and "exchange for," e.g., Matt. 20:2.

  5. Verbs of accusing and condemning may be found with the genitive as a direct object, e.g., Matt. 12:10.

E. *Genitive absolute (absolute = "loosened," "separated"):* A noun or pronoun with a participle stands out of grammatical connection with the rest of the sentence. Both are in the genitive. Translate the genitive with *"when" or "after,"* and the participle as a finite verb, e.g., "When/after the demon had been cast out" = ἐκβληθέντος τοῦ δαιμονίου (Matt. 9:33).

III. *Genitive of separation/ablative:* The genitive is the case of separation (e.g., ἀπό, ἐκ); the dative is the case of rest in a place (e.g., ἐν), and the accusative is the case of motion toward a place (e.g., εἰς). *Ablativus:* that which is borne away or separated. The point of departure is not only in the literal removal of one object from the vicinity of another but in any idea that implies departure from antecedent relations, such as derivation, cause, or origin.

Verbs of separation: include "to separate," "to hinder somebody from doing something," "to depart from," "be away from," "be in need of," "keep away from," "restrain oneself," "cease," "abstain," "miss," "lack," and "despair."

A. *Ablative/genitive of comparison:* e.g., "greater things *than* these will he do" = μείζονα τούτων ποιήσει (John 14:12).

B. *Ablative of means/genitive with substantivized verbal adjective/ genitive of source ("by," ὑπό):* may be used when the expression of means is accompanied by an implication of origin or source. Used to designate an agent with the passive voice. It expresses the active personal *agent* by which an action is performed; e.g., "There was great lamentation by [from] all" = ἱκανὸς . . . κλαυθμὸς ἐγένετο πάντων (Acts 20:37).

Accusative case (two basic types)

The accusative is probably the oldest and most widely used case. It indicates the direction, extent, or end of action. The accusative signifies that the object referred to is considered as the point toward which something is proceeding. It is the case of motion toward a place. It answers the question "How far?"

I. Substantival uses of the accusative.
   A. The simple accusative of the object.
      1. *Accusative of direct object:* noun as object (receiving the action) of a transitive verb. The action of the verb extends to the external object, passes over (transitive); e.g., "I speak truth" = ἀλήθειαν λέγω (John 8:45).
      2. *Accusative with the passive:* Verbs in passive voice may be transitive, such as verbs with meanings: "to speak well or ill of one," "abstain," "have mercy."

B. *Simple accusative of content/cognate accusative/accusative of the inner object:* When an accusative of the direct object contains the same idea signified by the verb, the limits set by the accusative are coextensive with the significance of the verb, the use being for emphasis. The action of the verb expresses itself in a word of the same root or a word similar in idea. (When an accusative is a cognate of the verb in etymology or meaning, a qualifying word or phrase is needed for the accusative to serve a purpose.). E.g, "I have fought the good fight" = τὸν καλὸν ἀγῶνα ἠγώνισμαι (2 Tim. 4:7).

C. *Double accusative:* Some verbs require more than one object to complete their meaning. Both accusatives are external objects.

   1. *Verbs that take a personal and an impersonal object:* "to teach," "remind," "inquire," "ask," "dress," and "undress"; e.g., "He will teach you all things" = ἐκεῖνος ὑμᾶς διδάξει (John 14:26).

   2. *Verbs that take a direct and a predicate object:* The second accusative may be in apposition with the first, following verbs like "to have as," "take as," "designate as," "call," and "regard as"; e.g., "No longer do I call you servants" = οὐκέτι λέγω ὑμᾶς δούλους (John 15:15).

   3. *Verbs that are causative and verbs of good and evil have two accusatives;* also known as a double accusative, e.g., "I adjure you by God" = ὁρκίζω σε τὸν θεόν (Mark 5:7).

II. *Adverbial accusative:* noun or pronoun in accusative case qualifies the verb in an indirect way. It is employed to denote a material object only in a mediate or remote way. It limits by indicating a fact indirectly related to the action rather than directly affected by the action. Adverbial accusatives essentially function as adverbs. An adverb is a word in a fixed case.

A. *Accusative of measure/extension of space:* answers the question "How far?"; e.g., "He was separated about a stone's throw" = ἀπεσπάσθη . . . ὡσεὶ λίθου βολὴν (Luke 22:41). The *accusative of duration* answers the questions "How long?" or "When?" with ὥρα.

B. *Accusative of manner:* for example, "freely you have received, freely give" = δωρεὰν ἐλάβετε, δωρεὰν δότε (Matt. 10:8).

C. *Accusative of reference/accusative with the infinitive:* the accusative is used with the infinitive in indirect discourse where the accusative is translated as the subject and the infinitive as a finite verb; e.g., "who labored for you *with reference to* many things" = ἥτις πολλὰ ἐκοπίασεν εἰς ὑμᾶς (Rom. 16:6); "This night before the rooster crows twice" = ταύτῃ τῇ νυκτὶ πρὶν ἢ δὶς ἀλέκτορα φωνῆσαι (Mark 14:30).

The *accusative of general reference* includes the *accusative absolute—a noun or pronoun with a participle both in the accusative case standing out of grammatical connection with the rest of the sentence.* Translate the participle as a finite verb; e.g., "you are acquainted" = γνώστην ὄντα σε (Acts 26:3).

D. *Accusative of inverse attraction:* The antecedent (substantive) is attracted into the case of the relative; e.g., "the bread that we break" = τὸν ἄρτον ὃν κλῶμεν (1 Cor. 10:16).

Infinitive (two basic types)

I. Verbal/adverbial uses of the infinitive.
   A. Idiomatic expressions with prepositions.
      1. εἰς τὸ (also πρὸς τό, τοῦ) + infinitive = "*in order to*" (to express purpose or result).[39]
      2. διά τό (also παρὰ τό) + infinitive = "*because*" (to express cause); e.g., "because of not having" ("because it had no") = διὰ τὸ μὴ ἔχειν (Matt. 13:5).
      3. *Time/infinitive in a temporal clause:* ἐν τῷ + present infinitive = "while," "as," "in"/"during the process of" (the infinitive denotes *contemporaneous* time); ἐν τῷ + aorist infinitive = "when"; e.g., "while they hear and see the signs" = ἐν τῷ ἀκούειν αὐτοὺς καὶ βλέπειν (Acts 8:6); πρίν/πρὶν ἤ (the infinitive expresses antecedent time); e.g., "*before* the cock crows twice" = πρὶν ἢ δὶς ἀλέκτορα φωνῆσαι (Mark 14:30). μετὰ τό + infinitive (the infinitive expresses subsequent time); e.g., "*after* I have risen" = μετὰ . . . του ἐγερθῆναί με (Matt. 26:32).
   B. Purpose and result.
      1. *Purpose:* Infinitives may express the aim of the action denoted by the finite verb. This usage is very common in the New Testament, especially with verbs of motion, giving, and sending. It was replaced by ἵνα. Equivalent of a final clause. May be infinitive + τοῦ or infinitive + preposition (εἰς, πρός, ὥστε); e.g., "and we have come *to* worship him" = καὶ ἤλθομεν προσκυνῆσαι αὐτῷ (Matt. 2:2).
      2. *Result:* often blending of purpose and result. May be actual, conceived, or intended result. Replaced by ὅτι. May be simple infinitive, infinitive + τοῦ, or infinitive + preposition (εἰς, ὥστε); e.g., "I shall be prospered to come to you" = εὐοδωθήσομαι . . . ἐλθεῖν πρὸς ὑμᾶς (Rom. 1:10).

---

39. See also genitive of the articular infinitive, above.

136 | In-Depth Study of the Text

  C. Infinitive absolute.

    The *absolute infinitive is found in letter greetings:* e.g., "greet-
    ings" = χαίρειν (Acts 15:23); "so to speak" = ὡς ἔπος εἰπεῖν
    (Heb. 7:9).

  D. *Imperatival infinitive/command:* extremely old, and not very
    frequent. It functions as a finite verb; e.g., "let us walk" = τῷ
    αὐτῷ στοιχεῖν (Phil. 3:16).

 II. Substantival uses of the infinitive.

  A. *As subject or object of verb/infinitive as complement of a verb:*
    The infinitive as a complement of a verb borders closely on an
    infinitive of purpose or result. It is used with such verbs as "to
    wish," "strive," "avoid," "ask," "summon," "be able," "know how
    to," and "permit."

    1. *Subject of a finite verb:* for example, "for to will is present
     with me" = τὸ γὰρ θέλειν παράκειταί μοι (Rom. 7:18).

    2. *Object of a finite verb:* A substantive object is essentially the
     complement of a verbal idea. Frequently, the infinitive can
     have a subject accusative or simply a different subject; e.g.,
     "And they sought to lay hold of him" = Καὶ ἐζήτουν αὐτὸν
     κρατῆσαι (Mark 12:12).

  B. *Infinitive in indirect discourse:* the practical equivalent of a
    clause, or the object of a verb of saying; e.g., "They answered
    how they did not know" = ἀπεκρίθησαν μὴ εἰδέναι πόθεν (Luke
    20:7).

  C. *Indirect object of a verb:* that for which or with reference to
    which the action or state of the governing verb is performed or
    exists; e.g., "My sister has been leaving me to serve alone" = ἡ
    ἀδελφή μου μόνην με κατέλιπεν διακονεῖν (Luke 10:40).

  D. *Epexegetical and appositional infinitive:* an infinitive may be
    in apposition with a noun or adjective or used with a verb
    ("epexegetical" = explanatory), especially with meanings such
    as "authority," "need," "ability," or "fitness"; e.g., "a rush to
    mistreat" = ὁρμὴ . . . ὑβρίσαι (Acts 14:5).

  E. *Articular infinitive:* article + infinitive. The article makes the
    phrase definite, not technically substantive. The word μή is
    always negative for the infinitive. Infinitive + preposition is
    always articular in the New Testament. The subject of the infini-
    tive is in the accusative case; e.g., "He did not consider *the being
    [the act of being]* equal with God" = οὐχ ἁρπαγμὸν ἡγήσατο
    τὸ εἶναι ἴσα θεῷ (Phil. 2:6).

Types of conditions (four basic types)[40]

Conditional sentences express the way and the mood in which the speaker *chooses* to represent the condition under consideration. They do not necessarily correspond to fact. Mode determines the type of Greek conditional sentence. It sets up a supposition that, if fulfilled, leads to certain results and various degrees of reality.

Subordinate clause	*Principal clause*
• Also known as a conditional clause • Comprises a protasis, beginning often with "if"	• Also known as a main or result clause • Comprises an apodosis or conclusion, which attains reality by reason of the protasis

I.   Condition that uses the indicative mood: always makes a *clear-cut assertion*. Condition is determined. (Classified according to function.)

A.   *First class/condition determined as fulfilled/simple condition/ present condition/εἰ with the indicative of reality/real condition:* condition = fact stated as "if." Predominately used with reference to a present or alleged reality. Condition *assumes* the reality of the condition. Indicative mode *states* it as a fact. It denotes a simple conditional assumption with emphasis on the reality of the assumption. This is the most common or normal condition.

εἰ (sometimes ἐάν)	+ indicative, any tense, especially unaugmented/ primary	Generally indicative (though sometimes imperative or subjunctive), never uses ἄν

For example, "If I by Beezeboul cast out the demons, by whom do your sons cast them out?" = εἰ ἐγὼ ἐν Βεελζεβοὺλ ἐκβάλλω τὰ δαιμόνια, οἱ υἱοὶ ὑμῶν ἐν τίνι ἐκβάλλουσιν (Matt. 12:27).

B.   *Second class/condition determined as unfulfilled/contrary-to-fact condition/εἰ with the augmented tense of the indicative/unreal condition:* The presumption is assumed to be contrary to fact. It always occurs in its full form, "an unreal case," the unreal (contrary-to-fact) indicative in conditional sentences.

εἰ	+ past/secondary tense of indicative (imperfect, aorist, pluperfect)	Usually ἄν + past/secondary indicative

---

40.   See also, "The Structural Relation of Clauses," above for a more detailed description. See further Robertson, *Grammar*, 1007–27.

138 | In-Depth Study of the Text

For example, "This fellow, if he were the prophet [he is not], he would know [as he does not]" = Οὗτος εἰ ἦν προφήτης, ἐγίνωσκεν ἂν (Luke 7:39).

II. *Condition that uses the subjunctive or optative mode:* A *doubtful or undetermined statement* is made whatever may be the actual fact or truth in the case. It expresses varying degrees of uncertainty or doubt. It has less doubt if subjunctive rather than optative is used.

A. *Third class/condition undetermined with prospect of determination/more probably future condition/ἐάν with the subjunctive/ minor degree of doubt:* It states the condition as a matter of doubt but with some expectation of realization and denotes that which under certain circumstances is expected from an existing general or concrete standpoint in the present "case of expectation." It is very common, a condition about something which has not yet happened: potential.

ἐάν/εἰ + subjunctive	Future indicative (usually); may also be present indicative or imperative

For example, "And this we will do, if God permits" = καὶ τοῦτο ποιήσομεν, ἐάνπερ ἐπιτρέπῃ ὁ θεός (Heb. 6:3).

B. *Fourth class/condition undetermined with remote prospect of determination/the less-probable future condition/indefinite future condition/εἰ with the optative/major or strong degree of doubt:* presents something as thought of as less probable, without regard for reality or unreality, and emphasizes the hypothetical character of the assumption; "a potential case." No complete New Testament example.

ἐάν/εἰ + optative (sometimes subjunctive; no negatives)	Optative (ἄν)

For example, "But even if you should suffer for righteousness' sake, you are happy" (condition only) = ἀλλ᾽ εἰ καὶ πάσχοιτε διὰ δικαιοσύνην, μακάριοι (1 Peter 3:14).

C. *Exceptions:*
   1. *Mixed condition:* One of four kinds of conditions is used in the condition, and another is used in the conclusion; e.g., "If you have . . . [first class], you would say [second class]" = Εἰ ἔχετε . . . , ἐλέγετε ἂν (Luke 17:6).
   2. *Implied, elliptical condition,* e.g., 1 Cor. 12:19.
   3. *Concessive clause:* Realization is secured *despite* the protasis. It consists of a conditional clause with the addition of καί or καὶ εἰ (ἐάν): "even if," "if also," "although," "though," "even

though," "but if," and "if"; e.g., "even if I judge" = καὶ ἐὰν κρίνω (John 8:16).

Participles (two basic types)

Participle versus infinitive[41]

Participle has pronounced adjective function	Infinitive is an indeclinable noun.
Participle generally contemplates action as real; e.g., "Begging, I am ashamed [and so shall stop it]."	Infinitive implies potential of action; e.g., "I am ashamed to beg [and so cannot do it]" (Luke 16:3).
Real object of governing verb is a person or thing whose act or state is described by the participle.	Infinitive real object of verb is an act or state.
Participle connects the action with the subject or individual;	Infinitive often connects the action with the verb;

The participle participates in both the verb and the adjective.

I. *As an adjective.*
   A. *Attributive/adjectival participle:* An articular participle is always attributive; e.g., "the healthful teaching" = τῇ ὑγιαινούσῃ διδασκαλίᾳ (1 Tim. 1:10). The participle may be, but usually is not, attributive without the article; e.g., "living water" = ὕδωρ ζῶν (John 4:10). The articular participle often appears in translation as the equivalent of a relative clause; e.g., "the one who steals" ("the stealing one") = ὁ κλέπτων (Eph. 4:28).
   B. *Predicate adjective:* Without the article the participle is most likely predicate. It may be used like an adjective in the predicate after a verb of being; e.g., "I was unknown *by* face" = ἤμην δὲ ἀγνοούμενος τῷ προσώπῳ (Gal. 1:22).
II. *As a verb/adverbial participle/predicate participle:* The participle is involved in the relation of the noun that it modifies to the action or state expressed in the main verb and exhibits predominantly verbal characteristics. Aorist and perfect participles usually denote antecedent action to the main verb. Present participles usually convey contemporaneous action to the main verb.
   A. *Supplementary or complementary participle:* The predicate completes the idea of the principal verb, which would otherwise not be clear; e.g., "that they may appear to be fasting" = ὅπως φανῶσιν . . . νηστεύοντες (Matt. 6:16).
      1. *The periphrastic conjugation (construction or use of the participle):* a common idiom. Participle + finite verb = a compound tense form. The periphrastic imperfect is most

---

41. Dana and Mantey, *Manual Grammar,* 221–23.

140 | In-Depth Study of the Text

common in the New Testament. The verb εἰμί is generally used, as is γίνομαι, ὑπάρχω, and ἔχω + a participle. May be subdivided into 6 types depending on the tense of the verb and the participle;[42] e.g., "He was teaching" = Ἦν . . . διδάσκων (Luke 13:10).:

Type of periphrastic participle	E.g.	verb	participle	effect
present	Col. 2:23	present	present	durative
imperfect	Mark 10:32	imperfect	present	durative
future	Mark 13:25	future	present	durative
perfect	Col. 1:21	present	perfect	intensive
pluperfect	Matt. 26:48	imperfect	perfect	intensive
future perfect	Heb. 2:13	future	perfect	

2. *In indirect discourse:* The participle as an adjective agrees with the substantive or pronoun and completes the idea; e.g., "which confesses Jesus Christ come in the flesh" ("*that* Jesus Christ has come in the flesh") = ὁ ὁμολογεῖ Ἰησοῦν Χριστὸν ἐν σαρκὶ ἐληλυθότα (1 John 4:2).

3. *The Hebraistic intensifying participle:* the effort in the LXX to reproduce the Hebrew infinitive absolute; e.g., "Let him die the death" = θανάτῳ τελευτάτω (Matt. 15:4).

B. *Circumstantial participle:* practically an additional clause, a sort of loose addendum to the sentence.[43] The point of contact may be with the subject, object, or any substantive or pronoun in the principle clause or an entirely independent construction; e.g., "They went forth *and* preached everywhere" = ἐκεῖνοι δὲ ἐξελθόντες ἐκήρυξαν πανταχοῦ (Mark 16:20).

1. *Temporal participle:* a participle used in the sense of a temporal clause, translated with "when," "after," or "while"; e.g., "he, coming, will rebuke" ("when he comes, he will rebuke") = ἐλθὼν ἐκεῖνος ἐλέγξει (John 16:8).

2. *Manner/modal participle:* A participle may signify the manner in which the action of the main verb is accomplished. It may be accompanied by ὡς, and it is often translated with "by"; e.g., "he went away grieved [by grieving]" = ἀπῆλθεν λυπούμενος (Matt. 19:22).

3. *Means/instrumental participle:* A participle may indicate the means by which the action of the main verb is accomplished. It is often translated with "by" or "by means of";

---

42. Dana and Mantey, *Manual Grammar,* 231–33; Robertson, *Grammar,* 374–76; Wallace, *Grammar,* 647–49.
43. In a sentence flow, I treat this as a phrase, not a clause.

e.g., "Who by being anxious is able?" = τίς . . . μεριμνῶν δύναται (Matt. 6:27).

4. *Cause/causal participle:* A participle may denote the ground of the action conveyed by the main verb, translated frequently with "because" and "since." It is very common in the New Testament; e.g., "We give thanks, having heard" ("We give thanks because we have heard") = Εὐχαριστοῦμεν . . . , ἀκούσαντες (Col. 1:3–4).

5. *Purpose participle/telic participle or result:* Purpose is denoted by the participle, ordinarily future. It is not frequent and translates with "to" or "in order to"; e.g., "he had come to worship" = ἐληλύθει προσκυνήσων (Acts 8:27).

6. *Condition/conditional participle:* A participle may function as the protasis of a conditional sentence. It is often translated with "if"; e.g., "from which, if you keep yourselves, you will do well" = ἐξ ὧν διατηροῦντες ἑαυτοὺς εὖ πράξετε (Acts 15:29).

7. *Concession/concessive participle:* A participle may denote a sense of concession, used either with or without the concessive participle. It is often translated with "though"; e.g., "For if, being enemies [though we were enemies], we were reconciled to God" = εἰ γὰρ ἐχθροὶ ὄντες κατηλλάγημεν τῷ θεῷ (Rom. 5:10).

C. *Genitive (or ablative) absolute.*[44]
D. *Accusative absolute.*[45]
E. *Independent participle/participle used as an imperative:* stands alone amid imperatives as if an imperative. There are few examples in the New Testament; e.g., "abhorring the evil" = ἀποστυγοῦντες τὸ πονηρόν (Rom. 12:9).

---

44. See the definition of genitive absolute under types of cases: genitive, above.
45. See the definition under types of cases: accusative, above.

142 | In-Depth Study of the Text

Grammatical Information Sheet: Blank

Text: Name & email:

Cite every word in your passage, no matter how small, include article with word modified, except if article functions as pronoun. Description is the basic grammatical form and parsing. The last column should include translation and as much grammatical information as helpful in interpretation. Use as many pages as necessary.

Ref.	Text Form	Lexical Form	Description	Use/Meaning

Grammatical Information Sheet of Philemon 4–6

Ref.	Text Form	Lexical Form	Description	Use/Meaning
v.4	Εὐχαριστῶ	Εὐχαριστέω	verb, 1st-person singular present active indicative	"I give thanks"
	τῷ θεῷ	Θεός, ὁ	noun, dative singular	"God" dative here is direct object of verb with strong idea of personal relation
	μου	ἐγώ	personal pronoun, genitive singular	"my"
	πάντοτε	πάντοτε	adverb	"always"
	μνείαν	μνεία, ἡ	noun, accusative singular	"remembrance, mention"
	σου	σύ	personal pronoun, genitive singular	"of you/your"
	ποιούμενος	ποιέω	participle present middle/passive	"making for myself" adverbial: manner or temporal
	ἐπὶ	ἐπί	preposition	"at" Ground meaning is "upon," a real resting upon, "period of prayer" in the time of /during. (ATR* 600, 603) What is difference between ἐπί, πρός, εἰς?
	τῶν προσευχῶν	προσευχή, ἡ	noun, genitive plural	"prayers"
	μου	ἐγώ	personal pronoun, genitive singular	"my"
v.5	ἀκούων	ἀκούω	participle, present active, masculine singular nominative	"hearing" adverbial: cause, probably modifies: ποιούμενος.
	σου	σύ	personal pronoun, genitive singular	"of you, your"
	τὴν ἀγάπην	ἀγάπη, ἡ	noun, accusative singular	"love"
	καὶ	καί	conjunction	"and"

144 | In-Depth Study of the Text

Ref.	Text Form	Lexical Form	Description	Use/Meaning
v.5	τὴν πίστιν	πίστις, ἡ	noun, accusative singular	"faith" could be hendiadys "faithful love"
	ἣν	ὅς, ἥ, ὅ	relative pronoun, feminine, modifies accusative singular	"which" "faith" and/or "love" introduces subordinate adjectival clause.
	ἔχεις	ἔχω	verb, present active indicative 2nd-person singular	"you have"
	πρὸς	πρός	preposition	"toward" (with accusative) root idea is "near, near by, facing." The acc. case implies extension. Faith "toward" Jesus and love "upon" people. Intimate. (ATR* 622, 624)
	τὸν κύριον	Κύριος	noun, accusative singular	"Lord"
	Ἰησοῦν	Ἰησοῦς	noun, accusative singular	"Jesus"
	καὶ	καί	conjunction	"and"
	εἰς	εἰς	preposition	"toward" aim/purpose The root ἐν-ς "lie within" +accusative, which normally suggests motion (ATR* 591, 594)
	πάντας	πᾶς	adjective, plural accusative masculine	"all"
	τοὺς ἁγίους	ἅγιος, α, ον	adjective, plural accusative; here used as noun	"saints"
v.6	ὅπως	ὅπως	conjunction	"so that, with the result that" introduces subordinate adverbial-result clause (not purpose)
	ἡ κοινωνία	κοινωνία, ἡ	noun, nominative singular	"fellowship" sharing partnership

Seek a Translation and Understand the Grammar of the Text | 145

Ref.	Text Form	Lexical Form	Description	Use/Meaning
v.6	τῆς πίστεώς	πίστις, ἡ	noun, genitive singular	"faith" can be objective gen. ("partnership for your faith" or subjective genitive "partnership of your faith")
	σου	σύ	personal pronoun genitive singular	"your"
	ἐνεργής	ἐνεργής, ές	adjective, nominative singular masculine + feminine	"effectual, effective, active, powerful," predicate adjective
	γένηται	γίνομαι	verb, subjunctive aorist middle 3rd-person singular	"might become"; subjunctive root idea is expectation, doubtful statement; aorist is usually punctiliar action (ATR* 848, 926)
	ἐν	ἐν	preposition	"in/within"; location is within the bounds marked by the word with which it occurs (ATR* 585)
	ἐπιγνώσει	ἐπίγνωσις, ἡ	noun, dative singular	"in knowledge"
	παντὸς	πᾶς	adjective, singular genitive masculine/neuter	"all"
	ἀγαθοῦ	ἀγαθός, όν	adjective, singular genitive masculine/neuter; here used as noun	"good [thing]"
	τοῦ	ὁ, ἡ, τό	article, singular genitive masculine/neuter; here used as noun	"the one" substantive article functioning as adjective modifying "good"
	ἐν	ἐν	preposition	"in"
	ὑμῖν (variant chosen)	σύ	personal pronoun plural dative	"you" (plural)
	εἰς	εἰς	preposition	"toward"
	Χριστόν	Χριστός, ὁ	noun accusative singular	"Christ"

*ATR= A. T. Robertson, *Grammar of the Greek New Testament.*

CHAPTER 5

UNDERSTAND THE MEANING
OF THE WORDS AND PHRASES

I. *Choose* a word or phrase to study. What looks important, unclear, interesting, odd/striking, natural/mundane, difficult to understand, and yet manageable in your text to study?
II. *Raise questions* about the meaning of your word/phrase.
III. *Find lexical forms.*
IV. *Locate* all the New Testament passages of the word family (noun, verb, adjective, adverb, etc.). If the word is not frequent in the New Testament, find related words using the same root.
V. *Study the context* of each use.
   A. *Begin with the text and its book or letter.* Study the sentence and immediate context for possible and impossible significances. Set limits and possibilities of meaning. Read the context. What is the trend of thought? Is the word being used literally or meta-phorically? How does literal use(s) of the word help give meaning to its metaphorical use(s)?
      1. Use *definitions/explanations* that the author gives.
      2. Learn about a word by looking for antonyms (opposite, contrast) or *repetition* (synonyms).
      3. *Subject* and *predicate* mutually explain one another.
      4. Author may have *examples* or outward manifestations of principles in action.
      5. *Modifiers* (adjectives, adverbs, prepositions, conjunctions, nouns) may help define a word.
   B. *Study the usage of the word elsewhere* in the New Testament using the same methodology. Keep in mind priority of context—in other words, understand a word in light of the following.

148 | In-Depth Study of the Text

      1. Sentence, paragraph, letter.
      2. Writings by the same author.
      3. The rest of the New Testament.

VI. *Study etymology.*[1]
   A. Does the word break down into clear parts?
   B. Find the "organizing" or root word (often verb). How does the meaning of roots help give significance to a word in its contexts? Find "related" synonyms or antonyms.

VII. *Classify the shades of meaning* found. Make up your own definitions or categories. Ask and check. What is the criteria you are using for categories? Are these categories exclusive of each other? Should some categories be subdivisions of other categories?

VIII. *Study further* the usage of the word in the Greek Old Testament and extrabiblical uses (contemporary Greek usage).
   A. Check Henry George Liddell and Robert Scott, comp., *A Greek-English Lexicon,* rev. Henry Stuart Jones (Oxford: Clarendon, 1996; hereafter referred to as LSJ). If time allows, check uses in LXX.
   B. As time allows, take a sampling of uses in the first through second century *or* pick a key author, such as Josephus, the Apocrypha, Philo, the Papyri, Strabo, Epictetus, or the Pseudepigrapha.
   C. Study and add to your classifications of the meanings of the word.

IX. *Compare* your findings with a Greek lexicon's classifications and, if time allows, with helpful secondary references. Do you have good reasons for your categories? Do you need to change some categories?

X. *Integrate your findings.* Write in essay form. Present your conclusion. What is the core or main meaning of your word? Summarize all the categories or uses of the word studied. Define each and give at least one example for each category. Footnote all other examples in each category. In which category does the meaning of the word in your text fit? How do uses of your word enlighten the text studied? How does the main meaning enlighten your particular passage? Give your reasons. Explain all that you learned from the immediate context.

---

1. Etymology is the true basis for a word's later meaning. In interpretation we are interested in a word's component parts or the earliest attested meaning of a word (Moisés Silva, *Biblical Words and Their Meaning: An Introduction to Lexical Semantics* [Grand Rapids: Zondervan, 1983], 39.) According to A. T. Robertson, Greek has about four hundred roots, the original stock of words, which are verbs and pronouns. Verbs, nouns, and pronouns are the earliest parts of speech. Some of these roots go back to a common Indo-Germanic stock. As for prepositions, Robertson recommends the interpreter hold on to the root idea or ground meaning and work out from that in each special context (Robertson, *A Grammar of the Greek New Testament in the Light of Historical Research* [Nashville: Broadman, 1934], 144–45, 600).

Explain how etymology, if helpful, helps explain the significance of your word or phrase. Clarify how usage of the word in your chosen text compares to broader uses of the word. Have you answered any questions you raised from your broader study of the word?

This step can be done by both Greek and translation readers.

INTRODUCTION

How do we communicate something completely different from the usual news, in other words, that God, the Creator of the universe, has become incarnate in the form of a creation, a human. We could create new words, but few people, if any, would understand them. As a result, we choose old words and give them new meanings. Words contain the minimum unit of written meaning and thought. Words plus structure result in meaning. Thus, the interpreter goes back and forth between words and sentences. As we tried to discover the purpose of a writer when writing a letter (see wider context, ch. 1), likewise we want to discover the meaning of a word for its writer when it was written to a specific group of readers. If we were to look up the meaning of a New Testament word in a contemporary dictionary, we might learn its definitions in English for the twenty-first century, but we need to know its meaning in first-century Greek. Again, context will help us.

For instance, what is faith? According to *Webster's Unabridged Dictionary,* faith is "confidence or trust in a person or thing" or "firm belief in something for which there is no proof."[2] But according to the writer of Hebrews, "Faith is confidence in what we hope for and assurance about what we do not see" (11:1 NIV) or "confidence, while hoping for oneself, certainty of matters not being seen" (author's translation). The English and New Testament meanings have some similarities but are not identical. Confidence is part of both definitions. The New Testament brings out more of the paradox: confidence versus hope and certainty versus being unseen. All of Hebrews 11 further explains the meaning of faith by illustrations and explanations.

Another example would be, What is eternal life? *Webster's Unabridged Dictionary* defines eternal as "without beginning or end, lasting forever; always existing."[3] Jesus defined eternal life as "that they may know you, the only true God, and Jesus Christ, whom you have sent" (John 17:3 NRSV). In the New Testament, for humans, eternal life has a beginning, but it lasts forever. It is embodied by a personal acquaintance with God and with whom God sent—namely, Jesus Christ.

Further, a word or phrase may be defined by its synonym or its antonym. For instance, Elizabeth told Mary: "Blessed are you among women." Why

---

2. *Random House Webster's Unabridged Dictionary* (2001), s.v. "faith."
3. *Random House Webster's Unabridged Dictionary* (2001), s.v. "eternal life."

150 | In-Depth Study of the Text

was she blessed? Because of her own righteousness? No, in this case, she was blessed because of the fruit of her womb, Jesus (Luke 1:42). She was the mother of her Lord (v. 43).

Another example would be, What does it mean to repent? We often think of *Webster's* second definition, "to feel such sorrow for sin or fault as to be disposed to change one's life for the better,"[4] and then we are surprised by Jonah 3:10: "God repented of the evil, that he had said he would do unto them; and he did it not" (KJV). How can God ever sin or have faults? But the Bible's use of "repent" here aligns more with *Webster's* first definition: "to feel sorry, self-reproachful, or contrite for past conduct."[5] In Jonah 3:10 "repent" simply signifies a change of decision. Rather than punish, God chose to forgive the Ninevites for their evil actions. God's character does not change, but God's decisions do.

The immediate literary context helps us to understand a writer's meaning. Linguist Kermit Titrud reminds us of the rule of maximum redundancy: "The best meaning is the least meaning. . . . The correct meaning in individual contexts is usually that which contributes the least new information to the total context."[6] Some important resources to do a word study follow.

WORD STUDY REFERENCES

New Testament Concordances

Kohlenberger, John R., III, E. Goodrick, and J. Swanson. *The Exhaustive Concordance to the Greek New Testament.* Grand Rapids: Zondervan, 1995. (*ECGNT*)

Kohlenberger, John R., III, E. Goodrick, and J. Swanson. *The Greek-English Concordance to the New Testament: With the New International Version.* Grand Rapids: Zondervan, 1997. (*GECNT*)

McReynolds, Paul R., ed. *Word Study Greek-English New Testament.* Wheaton, IL: Tyndale House, 1999.

Strong, James. *The Strongest Strong's Exhaustive Concordance of the Bible.* Edited by John R. Kohlenberger III and James A. Swanson. Grand Rapids: Zondervan, 2001. https://www.biblestudytools.com/concordances/strongs-exhaustive-concordance/.

Young, Robert. *Young's Analytical Concordance to the Bible.* Rev. ed. (with index lexicons). Nashville: Nelson, 1982. https://archive.org/details/analyticalconcor00inyoun/page/n3/mode/2up.

---

4. *Random House Webster's Unabridged Dictionary* (2001), s.v. "repent."
5. *Random House Webster's Unabridged Dictionary* (2001), s.v. "repent."
6. Kermit Titrud, "The Function of *Kai* in the Greek New Testament and an Application to 2 Peter," in *Linguistics and New Testament Interpretation: Essays on Discourse Analysis,* ed. David Alan Black with Katharine Barnwell and Stephen Levinsohn (Nashville: Broadman, 1992), 248; Silva, *Biblical Words,* 153–54.

Parallel or Interlinear Bible References

Aland, Barbara, Kurt Aland, Johannes Karavidopoulos, Carlo M. Martini, and Bruce M. Metzger, eds. *The Greek-English New Testament: UBS Fifth Revised Edition and New International Version.* Grand Rapids: Zondervan, 2015.

Brenton, Lancelot Charles Lee, trans. *The Septuagint Version of the Old Testament and Apocrypha with an English Translation and with Various Readings and Critical Notes.* Grand Rapids: Zondervan, 1972. (LXX)

Brown, Robert K., Philip Wesley Comfort, and J. D. Douglas. *The New Greek-English Interlinear New Testament: A New Interlinear Translation of the Greek New Testament.* 3rd ed. Wheaton, IL: Tyndale House, 1990.

Kohlenberger, John R., III, ed. *The Greek New Testament: UBS4 with NRSV and NIV.* Grand Rapids: Zondervan, 1993.

Kohlenberger, John R., III, ed. *The Precise Parallel New Testament.* New York: Oxford University Press, 1995. (Greek text plus seven versions.)

A parallel New Testament can be created with software by choosing the latest Greek text, a more literal translation, such as the NRSV, and a dynamic equivalent, such as the NIV.

Greek-English Lexicons

Bauer, Walter, Frederick William Danker, W. F. Arndt, and F. W. Gingrich, eds. *A Greek-English Lexicon of the New Testament and Other Early Christian Literature.* 3rd ed. Chicago: University of Chicago Press, 2000. (BDAG)

Liddell, Henry George, and Robert Scott. *A Greek-English Lexicon.* Edited by Henry Stuart Jones. 9th ed. Oxford: Clarendon, 1968. (LSJ)

Louw, Johannes P., and Eugene A. Nida, eds. *Greek-English Lexicon of the New Testament Based on Semantic Domains.* 2nd ed. 2 vols. New York: United Bible Societies, 1989.

Newman, Barclay M. *A Concise Greek-English Dictionary of the New Testament.* Rev. ed. Stuttgart: Deutsche Bibelgesellschaft, 2014. (This dictionary is also available attached to the United Bible Societies' Greek New Testaments.)

Thayer, Joseph H. *Thayer's Greek-English Lexicon of the New Testament.* Unabridged. Marshallton, DE: National Foundation for Christian Education, 1889. https://www.blueletterbible.org/resources/lexical/thayers.cfm.

Old Testament Concordances

Hatch, Edwin, and Henry Redpath. *A Concordance to the Septuagint.* 2 vols. Grand Rapids: Baker, 1983. https://archive.org/details/aconcordancetos00redpgoog. (HRCS)

152 | In-Depth Study of the Text

Kohlenberger, John R., III, and James Swanson. *The Hebrew-English Concordance to the Old Testament.* Grand Rapids: Zondervan, 1998. (*HECOT*)

Concordances to Greek Extrabiblical References

Biblia Patristica. 2 vols. Anatole: Recherche Scientifique, 1975. (*BiPa*)

Borgen, Peter, Kåre Fuglseth, and Roald Skarsten. *The Philo Index: A Complete Greek Word Index to the Writings of Philo of Alexandria.* Grand Rapids: Eerdmans, 2000.

Deissmann, Adolf. *Light from the Ancient East: The New Testament Illustrated by Recently Discovered Texts of the Graeco-Roman World.* 4th ed. New York: Harper, 1922.

Garcia Martinez, Florentino. *Dead Sea Scrolls.* Online ed. Leiden: Brill, 1994.

Goodspeed, Edgar. *Index Patristicus.* Peabody, MA: Hendrickson, 1993.

Grenfell, B., and A. Hunt, eds. *Oxyrhynchus Papyri.* 18 vols. London: Egypt Exploration, 1898–1994.

Horsley, G. H. R., ed. *New Documents Illustrating Early Christianity: A Review of the Greek Inscriptions and Papyri.* 10 vols. North Ryde, Australia: Ancient History Qumran Documentary Research Centre, Macquarie University, 2012. (New Docs)

Kraft, Heinrich. *Clavis Patrum Apostolicorum.* Munich: Korsel, 1963. (*CPAi*)

Mayer, Günter. *Index Philoneus.* Berlin: de Gruyter, 1974.

Moulton, James H., and G. Milligan. *The Vocabulary of the Greek Testament: Illustrated from the Papyri and Other Non-Literary Sources.* Peabody, MA: Hendrickson, 1930. (MM)

Perseus. Online data bank; www.perseus.tufts.edu.

Rengstorf, Karl Heinrich, ed. *A Complete Concordance to Flavius Josephus.* 4 vols. Leiden: Brill, 1973.

Thesaurus Linguae Graecae. Online data bank. (*TLG*)

Further Secondary Reading

Kittel, Gerhard, and Gerhard Friedrich, eds. *Theological Dictionary of the New Testament.* Translated by Geoffrey W. Bromiley. 10 vols. Grand Rapids: Eerdmans, 1964–76.

Silva, Moisés. *Biblical Words and Their Meaning: An Introduction to Lexical Semantics.* Grand Rapids: Zondervan, 1983.

Spicq, Ceslas. *Theological Lexicon of the New Testament.* Translated and edited by James D. Ernest. 3 vols. Peabody, MA: Hendrickson, 1994.

Terry, Milton. "The Use of Words in Various Contexts." In *Rightly Divided: Readings in Biblical Hermeneutics*, edited by Roy B. Zuck, ch. 10. Grand Rapids: Kregel, 1996.

EXAMPLE OF HOW TO DO
A WORD STUDY (PHILEMON 4–6)

In the sample exegesis paper on Philemon 4–6 (chapter 8), I picked these three words to study: "remembrance" (*mneia*), "active" (*energēs*), and "sharing" (*koinōnia*). *Koinōnia* is an obvious word to study because it contributes to a significant New Testament concept. Understanding *mneia* might help answer my question, How could Paul make a request when thanking God? "Active" (*energēs*) seems to clarify the meaning of "faithful love." After doing the syntactical (grammatical) study, these words needed clarification.

If you do not know Greek, an interlinear translation with Strong's numbering, such as Paul McReynolds's *Word Study Greek-English New Testament*, will help you find the lexical form.[7] For example, "sharing" or "partnership" in Philemon 6 in *Word Study* has the Greek font (κοινωνία) and the number 2842.[8] In the back of the same book, 2842 appears with a list of New Testament words.[9] There are nineteen occurrences of *koinōnia* in the Greek New Testament ("GO").[10] A related word is number 2844 ("R"), "*koinōnos*, partner." Numbers 2841 ("*koinōneō*, I am partner") and 2845 ("*koinōnikos*, partner") also are related to 2844 ("*koinōnos*, partner"). Number 2844 is also related to 2840 ("*koinoō*, I make common, I defile"). The root word is "*koinos*, common" (2839). Thus, the word study should include a study of five different words (2840–2844), yielding fifty-two total references (two verbs, two nouns, and an adjective).

If you know Greek, since you did the parsing already, you know the lexical form, *koinōnia*. You now need to find all the New Testament occurrences. *The Exhaustive Concordance to the Greek New Testament* or *The Greek-English Concordance to the New Testament: With the New International Version* can be used. One book quotes each sentence in Greek, the other in English. A square root sign (√) indicates the root word.[11] Thus, we learn that *koinoō, koinōneō, koinōnikos, koinōnos, koinōs* (the last adverb does not appear in the New Testament), and *koinōnia* are related to the root word *koinos*. These five words are the cognate family or word family. *Thayer's Greek-English Lexicon* stipulates in parentheses that the root word for *koinōnia* is *koinōnos*. Thayer then lists *koinos* as the root for *koinōnos*. For *koinos*, *Thayer's lexicon* lists the first meaning as "common," and it comes from "*sun*, with."[12]

---

7. A lexical form is the form found in a lexicon. You can use *Strong's Concordance,* but it involves much more work to amass all the Greek word family.
8. McReynolds, *Word Study*, 782. Learning the Greek alphabet helps students to better handle the Greek lexicons.
9. McReynolds, *Word Study,* 1378.
10. McReynolds, *Word Study,* xii.
11. Kohlenberger III et al. *The Exhaustive Concordance to the Greek New Testament*, 535.
12. Thayer, *Thayer's Greek-English Lexicon of the New Testament*, 351.

Using a computer to find the word family may take longer and usually is more complicated. If we simply key in the lexical form of *koinōnia*, we may find only the occurrences of that one word. We need to search on "lemma" or list all the principal parts of an irregular verb, such as *ginō* and *gnō* for *ginōskō*. On the computer, cite the Greek text and a literal translation for a parallel reference with which to work (e.g., NASB, NRSV).

Now that we have our word family, we are ready to study the context of each use. Looking at *koinōnia* in Philemon and our sentence flow, we learn that *koinōnia* is modified by "faith." (See chapter 4, "Sentence Flow of Philemon 4–6.") The phrase "the sharing of your faith" is modified by "the Lord Jesus" and "all the saints." "The sharing of faith" needs to become more "active" (Philem. 5–6). Not until I did the New Testament study did I learn that *koinōnia* could have several literal and metaphorical meanings. My notes on this word follow:

Word Study Notes: Philemon 4–6

koinōnia—communion, association, partnership

koinōneō—have/do in common with, share, take part in a thing with another (V = "verb")

koinōnos—companion, partner, joint-owner (H = "human")[13]

I. Economic meaning (partnership)
    A. *Literal* (financial sharing)
        "fishing partners": Simon, James, John (Luke 5:10) (H)
        "finances" (Rom. 15:26; 2 Cor. 8:4; 9:13; Heb. 13:16)
        "give financially" (V) (Rom. 12:13; 15:27; Gal. 6:6; Phil. 4:15; 1 Tim. 6:18)
    B. *Metaphorical* (which could include financial)
        1. "Christian partner" Titus and Paul (2 Cor. 8:23) (H)
           Philemon and Paul (Philem. 17) (H)—conditional, if Philemon welcomes Onesimus the same as he would Paul
        2. To "welcome" (Gal. 2:9; 2 John 11) (to welcome is to share evil deeds)
II. "Share/participate" ("have in common"—*koinos*)
    A. *Literal* (material)
        none between light and darkness (2 Cor. 6:14)
        participate in killing (Matt. 23:30) (H)
        flesh and blood (Heb. 2:14) (V)

---

13. LSJ, 969–70.

Koinoō mainly has a ceremonial meaning of "unclean" (Matt. 15:11, 18–20).

B. *Metaphorical.*
If you take the Lord's Supper, you "participate" in Christ's blood and body (1 Cor. 10:16).
"participate" in the gospel (Phil. 1:5)
"participate" in sufferings (Phil. 3:10; Heb. 10:33; 1 Peter 4:13) (V); (2 Cor. 1:7) (H)
"participate" in worship (1 Cor. 10:18, 20) (H), sin (1 Tim. 5:22) (V)
"participate" in glory (1 Peter 5:1)
"participate" in God's character (2 Peter 1:4)

III. Interpersonal Relations (intimacy).
A. Humans with humans
not teaching, maybe including the Lord's Supper and prayer (Acts 2:42; 1 John 1:3)
B. Humans with Jesus (1 Cor. 1:19); God (1 John 1:6).
C. Comes from the Holy Spirit (2 Cor. 13:13; Phil. 2:1).

Literally, *koinōnia* and its cognate words could refer to financial sharing or physical (material) sharing. If time allows, a study of the root word (*koinos*) may add insight into the meaning of the derivative word family. *Koinos* in the New Testament may have positive financial connotations, such as in Acts, where the believers sold their possessions and had "all in *common*" (2:44; also 4:32). Faith also could be held in common (Titus 1:4; Jude 3; my second category, "metaphorical"). A common, different use of *koinos* is for negative connotations as "not pure," such as unwashed hands.[14] Thus, I concluded, in Philemon the *koinōnia* word family is metaphorical and includes relational and material sharing. Philemon's "partnership" is conditional on whether he welcomes Onesimus in the same way as he would welcome Paul. Welcoming includes providing a guest room, which is a material benefit.

How do my findings compare with the categories given by BDAG?[15] BDAG lists four basic categories for *koinōnia:*

---

14. Mark 7:25; Acts 10:14, 28; 11:8; Rom. 14:14; Heb. 10:29; Rev. 21:27.
15. I have purposely left this step to the end because a bias may limit the contemporary interpreter's analysis. Of course, we must first check a lexicon to get a basic idea of the possible meanings of a Greek word. But if we do an in-depth study of the range of meanings first, we have no basis by which to choose the best rendering. For instance, an earlier version of Bauer, Arndt, and Gingrich's lexicon gives "Junias" as the translation of *Iounias.* It states *Iounias* is probably a "short form of the common Junianus." The possibility from a "purely lexical point of view, that this is a woman's name . . . is prob. ruled out by the context." Walter Bauer, William F. Arndt, and F. Wilbur Gingrich, *A Greek-English Lexicon of the New Testament and Other Early Christian Literature,* 1st ed. (Chicago: University of Chicago Press, 1957), 381. Yet the 2000 edition gives "Junia" as the translation and adds that the earlier edition "offers no evidence to support [H. Lietzmann's] statement that the context appears to

156 | In-Depth Study of the Text

1. "Close association involving mutual interests and sharing."
2. "Attitude of good will that manifests an interest in a close relationship."
3. "Sign of fellowship, proof of brotherly unity."
4. "Participation, sharing."[16]

Philemon 6 is listed under meaning number 4. Often BDAG separates literal and figurative uses, but not in this case. To me it appears as if the four categories are very similar, whereas listing the two basic literal meanings helps us better understand the metaphorical derivatives or counterparts.

LSJ includes the nouns *koinōnia and koinōnos* under the verb *koinōneō*. *Koinōnia* was also used of communion, even of marriage,[17] which adds light to my third group ("interpersonal relations" or "intimacy"). Marriage is an archetypal example of intimacy.

These steps are the basic ones I used for my sample exegesis paper in chapter 8, which I completed in one week, the average time a student or pastor might have. It felt complete or sufficient and manageable. If the paper were a doctoral-level academic study, I would have continued to research Old Testament and further contemporary Greek usages.[18]

The Old Testament is the authority for New Testament writers. If a New Testament writer cites an Old Testament passage, a contemporary interpreter needs to compare the New Testament word to its original Old Testament context to see if its original context might enlighten the New Testament meaning. I have always found this comparison helpful. (See "How to Study an Old Testament Quotation in the New Testament" in this chapter's appendix.)

The contemporary Greek world is also the world of the New Testament writers. Study of extrabiblical ancient references could be subsumed under a word study or done later in the Greco-Roman-Jewish background part of the study. The Greek Old Testament and Apocrypha[19] are easily available. Also, we

---

exclude her from consideration." Rather, "a woman named Junia is meant." Walter Bauer, Frederick William Danker, William F. Arndt, and F. Wilbur Gingrich, eds., *A Greek-English Lexicon of the New Testament and Other Early Christian Literature*, 3rd ed. (Chicago: University of Chicago Press, 2000), 480. Hereafter referred to as BDAG. For further information, see Aída Besançon Spencer, *Beyond the Curse: Women Called to Ministry* (Grand Rapids: Baker, 1985), 101–2.

16. BDAG, 552–53. For directions on how to use BDAG, see Gordon D. Fee, *New Testament Exegesis: A Handbook for Students and Pastors*, 3rd ed. (Louisville: Westminster John Knox, 2002), 84–89.

17. LSJ, 969–70.

18. I did a forty-page word study of *šərîrût*, often translated as "stubbornness," for a doctoral-level class. I then shortened the paper to twenty pages for a scholarly presentation, titled "Idolatry as Freedom: A Word Study of *Šərîrût*," and I shortened it still further to five pages, "*Šərîrût* as Self-Reliance," to be printed as a critical note for the *Journal of Biblical Literature* 100 (June 1981): 247–48. Each time I did the study, the thesis of my paper became more focused and shorter.

19. "Apocrypha" means "hidden," usually fifteen books not in the Hebrew canon (c. 250 BC–AD 100) but included in the Greek translation of the Hebrew Bible (the Septuagint [LXX]). These books are not canonical for Protestants but help us to understand ancient Jewish culture. The fourth-century church father Jerome wrote to Laeta about how to rear her daughter: "Let her avoid all apocryphal

can pick at least one additional ancient reference to study. Usually a sampling of Josephus's writings is helpful because, as a historian, he employs literal as well as metaphorical uses, whereas theologians such as Philo or Epictetus may have only metaphorical uses. Electronic and print versions are available (see word study references). The appendix has a listing and explanation of important ancient references in the *Thesaurus Linguae Graecae* (*TLG*).

The Greek Old Testament has fewer references for the *koinōnia* word family than does the New Testament (ten versus fifty-two). The Apocrypha has twelve references. Apparently the word family increases in importance from the time of the Old Testament to that of the New Testament. Moreover, in the Old Testament, *koinōnia* has mainly negative connotations, while in the New Testament it has mainly positive connotations. A major use of the Old Testament would fit under my second category: to have in common evil deeds, including killing, such as "Your rulers are rebels, associates of thieves" (Isa. 1:23 REB) or "Let not ungodly men lead you astray. . . . Come with us, *partake* in blood" (Prov. 1:10–11).[20] Interpersonal relations include political alliances (2 Chron. 20:35; 3 Macc. 2:31; 4:11), friendships, and marriage; for example, "Some friend is a *companion* at the table, and will not continue in the day of affliction" (Sir. 6:10), and "The LORD has borne witness against you on behalf of the wife of your youth. You have broken faith with her, though she is your partner, your wife by solemn covenant" (Mal. 2:14 REB).[21] How does this information enlighten our study of Philemon 4–6? Paul's "sharing of faith" has positive connotations and contrasts with the sharing of evil deeds elsewhere. Paul exhorted Philemon to be a genuine friend with Onesimus and all the saints, as he was toward Jesus and Paul himself.

HOW TO AVOID COMMON ERRORS

1. Remember to study the whole word family, not just the lexical form in the text. Better to study the whole word family in the one letter of your text than one lexical form in the whole of the New Testament.

---

writings. . . . Let her understand that they are not really written by those to whom they are ascribed, that many faulty elements have been introduced into them, and that it requires infinite discretion to look for gold in the midst of dirt." He added, however, "The letters of Athanasius and the treatises of Hilary she may go through without fear of stumbling" (*Letter* 57.107.12).

20. Sir Lancelot Charles Lee Brenton, trans., *The Septuagint Version of the Old Testament and Apocrypha with an English Translation and with Various Readings and Critical* Notes (Grand Rapids: Zondervan, 1972) [hereafter LXX]. See also Lev. 6:2; 2 Kings 17:11; Job 34:8; Prov. 28:24; Eccl. 9:4; Sir. 13:1–2, 7; 4 Macc. 7:6.

21. See also 3 Macc. 4:6; friendship: Sir. 6:10; 41:18; 42:3. More metaphorical uses are in Wisd. Sol. 6:23; 8:18; and 2 Macc. 14:25. Josephus's writings reinforce what we have learned elsewhere. He too used *koinōnia* to refer to political alliances (*War* 3.495), sexual intimacy (*Antiquities* 20.8; *Against Apion* 1.35; 2.198), and friendship (*Against Apion* 2.146; "We are born for *fellowship*" [*Against Apion* 2.281]). He added that the Jewish laws exhorted people "to *share* their possessions" (*Against Apion* 2.291). What the Christians practiced in Acts, Josephus believed was the Old Testament ideal.

158 | In-Depth Study of the Text

Balance your use of priority of context with time and space available for your research.

2. Different translations will pick one of many potential definitions for a word. Do not categorize the meanings of the word studied simply by repeating the translations used. Rather, read each context to get information about your word. You are not simply looking for brief translations but for more extended information, encyclopedic entries, including illustrations of the word studied. Gene Green summarized that a word study should include the basic logical entry of information essential to the concept *and* information incidental to the concept and open-ended that should then be organized by the interpreter.[22] In effect, you are doing a theological study of a concept from the basis of a word study. The categories you develop may vary, depending on the questions you raise.

3. Focus on the significance of the word, not its grammatical parsing. Parsing usually is irrelevant for semantics.

4. Cite the lexical, not the text, form of the word.

5. The literal root of a word must be compared to its use in context. Sometimes Greek writers consciously refer to or allude to or develop the root of a word, especially transparent words, in which form is related to meaning. Greek as a language is relatively transparent.[23]

6. Remember to interpret the way a literal use of a word enlightens the figurative or metaphorical use.

7. Do not assume a word means the same thing to the New Testament writer that it does to us or to the church language of today. Sometimes it does and sometimes it does not. For instance, when my husband was a seminarian, he was riding a train, studying Machen's *New Testament Greek for Beginners,*[24] when a passenger, who turned out to be a Greek native, grabbed his book and crossed out the ancient Koine Greek word for "bread" *(artos),* pointing out that word now referred only to "holy bread," not everyday bread, and it was too archaic to use today.

8. The same word may not mean the same thing throughout the Bible. Different writers at times use words in different ways. However, one word cannot have contradictory meanings in the same time period. There is a kernel of meaning (a ground meaning)[25] that underlies all its uses.

---

22. Gene Green, "Lexical Pragmatics and Biblical Interpretation," *Journal of the Evangelical Theological Society* 50, no. 4 (December 2007): 801–4.

23. Further, see Silva, *Biblical Words,* 49–51.

24. J. Gresham Machen, *New Testament Greek for Beginners* (Toronto: Macmillan, 1923).

25. Robertson, *Grammar of the Greek New Testament,* 580, 600.

Understand the Meaning of the Words and Phrases | 159

9. After an extensive word study is done, the findings need to be related to the text to clarify its interpretation.
10. The meanings of the word must be categorized. Do not simply list the different occurrences of the word.

APPENDICES

How to Study an Old Testament Quotation in the New Testament

1. Study the New Testament context of the quotation.
2. Find the Old Testament reference.
3. *Are there any textual issues that need to be decided? Compare the Masoretic and LXX texts.
4. Study the Old Testament context of the quotation.
5. How does the New Testament use the Old Testament?
    a. How does the Old Testament context deepen the meaning of the New Testament use?
    b. How does the omission, deletion, or addition of words affect the New Testament use?
6. *Which other sources refer to the Old Testament reference? Find and study the use of the Old Testament reference in early Judaism (e.g., LXX; Mishnah; Dead Sea Scrolls; Babylonian Talmud; Jerusalem Talmud; Tosefta; Old Testament Pseudepigrapha; other rabbinic works, such as midrashim and targumim; Josephus; Philo; and the rest of the New Testament).[26]
7. *How does the New Testament use compare and contrast with the use of the Old Testament and other sources in early Judaism?
8. Final conclusions

    (*optional extended study)

The following is a cover sheet which may be used to evaluate one's word study.

---

26. See chapter 7 for an explanation of these terms.

In-Depth Study of the Text

WORD STUDY COVER SHEET

Word Study of _____ To: _____
Date: _____   (*your name*)
Box/email: _____   Grade:_____

I. The following items are rated according to the following:
I=Inadequate   A=Adequate   G=Good   S=Superior

METHODOLOGY:
Comprehensive/Exhaustive ....I A G S
Accurate...I A G S
Insightful ....I A G S
Conclusions proved (supporting NT data,
    explanations, ancient sources).................................I A G S
Original (Primary sources studied —letter, NT,
    first-century references, secondary work is
    supplemental to own work ....I A G S
Thoughtful ....I A G S

COMPLETENESS:
Etymology/root ....I A G S
Word family studied ....I A G S
Categories presented...I A G S
Example(s) for each category...I A G S
Immediate contexts studied..I A G S
All uses footnoted / referred to in text ....I A G S
Clarified how usage of word in text
    compares to broader uses of word ....I A G S
Main meaning of word in text.......................................I A G S
Significance for text...I A G S
Sources quoted are given credit for work......................I A G S
Literal & figurative uses are noted & compared............I A G S
Overall lexical understanding.......................................I A G S

WORD STUDY COVER SHEET

WRITTEN PRESENTATION:
Well organized paper: Introduction .... I A G S
         Conclusion................................I A G S
         Application ....I A G S
Literary Style—clear and succinct................................I A G S
Spelling and grammar-correct..I A G S
Print is readable & double-spaced ....I A G S

II. *The following items need attention if checked:*
_____The paper is a series of research notes, not a unified essay.

_____The paper needs balance; do not give too much space to a less significant item but too little space to a major item.

_____Use Greek font *or* transliteration.

_____Correct length

_____The pages should be numbered consecutively throughout.

_____Use standard Bible abbreviations in parentheses and footnotes.

_____Cite Greek words out of context in their lexical entry form.

_____Accent Greek words.

_____Excessive use of the first and/or second person for a formal paper

_____Excessive use of the passive verb and "it is" without a clear antecedent

_____Use a consistent and/or correct form in footnotes and bibliography citations.

Comments:

162 | In-Depth Study of the Text

Selected Writings in the Thesaurus Linguae Graecae (TLG),[27] *Loeb Classical Library, and Old Testament Pseudepigrapha*

Author/Writing	Dates and Description	Sample Titles of Book and Sources (English-Greek)
100 BC–AD 100 New Testament era		
Epictetus of Hierapolis	c. AD 55–135, Stoic philosopher	(Loeb) *Discourses,* 2 vols.; *Enchiridion* (*TLG* 0557)
Flavius Josephus	AD 37–100, Jewish historian	(Loeb) 13 vols., *Jewish War; Jewish Antiquities; Life; Against Apion* (*TLG* 0526); http://www.earlyjewishwritings.com/josephus.html
Longinus	AD 1st cent., stylist	(Loeb) *On the Sublime* (*TLG* 0560)
New Testament/Novum Testamentum	AD 1st cent.	(*TLG* 0031)
Philo Judaeus of Alexandria	c. 20/30 BC–AD 45/50, Jewish philosopher	(Loeb) 10 vols. and two supplements (*TLG* 0018); earlyjewishwritings.com
Septuaginta	3rd cent. BC–AD 1st cent., Old Testament and Apocrypha	(*TLG* 0527)
Strabo of Amaseia	63 BC–AD 24, Greek historian, geographer, and philosopher	(Loeb) *Geography; Testimonia,* 8 vols.; 17 books (*TLG* 0099)
Pre–New Testament Greek		
Apollodorus of Athens	b. 180 BC, Athenian scholar, historical, mythological, and geographical works	(Loeb) 2 vols. (*TLG* 0549)
Aristotle	384–322 BC, Greek philosopher	(Loeb) 23 vols. (*TLG* 0086)
Bion of Phlossa	c. 100 BC, rhetorician	(Loeb) *Greek Bucolic Poets: Adonis, Achilles et Deidameiae*
Gaius Julius Caesar	c. 100–44 BC, Roman military and political leader	(Loeb) 3 vols., *Alexandrian War, African War, Spanish War, Gallic Wars, Civil Wars*
Callimachus	c. 305/310–240 BC, poet, critic, and librarian at Alexandria, Egypt	(Loeb) 2 vols. *Aetia, Iambi, Hecale and Other Fragments, Hymns, Epigrams* and more (*TLG* 0533)
Marcus Tullius Cicero	106–43 BC, Roman philosopher, lawyer, political theorist, and orator	(Loeb) 28 vols., *A. Rhetorical, B. Orations, C. Philosophical, D. Letters,* for example, *On the Nature of the Gods, Academics* (*TLG* 2165)

---

27.   The first category (100 BC–AD 100) is the most important time period for New Testament interpreters. The focus of this chart is the three-hundred-year period before and after the birth of Christ. My appreciation to librarian James Darlack for his assistance in developing this resource, especially the Old Testament Pseudepigrapha. References for the *TLG* chart: Maria C. Pantelia, *Thesaurus Linguae Graecae: A Bibliographic Guide to the Canon of Greek Authors and Works* (Oakland: University of California Press, 2022). Pantelia has listed more than twenty thousand works in *TLG* as of 2022. Also Johannes Quasten, *Patrology,* 4 vols. (Westminster, MD: Christian Classics, 1986); N. G. L. Hammond and H. H. Scullard, eds., *The Oxford Classical Dictionary,* 2nd ed. (Oxford: Clarendon, 1970).

Understand the Meaning of the Words and Phrases | 163

Author/Writing	Dates and Description	Sample Titles of Book and Sources (English-Greek)
Demetrius	1st cent. BC/AD 1st cent., Greek stylist	(Loeb) *On Style* (*TLG* 0613)
Demosthenes	384–322 BC, Greek statesman and orator	(Loeb) 7 vols., *Orations* (*TLG* 0014)
Diodorus Siculus (of Sicily)	1st cent. BC, Greek historian who wrote forty books on the history of Egypt, Mesopotamia, India, Scythia, Arabia, North Africa, Greece, and Europe	(Loeb) 12 vols., *History* (*TLG* 0060)
Dionysius of Halicarnassus	60–c. 7 BC, Greek historian and teacher of rhetoric	(Loeb) *Roman Antiquities, Critical Essays* (*TLG* 0081)
Herodotus	c. 484–425 BC, considered "Father of History" of Western culture	(Loeb) *Persian Wars*, 4 vols. (*TLG* 0016)
Hippocrates (Asclepiod of Cos)	5th cent. BC, Greek physician	(Loeb) 9 vols., *Ancient Medicine*
Livy (Titus Livius)	59 BC–AD 17, Roman historian	(Loeb) *History of Rome,* 14 vols.
Manetho	3rd cent. BC, Egyptian historian and priest	(Loeb) *History of Egypt and Other Works* (chronology of pharaohs) (*TLG* 2583)
Moschus of Syracuse	c. 150 BC	(Loeb) *Greek Bucolic Poets* (*TLG* 0035)
Cornelius Nepos of Gaul	c. 99–24 BC, Roman biographer	(Loeb) *On Great Generals, On Historians*
Parthenius of Nicae	1st cent. BC, Greek poet	(Loeb) *Daphnis and Chloe, Parthenius*
Plato	c. 428–348 BC, Greek philosopher	(Loeb) 12 vols., *Timaeus* (*TLG* 0059)
Pliny the Elder (Gaius Plinius)	AD 23–79, Roman author and natural philosopher	(Loeb) *Natural History,* 10 vols.
Polybius of Megalopolis	c. 203–120 BC, Greek historian of the rise of Rome	(Loeb) *Histories,* 6 vols. (*TLG* 0543)
Posidonius	c. 135–51 BC, Greek Stoic philosopher, geographer, teacher	*Histories* (*TLG* 1961)
Post–New Testament Greek[28]		
Appian (Appianus) of Alexandria	c. AD 95–165, procurator, orator, Roman historian	(Loeb) *Roman History,* 4 vols. (*TLG* 0551)
Arrian of Bithynia (Flavius Arrianus)	c. AD 86–146, Roman historian and philosopher	(Loeb) *Anabasis of Alexander,* 2 vols. (*TLG* 0074)
Augustine (Aurelius Augustinus)	AD 354–430, Bishop of Hippo Regius, philosopher, theologian	(Loeb) *City of God,* 7 vols., *Confessions,* 2 vols., *Select Letters*

---

28. The post–New Testament Greek writers may be helpful for later Christian use of a word.

164 | In-Depth Study of the Text

Author/Writing	Dates and Description	Sample Titles of Book and Sources (English-Greek)
Barnabas	c. AD 70–135, teacher, anonymous	(Loeb) *Apostolic Fathers,* vol. 1 + ed. Michael W. Holmes[29] *Epistle* (*TLG* 1216)
Celsus	AD 2nd cent., Greek Neoplatonic philosopher and polemical writer against Christianity	*The True Word* cited by Origen in *Contra Celsus* (*TLG* 1248)
Clement of Alexandria (Titus Flavius Clemens)	c. AD 150–216, teacher	(Loeb) *Protrepticus* (*The Exhortation to the Greeks*), *Paedagogus* (*Tutor*), *Stromata* (*Carpets*), *The Rich Man's Salvation* (*TLG* 0555)
Clement of Rome	c. AD 1st cent., bishop of Rome (2 Clement is anonymous)	(Loeb) *Epistle to the Corinthians* in *Apostolic Fathers,* vol. 1 + ed. Michael W. Holmes; *1 Clement* (*TLG* 1271)
The Didache (*Teaching of the Twelve Apostles*)	c. AD 100–150, church manual, anonymous author(s)	(Loeb) *Apostolic Fathers,* vol. 1 (*TLG* 1311) + ed. Michael W. Holmes
Dio Cassius (Cassius Dio Cocceianus)	AD 160–230, Roman historian of Nicaea, author of an 80-vol. history of Rome	(Loeb) 9 vols., *Roman History* (*TLG* 0385)
Dio Chrysostom	AD 40–120, Greek orator, philosopher, and Roman historian	(Loeb) 5 vols., *Discourses* (*TLG* 0612)
Laërtius Diogenes	c. AD 3rd cent., biographer of Greek philosophers	(Loeb) *Lives of Eminent Philosophers*, 2 vols. (*TLG* 0004)
Eusebius of Caesarea	c. AD 263–339, bishop of Caesarea and church historian	(Loeb) *Ecclesiastical History*, 2 vols., *Preparation for the Gospel* (*TLG* 2018)
Galenus of Pergamum	c. AD 129–99, physician and philosopher	(Loeb) *Method of Medicine*, 3 vols., *Natural Faculties* (*TLG* 0057)
Heron of Alexandria	c. AD 62, mathematician and inventor	(Loeb) *Greek Mathematical Works* (*TLG* 0559)
Ignatius	d. c. AD 98–117, bishop of Antioch, wrote on way to martyrdom	(Loeb) *Apostolic Fathers* + ed. Michael W. Holmes, *Letters* (*TLG* 1443)
Irenaeus	c. AD 130–202, theologian, bishop of Lyons	*Against Heresies, Demonstration of the Apostolic Preaching, Proof of the Apostolic Preaching* in *Ancient Christian Writers; Ante-Nicene Christian Library* 5, 9 (TLG 1447)
Jerome (Eusebius Hieronymus)	c. AD 347–420, priest, apologist, translator of the Latin Vulgate, and author of OT and NT commentaries	*De Viris Illustribus* (*On Famous Men*), *Early Christian Biographies, Commentary on Ephesians, Early Latin Theology* in series *Fathers of the Church, Homilies of Saint Jerome*

---

29. *The Apostolic Fathers: Greek Texts and English Translations,* ed. and trans. Michael W. Holmes, 3rd ed. (Grand Rapids: Baker, 2007), has in one volume what appears in two volumes of *The Apostolic Fathers,* Loeb Classical Library (also in Greek and English). See also *Africanus Journal* vol. 1, no. 1 (April 2009), 3 for his life and further references.

Understand the Meaning of the Words and Phrases | 165

Author/Writing	Dates and Description	Sample Titles of Book and Sources (English-Greek)
Julius Africanus	AD 2nd–3rd cent., historian	Also cited by Eusebius (*TLG* 2956)[30]
Justinus Martyr	c. AD 100–165, Christian philosopher	*Apologies, Dialogue with Trypho* (*TLG* 0645)
Lucian of Samosata	c. AD 120–80, orator, philosopher	(Loeb) 8 vols., *How to Write History*
Oppian of Cilicia	c. AD 2nd cent., poet	(Loeb) *Halieutica* (*On Fishing*); *Cynegetica* (*TLG* 0023)
Pausanias of Lydia	c. AD 150, Greek traveler and geographer	(Loeb) *Description of Greece,* 5 vols. (*TLG* 0525)
Pliny the Younger (Gaius Plinius Caecilius Secundus)	c. AD 61–112, lawyer, praefector	(Loeb) *Letters,* 10 vols.
Plutarch of Chaeronea (Mestrius Plutarchus)	c. AD 46–120, Roman historian, biographer, essayist, Middle Platonist	(Loeb) *The Parallel Lives,* 11 vols., *Moralia,* 16 vols. (*TLG* 0007)
Polycarp	After Ignatius's death (2nd cent.)	(Loeb) *Letter to the Philippians* + ed. Michael W. Holmes (*TLG* 1622)
Shepherd of Hermas	Written c. 1st–2nd cent.	(Loeb) *Visions* + ed. Michael W. Holmes
Suetonius (Gaius Suetonius Tranquillus)	c. AD 69–122, equestrian and historian during Roman Empire who wrote biographies of twelve successive rulers, from Julius Caesar to Domitian	(Loeb) Vol. 1: *Lives of the Caesars: Julius, Augustus, Tiberius, Gaius, Caligula*; vol. 2: *Lives of the Caesars: Claudius, Nero, Galba, Otho, and Vitellius, Vespasian, Titus, Domitian; Lives of Illustrious Men; Lives of Pliny the Elder and Passienus Crispus* (*TLG* 1760)
Cornelius Tacitus	c. AD 56–117, senator and historian of the Roman Empire	(Loeb) Vol. 1: *Agricola, Germania, Dialogue on Oratory*; vols. 2–3: *Histories 1–5;* vols. 3–5: *Annals 1–16*
Pseudepigraphal[31] Writings Pre–New Testament		
Apocalypse of Enoch	2nd–1st cent. BC, Gen. 5:24	*OTP*[32] 1:5–89 (*TLG* 1463)
Jubilees	2nd cent. BC, Exod. 24:18, retelling accounts of Adam, Noah, Abraham, Jacob, and Moses	*OTP* 2:35–142 (*TLG* 1464)
Letter of Aristeas	3rd cent. BC–AD 1st cent., background for LXX	*OTP* 2:7–34 (*TLG* 1183)
Testaments of the Twelve Patriarchs	2nd cent. BC, final utterances of twelve sons of Jacob	*OTP* 1:775–828 (*TLG* 1700)

---

30. Content of note is in next comment.
31. The Pseudepigrapha are false or fictional writings that often develop biblical narratives. This list includes Pseudepigraphal writings that are also in TLG. It is not a complete list of all Greek Pseudepigrapha that have been collected. The dates are tentative.
32. James H. Charlesworth, ed., *The Old Testament Pseudepigrapha,* 2 vols. (Garden City, NY: Doubleday, 1983–85). Cited as *OTP* in this chart. The numbers cited are the volume number and page numbers.

166 | In-Depth Study of the Text

Author/Writing	Dates and Description	Sample Titles of Book and Sources (English-Greek)
Pseudepigraphal Writings Post–New Testament (1st-2nd centuries)		
Apocalypse of Adam	AD 1st–4th cent., Gnostic revelation	*OTP* 1:707–19 (*TLG* 1153)
Apocalypse of Baruch (2 Baruch)	AD 2nd cent. (after AD 70)	*OTP* 1:615–52 (*TLG* 1155)
Apocalypse of Baruch (3 Baruch)	AD 1st–3rd cent.	*OTP* 1:653–79 (*TLG* 1154)
Apocalypse of Elijah	AD 1st–4th cent. composite	*OTP* 1:721–53 (*TLG* 1156)
Apocalypse of Zephaniah	1st cent. BC–AD 1st cent. fragments	*OTP* 1:497–515 (*TLG* 1160)
Apocryphon of Ezekiel	1st cent. BC–AD 1st cent. fragments	*OTP* 1:487–95 (*TLG* 1161)
Jannes and Jambres	AD 1st–3rd cent.[33]	*OTP* 2:427–42 (*TLG* 1859)
Joseph and Aseneth	1st cent. BC–AD 2nd cent., Gen. 41:45	*OTP* 2:177–247 (*TLG* 1451)
Life of Adam and Eve (Apocalypse of Moses)	AD 1st cent.	*OTP* 2:249–95 (*TLG* 1747)
Lives of the Prophets	AD 1st cent.	*OTP* 2:379–99 (*TLG* 1750)
Martyrdom and Ascension of Isaiah	2nd cent. BC–AD 4th cent., composite, Jewish and Christian	*OTP* 2:143–76 (*TLG* 1483)
Prayer of Joseph	AD 1st cent., Gen. 48, angels Israel and Uriel	*OTP* 2:699–714 (*TLG* 1552)
Prayer of Manasseh	2nd cent. BC–AD 1st cent., 2 Kings 21	*OTP* 2:625–37 (*TLG* 1858)
Pseudo-Phocylides	1st cent. BC–AD 1st cent.	*OTP* 2:565–82 (*TLG* 1605)
Sibylline Oracles	2nd cent. BC–AD 7th cent., older woman uttering ecstatic prophecies	*OTP* 1:317–472 (*TLG* 1551)
Testament of Abraham	AD 1st–3rd cent.	*OTP* 1:871–902 (*TLG* 1701)
Testament of Job	1st cent. BC–AD 1st cent.	*OTP* 1:829–68 (*TLG* 1702)
Testament of Moses	AD 1st cent. before AD 70	*OTP* 1:919–34 (*TLG* 1201)
Testament of Solomon	AD 1st–3rd cent.	*OTP* 1:935–87 (*TLG* 2679)

---

33. Paul was not quoting this work in 2 Tim. 3:8. For more information, see Aída Besançon Spencer, *2 Timothy and Titus*, New Covenant Commentary Series (Eugene, OR: Cascade, 2014), 123–24.

CHAPTER 6

UNDERSTAND THE MEANING OF THE TEXT BY A STYLISTIC ANALYSIS

STUDY UNUSUAL WORD ORDER AND FIGURES OF SPEECH[1]

I. *Identify* the figures of speech.
  A. Using the sentence flow as a help, note unusual Greek word order.
  B. Find and correctly identify other figures of speech.[2]
    1. Determine whether a word is being used literally or figuratively.
    2. Decide what kind of figure of speech it is.
II. *Analyze* each figure of speech.
  A. Determine degree of development.
  B. Analyze how your stylistic features relate to the immediate context and the overall plan of the letter.
  C. Determine the literal concept to which each image alludes.
  D. Analyze the properties of the image.

---

1. For further reading, see Aída Besançon Spencer, *Paul's Literary Style: A Stylistic and Historical Comparison of II Corinthians 11:16–12:13, Romans 8:9–39, and Philippians 3:2–4:13* (Lanham, MD: University Press of America, 1998), app. 2, ch. 2, 21–27, 33–41; Demetrius, *On Style*, ed. and trans. Doreen C. Innes, Loeb Classical Library (Cambridge: Harvard University Press, 1995); A. Berkeley Mickelsen, *Interpreting the Bible* (Grand Rapids: Eerdmans, 1963), chs. 8–11; T. Norton Sterrett and Richard L. Schultz, *How to Understand Your Bible*, 3rd ed. (Downers Grove, IL: InterVarsity Press, 2010), chs. 13–18; Margaret Parker, *Unlocking the Power of God's Word* (Downers Grove, IL: InterVarsity Press, 1991), chs. 1–4; William W. Klein, Craig L. Blomberg, Robert L. Hubbard Jr., *Introduction to Biblical Interpretation*, rev. ed. (Nashville: Nelson, 2004), ch. 8; George B. Caird, *The Language and Imagery of the Bible* (Grand Rapids: Eerdmans, 1997), ch. 8, 144–59; Bob Smith, *Basics of Bible Interpretation*, A Discovery Bible Study Book (Waco, TX: Word, 1978), chs. 7–9; E. W. Bullinger, *Figures of Speech Used in the Bible: Explained and Illustrated* (Grand Rapids: Baker, 1968).
2. For definitions, see the appendix at the end of this chapter.

168 | In-Depth Study of the Text

      E. Analyze the properties that the image has in common with the concept in your passage, and determine the degree of correspondence between them.

III. Suggest what is the *effect* or *function* of each stylistic feature in your passage.

IV. Write a tentative paragraph or page(s) in essay form or intersperse findings in a verse-by-verse presentation of grammar, semantics, and stylistic analysis. Use only data that enhances the overall purpose of your paper.

This step can be done principally by Greek readers, and by translation readers if using a literal Bible version.

INTRODUCTION

How might we win over a Christian group whom we have known for many years that now rebels against us? Paul, the "wise fool," used irony and other figures of speech to transfer the Corinthians' allegiance from esteeming their oppressive heroes, the super apostles, back to their liberating Christlike spiritual father, Paul. Were the Corinthians indeed "wise" in allowing the super apostles to enslave, exploit, and strike them? Is that kind of leadership "strength" (2 Cor. 11:16–21)?[3]

Another aspect of a passage to study is style, what writers or speakers do to reinforce their cognitive message by their manner of writing. Style is the choices an author makes (whether consciously or subconsciously) among linguistic possibilities (usually but not always choices among grammatical possibilities). Style is different from grammar (the study of the form of words and the manner of their combination in phrases, clauses, and sentences) or semantics (the meanings of words), yet every grammatical and semantic choice has stylistic implications. Two aspects of style study are especially helpful in exegesis: word and clause order and figures of speech.

After identifying figures of speech in your text by studying the Greek text (together with your own parallel literal translation), develop an intuitive hypothesis about the significance of how the stylistic feature(s) relate to the whole passage. Once a literal translation is complete, someone without knowledge of Greek could study figures of speech as well (if [s]he can recognize Greek letters).

---

3.   See further Aída Besançon Spencer, *2 Corinthians*, People's Bible Commentary (Abingdon, UK: Bible Reading Fellowship, 2001), 194–95.

IDENTIFY UNUSUAL WORD ORDER

Begin by looking at any unusual Greek word order. Compare your sentence flow with the Greek text. Normal Greek word order is similar to English word order, except for modifiers. Unlike English, modifiers in Greek tend to follow the word being modified. The ancient rhetorician Demetrius gave his readers a sample normal (or simple) Greek sentence word order: "Epidamnus is a city on your right as you sail into the Ionian gulf" (*On Style,* 199). But the order in Greek can be varied even more than in English for purposes of emphasis, rhythm, expression of emotion, or clarity of argument. (See "Greek Word and Clause Order" in appendices at the end of this chapter.)

In the sample exegesis of Philemon 4–6 (chapter 8), the first basic sentence is in normal word order: "I am giving thanks [subject and verb] to my God [indirect object] always [adverb]" (v. 4). Normally a participle will precede its object, but not here ("remembrance of you—making"). The word or words brought forward usually are then emphasized. Also, any two words in contrast can be brought sharply together. Otherwise, the beginning and, less frequently, the end of a sentence are the places of emphasis. *Mneia* ("remembrance"), the object, is emphasized, rather than the participle ("making"). This is one reason why I chose to do the word study of *mneia.* Paul emphasized it. Pronouns tend to follow the word modified, as in "God—of me" or "remembrance—of you" (v. 4), but in verse 5 the pronoun precedes the noun it modifies ("of you—the love"). The pronoun is singular, bringing out that Paul was especially addressing the first person addressed in the letterhead: Philemon (v. 1). Also, in verse 6, the complement/direct object precedes the verb "might become" (*genētai*), emphasizing "active/effective." That is what Paul wanted, not just a "sharing of faith," but a more effective one. The adjective "all/every" (*pantos*) precedes its noun "good" (*agathou*). Paul wanted Philemon to know not just "good" but *every* good.

The changes to a normal word order thus give emphasis to the content of those words. If Paul were speaking, he might have shouted these particular words: *remembrance* of you, *your* love, *active* sharing, *every* good. As commentators, we too will want to explain these particular words. Changes in word order are transposition sentence changes. They do not add or delete or substitute words, but they transpose or rearrange elements of a sentence in a different order.[4]

IDENTIFY OTHER FIGURES OF SPEECH

Figures of speech may be grouped by the way they affect the whole sentence: addition, omission, substitution, and transposition. Addition changes in a sentence include the addition of a word, phrase, or clause, such as parallelism,

---

4. See Spencer, *Paul's Literary Style,* 23–25.

170 | In-Depth Study of the Text

polysyndeton, pleonasm, anaphora, or chiasm.[5] Omission changes in a sentence include the deletion of a word, phrase, or clause, such as ellipses and asyndeton. Asyndeton and polysyndeton are opposites. In asyndeton, conjunctions between a series of related words, phrases, or clauses are deliberately omitted, while in polysyndeton they are used two or more times in close succession in a pattern, between clauses, words, or phrases.[6]

In substitution sentence changes, one element of a sentence is chosen over another. Figurative changes are metaphor, simile, personification, synecdoche, meiosis, irony, hyperbole, and hendiadys.[7] A figurative sentence change includes those with an image where something represents something else. Sometimes meiosis and litotes are defined differently by different authors. For most interpreters the difference does not affect analysis, so I have subsumed litotes under meiosis; both are a deliberately employed understatement, presenting something as less than it really is in order to assert the affirmative or to avoid an arrogant display. When Paul told the tribune that he was a citizen and came from Tarsus, "no insignificant city," he implied that Tarsus was a significant city and therefore the tribune should treat him with respect (Acts 21:39).

There are many other figures of speech, but these are the ones I have found to be more common in the New Testament. They are all defined in the appendix "Definitions of Frequent New Testament Rhetorical Terms" at the end of this chapter.[8]

As well as transposition sentence changes, the sample exegesis paper of Philemon 4–6 in chapter 8 has addition, omission, and substitution sentence changes. Not all texts will have all types of sentence changes, but normally they have some of them. Pleonasm has both a general and a narrow definition. The word *pleonasm* comes from the Greek *pleon* ("more") and thus refers to any doubling or repetition of words of similar meaning, thoughts of similar content, and all forms of addition. More narrowly, it refers to doubled synonyms (such as "in trouble and hardship") and parenthetical asides (such as "I think" or "I say," 2 Cor. 11:21, 27). You need to find the most specific term that applies to each case of addition.

Pleonasm (General = Repetition)		
Polysyndeton	Parallelism	Pleonasm
repetition of conjunctions	repetition in a pattern ↓	specific = doubled items, parenthetical aside
	chiasm — one type of repetitive pattern — anaphora — repetition of first word(s) in a sequence	

---

5. See "Definitions of Frequent New Testament Rhetorical Terms" in appendix of this chapter.
6. Spencer, *Paul's Literary Style,* 22–23.
7. Spencer, *Paul's Literary Style,* 25–28.
8. See also Spencer, *Paul's Literary Style,* app. 2, 187–212.

The pleonasm in Philemon 5 is the repetition of the article preceding "love" (*agapēn*) and "faith" (*pistin*). The repetition of the article emphasizes each noun and differentiates between them. But in this case, I suggested they may be a hendiadys: the second adjective modifying the first noun, "faithful love" (v. 5). Verse 6 does not have a full parallelism, where one clause or sentence is parallel to another (article opposed to article, connective to connective, like to like from the beginning to the end),[9] but one prepositional phrase ("in you," [*en hymin*]) is parallel to another prepositional phrase ("into/toward Christ" [*eis Christon*]). Both refer to the pronoun ("the one"). To what "good knowledge" did Paul refer? It was the one among the believers in that local church and also the one directed to Christ. These horizontal and vertical aspects are repeated several times in our text (vv. 5, 6).

A common type of omission is an ellipsis—that is, the deliberate omission of a word or words necessary to complete or clarify a construction but implied by the context. Normally we would expect "good" to be repeated: "knowledge of all good, the *good* among you, toward Christ," but Paul chose to eliminate the second "good." The focus, then, is on the two prepositional phrases that describe "good" (v. 6).

In looking for substitution sentence changes, the first step is to determine whether a word was being used literally or figuratively. A word is an image or is "figurative" if it is impossible literally. A word used literally refers to one of the five senses (sight, touch, hearing, smell, taste) or to a concept. Being truer has nothing to do with figurative or literal language. Figurative and literal language has to do with the manner of expression. For example, "I am as wealthy as Solomon" or "I have a million dollars" are two different ways to express a similar idea, which is that one claims to be wealthy, something that may be true or false. Some lexicons, such as BDAG, list the definitions of a word under "literal" and "figurative," which allows us to determine that both are possible. LSJ and Thayer's lexicon list the literal use of a word first. The lexicon does not analyze the analogy being made between metaphorical language and its concept; only the interpreter can do that with each text in its context.

Metaphors and similes are almost identical types of figures of speech. The only difference is whether a conjunction is used, such as "like" or "as," to make the comparison implicit or explicit. Each is a comparison between two things of unlike nature that yet have something in common so that one or more properties of the first are attributed (or carried over) to the second.[10]

There are five steps in the analysis of an image, such as a metaphor:

1. Correctly identify the image.
2. Correctly identify the concept to which the image refers.

---

9. Spencer, *Paul's Literary Style*, 198. True parallelism is structured precisely, whereas parallel *thought* is more general. The same is true of chiasm versus chiastic thought.
10. Spencer, *Paul's Literary Style*, 195–97, 207.

172 | In-Depth Study of the Text

3. Study the properties of the image.
4. Study the properties the image has in common with the concept.
5. Analyze the effect or function of the image in the text being studied.

In correctly identifying the image and its concept, we must consider the degree of development, the extent to which the author developed the ramifications of a certain comparison. For instance, the metaphor *koinōnia* appears only once in the sentence (Philem. 4–6), while, in contrast, Paul used an extended personification throughout Romans 8:19–22 when comparing creation to an enslaved pregnant woman: "eager expectation of creation awaits eagerly ... to frustration the creation became subject, not willingly but by the one who subjected it, upon the hope that also the creation itself will be set free from the destructive slavery to the glorious freedom ... all the creation groans together and suffers agony together until the present." Personification is a type of metaphor in which abstractions (qualities, ideas, or general terms), inanimate objects, or nonhuman living things are invested with human qualities or abilities, especially with human feelings. In Romans 8, nonhuman creation is invested with human feelings as well as the abilities of eagerness, frustration, enslavement, willingness, hope, freedom, and the agony of childbirth. This extended personification dramatizes present sufferings felt by humans. Even creation mirrors our feelings!

A business partnership, enslavement, and childbearing are all activities that are understandable, not that different now as before, but sometimes the ancient image needs to be studied. For example, "The law became our instructor [*paidagōgos*] until Christ" (Gal. 3:24). We need to learn more about ancient pedagogues to help us understand the role of the law before faith came.[11]

Before we suggest an effect or function of an image in our text, we must analyze the properties the image has in common with the concept. This is the degree of correspondence, the extent of likeness between an image and a referent. All images are analogies, and we would misinterpret the author if we stretched an analogy beyond the "intended point of comparison."[12] A common example of overextending the degree of correspondence occurs in Luke 18:1–8. How is God like the unjust judge? Simply, both are in a position to vindicate the oppressed—and that's it! Beyond that fact, the comparison ceases and contrast takes over. Otherwise, one would conclude God is unjust like the unjust judge, but God is always just.

Parables[13] are usually extended similes, as, for example, Matthew 13:45–46: "The reign of the heavens [which is the concept being explained] is like [the word of comparison is *homoia*] a human merchant seeking good pearls,

---

11. See further Aída Besançon Spencer, *Beyond the Curse: Women Called to Ministry* (Grand Rapids: Baker, 1985), 68.
12. Caird, *Language and Imagery*, 145.
13. See also Craig L. Blomberg, *Interpreting the Parables* (Downers Grove, IL: InterVarsity Press, 1990).

and after he found one pearl of great value, after he left he sold all that he had and bought it [the last part is the extended image]." All merchants do not describe God's reign but only the ones who sell everything to buy one pearl of great value. Heaven's reign is like the image in that it is valuable and worth all one has, but it is unlike the concept in that one cannot buy it and heaven's reign is not profit motivated.

Allegories, in contrast, are usually extended metaphors, such as Ephesians 6:13–17. Paul used a point-by-point comparison: belt and truth, breastplate and righteousness, feet and peace, shield and faith, helmet and salvation, sword and the Word. To understand better Paul's extended image, a study of ancient Roman foot soldiers is insightful.

As with all images, we need to analyze the image, concept, and analogy between them and the function of the stylistic feature in its context. In narratives, such as the Gospels and Acts, the immediate context is the specific historic situation. For example, Jesus's parable in Luke 20:9–18 is addressed especially to "the chief priests and the scribes, together with the elders" at the temple court. And they knew the parable was directed against them (20:1, 19). Thus, we have two levels to study: how the tenants were analogous to these religious leaders and how this parable fits within Luke's arrangement of Jesus's life. Why did Luke make sure he cited this parable in his life of Jesus?

Edward P. J. Corbett wrote, "It does not take much intelligence to gather the data; it takes only patience and accuracy. But it does take intelligence and perhaps a good measure of imagination to be able to see the rhetorical function of a particular function of a particular stylistic feature."[14] In biblical studies, we compare the stylistic features to the context of the letter, the author's overall purpose, the historical situation or occasion, and the audience. The stylistic techniques supplement the cognitive information being shared between the writer and the readers. Augustine promised, "The more these things seem to be obscured by figurative words, the sweeter they become when they are explained" (*On Christian Doctrine* 4.7.15). Ben Witherington summarizes: "If early Christianity really was an evangelistic religion wanting to persuade a Greek-speaking world about the odd notion that a crucified manual worker from Nazareth rose from the dead and was King of kings and Lord of lords, this was going to take some serious 'persuasion,' and the chief tool in the arsenal of all well-known persuaders, orators, rhetoricians in the Greco-Roman world was rhetoric."[15]

---

14. Edward P. J. Corbett, "A Method of Analyzing Prose Style with a Demonstration Analysis of Swift's *A Modest Proposal*" in *Style in English*, ed. John Nist, Bobbs-Merrill Series in Composition and Rhetoric (New York: Bobbs-Merrill, 1969), 27.

15. Ben Witherington III, "'Almost Thou Persuadest Me . . .': The Importance of Greco-Roman Rhetoric for the Understanding of the Text and Content of the NT," *Journal of the Evangelical Theological Society* 58, no. 1 (March 2015): 69.

HOW TO AVOID COMMON ERRORS

1. Beware of using the heading "grammar, semantics, and stylistic analysis" but actually not having any style observations or analysis.
2. Do not simply identify a few figures of speech; analyze how the stylistic features enlighten the significance of the passage.
3. A few students may see style as irrelevant to life and to interpretation. Richard A. Lanham has written an apologetic for the necessity of style in composition courses that may help explain the importance of being aware of style. I suggest students read the chapters beginning at the start until they are convinced.[16]
4. Do not simply state that certain words are stressed. Analyze further how the rhetorical features affect the total meaning of the passage.

APPENDICES

Greek Word and Clause Order[17]

I. *Normal Greek word order:* subject-verb-object (or complement) + modifying phrases and clauses; e.g., Ἐπίδαμνος ἐστι πόλις ἐν δεξιᾷ ἐσπλέοντι εἰς τὸν Ἰόνιαν κόλπον (Demetrius, *On Style* 4.199).
   A. Minor words generally come close to the word they belong to in sense.
   B. *Adjectives:* are near the subject they modify and usually after it. Two adjectives in the same case with repeated articles show emphasis. Usually one article is used for adjectives referring to the same noun (e.g., John 8:16; 2 Cor. 6:2; 12:4).
   C. *Prepositional phrases:* usually follow verb and object (e.g., 2 Cor. 11:21).
   D. *Clauses:* A dependent clause usually follows the main clause. The order of clauses is also dependent on the flow of thought. Often dependent clauses may precede a main clause to emphasize reason (e.g., Rom. 8:9).
   E. *Conjunctions:* are usually next to the verb. Subordinating conjunctions begin dependent clauses. Elements before a conjunction are emphasized.

---

16. See Richard A. Lanham, *Style: An Anti-Textbook* (New Haven, CT: Yale University Press, 1974).
17. Resources for explaining word order are A. T. Robertson, *A Grammar of the Greek New Testament in the Light of Historical Research* (Nashville: Broadman, 1934), chs. 10, 11, 417–25; F. Blass, A. DeBrunner, and Robert Funk, *A Greek Grammar of the New Testament and Other Early Christian Literature* (Chicago: University of Chicago Press), ch. 13, 248–53; Kenneth James Dover, *Greek Word Order* (Cambridge: Cambridge University Press, 1960).

F. *Genitives:* generally follow the word they modify (i.e., phrasal modifier). The phrasal modifier is more common than the attributive modifier. In the attributive modifier, if the adjective comes between the article and the noun, the phrase is a unified concept (e.g., Phil. 3:9).

G. *Vocatives:* often at the beginning of a sentence.

H. *Adverbs:* generally take the second place in a sentence or follow the verb (e.g., 2 Cor. 11:19).

I. *Negatives:* generally come before the words they negate.

J. *Pronouns:* tend to come early in a sentence or immediately after the verb. They never begin a clause. Pronominal subjects are usually not mentioned (e.g., 2 Cor. 11:21; Rev. 1:8).

K. *Postpositives, prepositions, particles, enclitics:* never or rarely begin a clause.

II. *Principles:* The normal Greek order of a sentence can be varied for purposes of emphasis or euphony and rhythm to express emotion or clarity of argument. Generally words are moved forward for emphasis. Also, placing them at the beginning and at the end of a sentence may be used for emphasis (except for chiasm or antithesis). Any two words (such as two genitives) in contrast can be brought sharply together.

Sentence Changes in Philemon 4–6

Addition	Omission	Substitution	Transposition
v. 4			object precedes participle: μνείαν ... ποιούμενος (focus on remembering, not making)
v. 5 pleonasm—repetition of article differentiates two qualities of "love" and "faith" hendiadys—"faithful love" "Love" is emphasized as first word, but repetition of article and later use of "faith" focus on it too.		metaphor κύριον (a common metaphor, but in this context, contrast with Philemon is significant)	pronoun precedes noun and indicates reader, Philemon: σου ... ἀγάπην (why? σου modifies both nouns) adjective precedes noun: πάντας τοὺς ἁγίους (emphasizes "all")
v. 6 parallel prepositional phrases ἐν ἡμῖν and εἰς Χριστόν (contrast and combine two ideas)	ellipsis of ἀγαθοῦ after τοῦ (focus then is on two prepositional phrases that follow)	metaphor κοινωνία (economic and interpersonal literal base also is found in metaphor)	ἐνεργὴς γένηται object/complement precedes verb (emphasizes ἐνεργὴς— "effective") adjective/modifier precedes noun modified: παντὸς ἀγαθοῦ (emphasizes "every")

176 | In-Depth Study of the Text

Definitions of Frequent New Testament Rhetorical Terms[18]

anaphora (addition sentence change). The first word or group of words of succeeding (at least two) clauses, phrases, lines, or sentences are repeated; e.g., repetition of "by faith" (*pistei*) (Heb. 11:3, 4, 5, 7, 8, 9, 11, 17, 20, 21, 22, 23, 24, 27, 28, 29, 30, 31).

asyndeton (omission sentence change). The deliberate omission of conjunctions between a series of related words, phrases, or clauses separated by commas; for example, no conjunction in 1 Corinthians 3:12.

chiasm (addition sentence change). A reverted type of parallelism, an inversion of the second of two parallel phrases or clauses. It is a diagonal arrangement, usually of one to four clauses or phrases in a sequence in a well-rounded sentence or *period*. The first clause corresponds with the fourth, and the second with the third, as in the sequence ABBA, ABCD-DCBA, or even ABCBA; for example, "Meats for the belly, and the belly for meats" (1 Cor. 6:13). Also, a theme may be developed in a chiastic thought pattern in larger contexts.

ellipsis (omission sentence change). The deliberate omission of a word or words necessary to complete or clarify a construction but which is implied by the context; for example, "Wives, to your husbands, as to the Lord" (Eph. 5:22).

hendiadys (substitution sentence change). Expression of an idea by two nouns in the same case connected by "and" instead of a noun and its qualifier or by two verbs connected by "and," where one word is subordinate to the other; for example, "[I am on trial] concerning hope and resurrection" = "the resurrection hope" (Acts 23:6).[19]

hyperbole (substitution sentence change). Self-conscious use of exaggerated or extravagant terms to gain heightened effect or emphasis that is not intended to be understood literally; for example, "But there are also many other things which Jesus did; were every one of them to be written, I suppose that the world itself could not contain the books that would be written" (John 21:25 RSV).

irony (substitution sentence change). The intended use of a word or words to express a meaning directly opposite the literal meaning of the word or words; for example, "For in what were you worse off than the remaining churches, except that I myself was not a burden to you? Forgive me this injustice" (2 Cor. 12:13).

---

18. Definitions can be found in more depth in Spencer, *Paul's Literary Style*, 186–212; Richard A. Lanham, *A Handlist of Rhetorical Terms*, 2nd ed. (Berkeley: University of California Press, 1991).

19. This example comes from Max Zerwick and Mary Grosvenor, *A Grammatical Analysis of the Greek New Testament* (Rome: Editrice Pontificio Istituto Biblico, 1996), xx; see also Bullinger, *Figures of Speech*, 657–72.

meiosis (substitution sentence change). A deliberately employed understatement, presenting something as less than it really is. As a form of *meiosis, litotes* is a deliberate use of understatement to assert an affirmative by denying its opposite in order to enhance the impressiveness of what is said or to intensify the affirmative; for example, "Paul said, 'I am a Jew, from Tarsus in Cilicia, a citizen of no insignificant city'" (Acts 21:39).

metaphor (substitution sentence change). An implied or implicit comparison between two things of unlike nature that yet have something in common so that one or more properties of the first are attributed to the second; the substitution of one thing for another; for example, "If in the tongues of humans and of angels I speak, but I have not love, I have become a roaring gong or a clanging cymbal" (1 Cor. 13:1).

parallelism (addition sentence change). The repetition of a syntactic or structural pattern. Article is opposed to article, connective to connective, like to like, from the beginning to the end (Demetrius, *On Style* 23). There are two basic types: synonymous (the second line expresses an identical or similar thought to the first line) and antithetic (the second line expresses a thought in sharp contrast to that which was declared in the first line). Parts of a sentence can also be parallel. Parallelism is structural in form; for example, "Blessed [are] the ones hungering now, for you will be satisfied; blessed [are] the ones weeping now, for you will laugh" (Luke 6:21). Also, thoughts can be parallel.

personification (substitution sentence change). To invest abstractions (qualities, ideas, or general terms), inanimate objects, or nonhuman living things with human qualities or abilities, especially with human feelings. *Apostrophe* is addressing a personified abstraction or an absent person; for example, "Therefore, do not be anxious about tomorrow, for tomorrow will be anxious for itself" (Matt. 6:34a).

pleonasm (addition sentence change). The doubling and repetition of words of similar meaning, of thoughts of similar content, as well as of all forms of addition. Narrow or specific pleonasm is the doubling of items and parenthetical asides; for example, "in dangers from rivers, in dangers from robbers, in dangers from kin, in dangers from Gentiles, in dangers in city, in dangers in wilderness, in dangers in sea, in dangers among false brothers and sisters, in trouble and hardship" (2 Cor. 11:26b–27a).

polysyndeton (addition sentence change). The same or even different conjunctions or connecting particles are deliberately used at least two times in close succession between each clause, word, or phrase; for example, "Worthy is the Lamb, the slaughtered one, to receive the power and riches and wisdom and might and honor and glory and praise" (Rev. 5:12).

simile (substitution sentence change). An explicit comparison using "like" or "as" between two things of unlike nature that yet have something in common so that one or more properties of the first are attributed to the second; the substitution of one thing for another; for example, "For just

178 | In-Depth Study of the Text

as the lightning flashing lights up the sky from one side to another, in the same way the Son of Man will be in his day" (Luke 17:24).

synecdoche (substitution sentence change). The whole (a more inclusive term) is known from a small part (a less inclusive term) or a part for the whole. In *metonymy* ("change of name"), a form of synecdoche, the name of one object or concept is used for that of another to which it is related, or of which it is a part. For instance, a proper name can be substituted for one of its qualities, a cause for effect, or vice versa;[20] for example, "Give us our daily bread for today" (Matt. 6:11).

Sentence Changes: Summary of Frequent Rhetorical Terms

Addition	Omission	Substitution	Transposition
Anaphora—first word(s) of two or more clauses, phrases, or sentences are repeated.	*Asyndeton*—no conjunctions between words, phrases, or clauses.	*Hyperbole*—exaggerated or extravagant terms self-consciously used.	*Word Order*
Chiasm—inversion of second of two parallel phrases or clauses in a period.	*Ellipsis*—word(s) omitted.	*Irony*—word(s) say opposite of the intended and literal meaning.	
Parallelism—repetition of a syntactical or structural pattern.		*Meiosis*—understatement, something less than it really is; to assert affirmative by denying its opposite (*litotes*).	
Pleonasm—doubling and repetition of words of similar meaning, thoughts (doubling of items; parenthetical asides).		*Metaphor*—implied or implicit comparison between two unlike things.	
Polysyndeton—same or different conjunctions or particles used at least two times between words, phrases, or clauses.		*Personification*—invest abstractions, inanimate objects, nonhuman things with human qualities or abilities, especially feelings.	
		Simile—explicit comparison between two unlike things using "like" or "as." Greek ὡς, ὥσπερ, οὕτως, ὁμοίως, καθώς, ὃν τρόπον, ὡσεί, ὅμοιος, ὁμοιόω, ἔοικα.	
		Synecdoche—the whole known from a part or a part from the whole (*metonymy*).	

---

20. *Random House Webster's Unabridged Dictionary* (2001), s.v. "synecdoche"; Lanham, *Handlist*, 102, 148.

CHAPTER 7

STUDY FURTHER CONTEXTUAL RESOURCES: JEWISH AND GRECO-ROMAN BACKGROUND

CONTEXTUAL RESOURCES: BACKGROUND[1]

I.   *Identify.* Determine how knowing the ancient Jewish and/or the Greco-Roman historical-cultural background might enlighten your text, such as context and content of Old Testament quotations, allusions, or other questions, information for cultural/historical/ geographic, linguistic, or literary background.

II. *Decide if the study will be topical or semantic.* Will it cover subject matter or be a word study or be some of both? Will the Jewish or Greco-Roman background be more important? Or are both relevant? Narrow the topic to be studied to what can be accomplished in the time/space allotted.

III. *Investigate.* Gather parallel or counter-parallel texts from ancient primary sources. Use book indexes. Write or paraphrase

---

1. See also Gordon D. Fee, *New Testament Exegesis: A Handbook for Students and Pastors,* 3rd ed. (Louisville: Westminster John Knox, 2002), 96–111; T. Norton Sterrett and Richard L. Schultz, *How to Understand Your Bible*, 3rd ed. (Downers Grove, IL: InterVarsity Press, 2010), ch. 11; William W. Klein, Craig L. Blomberg, and Robert L. Hubbard Jr., *Introduction to Biblical Interpretation*, 3rd ed. (Grand Rapids: Zondervan, 2017), 312–23; Craig L. Blomberg with Jennifer Foutz Markley, *A Handbook of New Testament Exegesis* (Grand Rapids: Baker Academic, 2010), 64–78, 270; Richard J. Erickson, *A Beginner's Guide to New Testament Exegesis: Taking the Fear Out of Critical Method* (Downers Grove, IL: InterVarsity Press, 2005), ch. 5, 229–31; Billie Jean Collins et al., *The SBL Handbook of Style,* 2nd ed. (Atlanta: SBL Press, 2014), ch. 8, app. C. For further reading, see David S. Dockery, Kenneth A. Mathews, and Robert B. Sloan, *Foundations for Biblical Interpretation: A Complete Library of Tools and Resources* (Nashville: B&H, 1994), chs. 23–25; Roy B. Zuck, ed., *Rightly Divided: Readings in Biblical Hermeneutics* (Grand Rapids: Kregel, 1996), chs. 14–17.

180 | In-Depth Study of the Text

Jewish/Greco-Roman texts. Find a variety of types of texts. Date references cited when possible. Make sure you correctly cite ancient references. (Cite by author, title of book, chapter, and paragraph number, not page number.) Separately, keep a full bibliography of editions used. If a word is studied, underline the pertinent word in each quotation.

IV. *Evaluate.* After each ancient reference, wherever possible, briefly cite in brackets the significance of the reference for your text. Be aware of the date and context of the ancient text.

V. *Summarize in a paragraph or two how these different references enlighten your text.* When writing up these references for the exegesis paper, write at the start what you learned from the study. In other words, present your conclusion in one to two sentences. Then present and cite the most important ancient references. Footnote other less important ancient references. Use the same format as writing a word study.

This step can be done by both Greek and translation readers.

INTRODUCTION

In exegesis we learn to ask questions of the text that lead us to understanding. We have basically three kinds of questions:

1. Content: What does the author say? (referring to grammar and semantics)
2. Composition: How does the author say it? (referring to style)
3. Context

Context may be subdivided into (1) literary (around the text—paragraph, letter, genre) and (2) historical (beyond the literary text). "Historical" may refer to the occasion for a letter or book (who wrote it, to whom, when, from where, why) and the culture of the author and readers. In effect, the content and composition of a text are clarified by the historical and cultural contexts. Or we may say, the historical and cultural contexts clarify the content and composition of a text. New Testament background includes these interrelated broad areas:

1. History: information on historical events and individuals
2. Geography: information on places
3. Culture

"Culture" is an agricultural image. Having a rich soil helps a seed to grow. Similarly, the metaphorical "culture" affects the growth of an idea or communication. Anthropologist Adamson Hoebel defined "culture" as an "integrated system of learned behavior patterns which are characteristic of the members of a society and which are not the result of biological inheritance."[2] Culture includes material and social culture (ways of living). Elements of background that are important in biblical studies may be summarized in the following chart.

ELEMENTS OF BACKGROUND

Elements of Background	Old Testament	New Testament	New Testament Letters
I. Historical factors	Earlier occurrences in OT, Near East, Mesopotamia, Canaan, Israel, Egypt, Syria, Assyria, Babylonia, Media, Persia	OT, Israel, Jewish groups (such as Samaritans, Pharisees, Sadducees, Herodians, scribes, common people), Hellenistic, Roman	OT, life of Jesus
II. Geographical factors (physical features)		Judea, Galilee, Rome	Galilee, Judea, Rome
III. Culture			
A. Material culture (e.g., implements, tools, objects, buildings, weapons, garments)			
B. Social culture (ways of living)			
1. Social relational (e.g., marriage, burial, family customs)			
2. Religious practices and perspectives (worldviews, morals)		Jewish groups (such as Pharisees, Sadducees, Samaritans), pagans	Also, e.g., Artemis
3. Politics (e.g., law, government)	Israel, Egypt, Assyria, etc.	Judea, Rome	Judea, Rome
4. Economics (e.g., property, money, commerce, debt)			
5. Language and literature	Hebrew, Aramaic	Hebrew, Aramaic, Greek, Latin	Hebrew, Aramaic, Greek, Latin
6. Art and architecture		Greek, Roman	Greek, Roman

---

2.   E. Adamson Hoebel, *Anthropology: The Study of Man* (New York: McGraw-Hill, 1966), 5; see also the discussion on culture by A. Berkeley Mickelsen, *Interpreting the Bible* (Grand Rapids: Eerdmans, 1963), 159–76.

182 | In-Depth Study of the Text

When my husband and I were first married, we lived in Trenton, New Jersey. One day a group of young Europeans rang the doorbell of our apartment, representing the "Moonies," members of the Unification Church. The group had not yet become famous. My husband, as a theologian, wanted to learn more about them and asked about their teachings. Shortly, he was given their teaching manual on the *Divine Principle* by Sun Myung Moon. We were surprised to see that it was written as an abstract discourse. In contrast, the Bible has not been written as a philosophical treatise. Rather, since God is a God who created and intervenes and moves history, God's Word is composed of a series of historical accounts, along with poems, prophecies, proverbs, letters of advice, and so on, given in many different historical times and places. The New Testament was written in Koine Greek, the international everyday language of its time, and in the culture of its authors. Some of the background material is explained in the New Testament itself. Reading and rereading the Bible is helpful. As Norton Sterrett explained, "The more familiar you become with the whole Bible, the more you will grow in your background knowledge."[3]

For instance, Mark, who traditionally is said to have written his gospel to Romans, explained Jewish practices, such as "eating with defiled hands": "that is, without washing them. (For the Pharisees, and all the Jews, do not eat unless they wash their hands, thus observing the tradition of the elders, and they do not eat anything from the market unless they wash it, and there are also many other traditions that they observe: the washing of cups and pots and bronze kettles)" (Mark 7:2–4 NRSV). We can learn more about this practice by reading the Mishnah (a collection of Jewish rabbinical rules and discussions written down in the first century).[4] At other times, common cultural assumptions are assumed and not explained. What is a "narrow gate" (Matt. 7:13) or a "holy kiss" (Rom. 16:16)? We are separated from the first century by time, geography, language, culture, customs, and worldview. But we can bridge that gap because the ultimate author of this ancient collection of books, "The Book," is God, who is still alive and present to us through the Holy Spirit. That is why prayer or communication with God is so important for the effective exegete.

In addition, we, like the New Testament writers, are human. We still have social relations, religious practices, politics, economies, languages, literature (whether in print or online), art, and architecture. We live in community, as they did. Like them, we may feel lonely or loved, admired or isolated, confident and/or embarrassed, and so on. As Shylock defended himself, we too can say that we twenty-first century readers are like the

---

3.   Sterrett and Schultz, *How to Understand Your Bible,* 94. The appendix at the end of this chapter includes a Bible reading plan (in the form of a bookmark) that is basically in chronological order. Good marginal references can help find appropriate passages.

4.   See Mishnah, Yadaim ("Hands").

Study Further Contextual Resources: Jewish and Greco-Roman Background | 183

first-century readers in that we have "hands, organs, dimensions, senses, affections, passions. . . . If you prick us, do we not bleed? If you tickle us, do we not laugh? If you poison us, do we not die? And if you wrong us, shall we not revenge?"[5] If we are sympathetic and open to God's presence in our time and world, we become like the earliest believers as God transforms us, and we become better able to understand God's perspective in an earlier era.

For example, which practices described in the book of Acts are authoritative for us today? We look for God's perspective. God's perspective is apparent by the end of events, by the explicit and implicit commentary by Luke, by the models of people, and is reinforced in the teaching sections of the New Testament letters. Should we approve the killing of Christians, as Saul did in Acts 8:1–3; 9:1–2? No, because we learn that Saul had been in fact persecuting Jesus, God incarnate (Acts 9:3–20)!

We can learn the original languages of the New and Old Testaments, Greek and Hebrew, and learn more about their culture and customs. Harold Mattingly explained that "language" is "much more than vocabulary and grammar." It includes "forms of thought that crystallize round certain words or phrases but are not fully expressed in them, when much more is suggested than actually said. It may include general ideas, . . . pictorial language, the language of symbolism, comparable to written language but not capable of exact translation into it."[6] Excellent resources have been available through these many centuries to help us better understand ancient Jewish, Greek, and Roman cultures.

The more we learn about the ancient Jewish, Greek, and Roman setting, the more likely we can ask the right questions of our text. Nevertheless, we can use whatever resources we have to obtain additional insight into a text's meaning. Since we are beginning with a specific text, an inductive approach is helpful. First, we need to *identify* something that needs to be investigated: a word, custom, practice, institution, person, event, or place. Is the Old Testament cited or some Jewish practice assumed? Second, we need to *decide* if the Jewish or Greco-Roman background is more important, or would a topical or semantic study be most helpful? Our third step is to *investigate* our topic from ancient primary sources and, fourth, to *evaluate* its relationship to our text. Is it similar? Different? Some books have indexes of words while others have indexes of subject matter. If your time is limited, I have found most helpful Josephus's historical works and the Mishnah.

During the evaluation process, we may find three types of literary parallels: abstract, specific, or exact.

---

5.   William Shakespeare, *The Merchant of Venice* 3.1.57–59, 63–66.
6.   Harold Mattingly, *The Man in the Roman Street* (New York: Norton, 1966), 28.

184 | In-Depth Study of the Text

THREE TYPES OF LITERARY PARALLELS

1. *Abstract or imperfect or alleged or seeming parallel.* Passages appear similar but may be different contexts.
2. *Specific or applied parallel.* Direct organic literary connection provides the parallels, a relationship of dependence shown by word-for-word similarity and similar content or ideas.
3. *True or exact parallel—source and derivation.* Literary connection flowing in a particular direction can be significant or devoid of significance if merely a result of broad commonalities.

Samuel Sandmel popularized the term *parallelomania* as "that extravagance among scholars which first overdoes the supposed similarity in passages and then proceeds to describe source and derivation as if implying literary connection flowing in an inevitable or predetermined direction."[7] Our goal as exegetes is rarely steps 2 and 3 above, proving one document is the source of another, unless the second document cites the first one, is later, and has word-for-word similarity. Rather, the goal is to learn what ideas and practices were around or preceded the writing we are studying. We need to understand all the ancient texts in their own literary and historical contexts as we do the New Testament. God's direct revelation, the Old Testament, is more likely a source for the New Testament than other second-temple (first-century) references. Yet God's truth may be found not only in the Bible but also in other texts.

For my sample exegesis paper in chapter 8, I decided to get a sampling of ideas about slavery as background for Paul's treatment of Onesimus. I thought both the Jewish and Greco-Roman backgrounds might be enlightening. Subject matter indexes were helpful. A commentary on Philemon[8] also led me to several primary references. (See the appendix to this chapter "Philemon: Examples of the Place of Slaves in the Rabbinic and Greco-Roman Worlds." p. 195) I summarized my findings in the sample Philemon 4–6 exegesis paper (chapter 8) under the explanation of what preparing a guest room might signify, where I describe the unequal status of slaves for Jews and Greeks.

What ancient literature is available?[9]

---

7. Samuel Sandmel, "Parallelomania," *Journal of Biblical Literature* 81, no. 1 (March 1962): 1; see also Aída Besançon Spencer, "'Parallelomania' and God's Unique Revelation," *Africanus Journal* 1, no. 1 (2009): 31–40.
8. Markus Barth and Helmut Blanke, *The Letter to Philemon: A New Translation with Notes and Commentary,* Eerdmans Critical Commentary (Grand Rapids: Eerdmans, 2000).
9. See also the online *TLG* in the appendix of chapter 5.

REFERENCES FOR THE STUDY OF ANCIENT LITERATURES

References for the Literature of the Ancient Jewish World

I. Biblical[10]

A. *Old Testament and the Septuagint.* The Old Testament was written largely in Hebrew. The Septuagint (LXX)[11] is its translation into Greek (c. 250–100 BC).

Brenton, Lancelot C. L. *The Septuagint: Greek and English.* Grand Rapids: Zondervan, 1851. Reprint of version by Samuel Bagster.

Brown, A. Philip, II, and Bryan W. Smith. *A Reader's Hebrew Bible.* Grand Rapids: Zondervan, 2008. Hendrickson has a variety of editions.

Kohlenberger, John R., III, and James Swanson. *The Hebrew-English Concordance to the Old Testament.* Grand Rapids: Zondervan, 1998.

Lanier, Gregory R., and William A. Ross, eds. *Septuaginta: A Reader's Edition.* 2 vols. Peabody, MA: Hendrickson, 2018.

Rahlfs, Alfred, and Robert Hanhart, eds. *Septuaginta.* Stuttgart: Deutsche Bibelgesellschaft, 2006.

B. *Apocrypha.* Fifteen "hidden" books included in the LXX but not canonical for Jews or Protestants,[12] literature of different genres: historical narratives (1 Maccabees [covers 175–135 BC], 2 Maccabees [covers 175–111 BC], 1 Esdras [c. 150 BC]); fictional narratives (Tobit [c. 200–175 BC], Judith [c. 150 BC], Rest of Esther [c. 100 BC], Daniel and Susanna [100–25 BC], Daniel, Bel, and the Snake [c. 100 BC]); apocalypse (2 Esdras [AD 100–300]); wisdom literature (Wisdom of Solomon [c. 150–50 BC], Ecclesiasticus or the Wisdom of Jesus Son

---

10. For a description of the Jewish, Greek, and Latin literature, see Emil Schürer, *The History of the Jewish People in the Age of Jesus Christ (175 B.C.–A.D. 135): A New English Version,* rev. and ed. Geza Vermes, Fergus Millar, Pamela Vermes, and Matthew Black, vol. 1 (Edinburgh: T&T Clark, 1973), 17–122; David W. Chapman and Andreas Köstenberger, "Jewish Intertestamental and Early Rabbinic Literature: An Annotated Bibliographic Resource Update (Part 1)," *Journal of the Evangelical Theological Society (JETS)* 55, no. 2 (June 2012): 235–72; (pt. 2), *JETS* 55, no. 3 (September 2012): 457–88; Philip Walker Jacobs, *A Guide to the Study of Greco-Roman and Jewish and Christian History and Literature* (Lanham, MD: University Press of America, 1994); Joseph A. Fitzmyer, *An Introductory Bibliography for the Study of Scripture,* Subsidia Biblica 3 (Rome: Istituto Biblico, 1990).

11. For a list of acceptable abbreviations, see Collins et al., *The SBL Handbook of Style,* 124–68. An earlier edition is available online: https://www.sbl-site.org/assets/pdfs/pubs/SBLHSsupp2015-02.pdf.

12. Even the early church theologian Jerome advised Laeta that the apocryphal writings "are not really written by those to whom they are ascribed, that many faulty elements have been introduced into them, and that it requires infinite discretion to look for gold in the midst of dirt" (*Letter* 57.12).

186 | In-Depth Study of the Text

of Sirach [c. 180 BC]; Baruch [c. second century BC], Prayer of Azariah and the Song of the Three [200–100 BC], Prayer of Manasseh [100–90 BC]), sermon (Letter of Jeremiah [c. 300–110 BC]).[13]

First Maccabees is helpful for historical data, Ecclesiasticus for theology by an Alexandrian Jew, and the Daniel stories for early mysteries.[14] The Revised English Bible has a readable version of 1 Maccabees.

> Charles, R. H. *The Apocrypha and Pseudepigrapha of the Old Testament in English.* 2 vols. Oxford: Clarendon, 1913. Volume 2 has an index.
>
> Hatch, Edwin, and Henry A. Redpath. *A Concordance to the Septuagint and the Other Greek Versions of the Old Testament.* 2 vols. Grand Rapids: Baker, 1983.

C. *Pseudepigrapha.* Most of the remaining unclassified intertestamental literature ("false titles"), except for the Dead Sea Scrolls, is included in this category. These works shed light on the ancient thought world. Those written before the first century AD include the Treatise of Shem (first century BC), Testaments of the Twelve Patriarchs (second century BC–AD second century), Letter of Aristeas (c. 170 BC), Jubilees (161–140 BC), Ahiqar (seventh–sixth centuries BC), 3 Maccabees (first century BC), and fragments by different writers.

> Charlesworth, James H., ed. *The Old Testament Pseudepigrapha.* 2 vols. Garden City, NY: Doubleday, 1983. Reprint, Peabody, MA: Hendrickson, 2010.
>
> Delamarter, Steve. *A Scripture Index to Charlesworth's The Old Testament Pseudepigrapha.* New York: Sheffield, 2002.

II. Hellenistic Jewish Writers

A. *Flavius Josephus.* Jewish historian and apologist, born in Jerusalem (c. AD 37–100). He wrote *Jewish Antiquities, The Jewish War, Life,* and *Against Apion.* His works can be found in Greek

---

13. All dates are approximate. For the apocryphal dates, see R. K. Harrison, *Introduction to the Old Testament* (Grand Rapids: Eerdmans, 1969), 1196–97, 1200, 1211, 1216, 1218, 1225, 1232, 1240, 1242. See also Bruce M. Metzger, *An Introduction to the Apocrypha* (New York: Oxford University Press, 1957). For the pseudepigraphal dates, see James H. Charlesworth, ed., *The Old Testament Pseudepigrapha,* 2 vols. (Garden City, NY: Doubleday, 1983, 1985), 1:474–75, 777–78; 2:8–9, 43–44, 482, 510–12. See also the chart in the appendix to chapter 5: "Selected Writings in the *TLG,* Loeb Classical Library, and Old Testament Pseudepigrapha."

14. For a discussion of the Daniel stories, see William David Spencer, *Mysterium and Mystery: The Clerical Crime Novel* (Carbondale, IL: Southern Illinois University Press, 1989), ch. 1.

with parallel English translations and subject indexes in the Loeb Classical Library (LCL) series (a general subject index may be found in book 20 of the *Jewish Antiquities*, book 2 of *The Jewish War, Life,* and *Against Apion*, as well as Greek word indexes in *TLG* and Perseus). Translations of his works into English are available at www.sacred-texts.com/jud/josephus/index.html.

Josephus. *The New Complete Works of Josephus.* Translated by William Whiston. Edited by Paul L. Maier. Rev. ed. Grand Rapids: Kregel, 1999.

Josephus. *The Works of Josephus: Complete and Unabridged.* Translated by William Whiston. Peabody, MA: Hendrickson, 1987.

Rengstorf, Karl Heinrich, ed. *A Complete Concordance to Flavius Josephus.* 4 vols. Leiden: Brill, 1973.

B. *Philo.* Jewish philosopher, apologist, and historian, born in Alexandria, Egypt (c. 20 BC–AD 42/50), known for his allegorical exegesis. The LCL has twelve volumes by Philo in Greek and English. Volume 10 has indices.

Borgen, Peter, Kåre Fuglseth, and Roald Skarsten. *The Philo Index: A Complete Greek Word Index to the Writings of Philo of Alexandria.* Grand Rapids: Eerdmans, 2000.

Mayer, Günter. *Index Philoneus.* Berlin: de Gruyter, 1974. Includes Greek word concordance.

Philo. *The Works of Philo: Complete and Unabridged.* Translated by C. D. Yonge. Peabody, MA: Hendrickson, 1993. http://www.earlychristianwritings.com/yonge/. Includes subject and Scripture indexes.

III. *Rabbinic literature.* This is the literature of the scribes and rabbis and may be dated by the dates of the rabbis.

A. *Mishnah.* Oral rabbinic traditions "repeated" up to AD 200, mostly "halachic" teaching, to help fulfill the law. The Mishnah has six orders on seasons, women, damages, holy things, and purities. It includes some "haggadah," teaching to encourage or exhort.

Danby, Herbert. *The Mishnah.* Oxford: Oxford University Press, 1933. Includes subject and Scripture indexes, a list of rabbinical teachers and their dates, and a glossary. Reprint, Peabody, MA: Hendrickson, 2012.

Gianotti, Charles R. *The New Testament and the Mishnah: A Cross-Reference Index.* Grand Rapids: Baker, 1983. Includes

188 | In-Depth Study of the Text

cross-references between the New Testament and the Mishnah, taken from Strack-Billerbeck (see below).

Neusner, Jacob. *The Mishnah: A New Translation*. New Haven, CT: Yale University Press, 1988.

Strack, Hermann L., and Paul Billerbeck. *A Commentary on the New Testament from the Talmud and Midrash*. Edited by Jacob N. Cerone. Translated by Andrew Bowden and Joseph Longarino. 3 vols. Bellingham, WA: Lexham, 2022. Refers readers to potential parallel rabbinic literature, but the parallels may not be exact.

https://www.sefaria.org/texts/Mishnah

B. *Talmud*. Mishnah and commentary (Gemara) by the rabbis.
   1. *Jerusalem/Palestinian Talmud*. Commentary by rabbis living in Israel, especially Galilee, c. AD 400s.

Guggenheimer, Heinrich, ed. *The Jerusalem Talmud*. 22 vols. New York: de Gruyter, 2000–2020.

Neusner, Jacob, ed. *The Talmud of the Land of Israel*. 35 vols. Chicago: University of Chicago Press, 1982–1994. Encompasses the Jerusalem Talmud.

   2. *Babylonian Talmud*. Commentary by rabbis in Babylonia that condenses and supersedes the Jerusalem Talmud, c. AD 500s.

Epstein, Isidore, and Judah Slotki, eds. *The Babylonian Talmud*. 18 vols. London: Soncino, 1935–1990. Includes a one-volume index. http://come-and-hear.com/talmud/index.html.

Neusner, Jacob, ed. *The Talmud of Babylonia: An American Translation*. 36 vols. Chico, CA: Scholars Press, 1984–90.

C. *Tosefta*. A collection of traditions that "supplement" and follow the plan of the Mishnah but never obtained Mishnah's authority.

Neusner, Jacob, trans. *The Tosefta*. 6 vols. New York: KTAV, 1977–1986. The set has a general index. Reprint, Peabody, MA: Hendrickson, 2014.

D. *Midrashim*. Biblical interpretation and exposition that "searches out" the biblical meaning, passage by passage. Midrashim are available in individual volumes, such as Jacob Z. Lauterbach, trans., *Mekhilta de-Rabbi Ishmael*, 3 vols. (Philadelphia: Jewish Publication Society, 1961), which has an index.

E. *Targum*. Aramaic paraphrases or translations of the Old Testament.

Sperber, A., ed. *The Bible in Aramaic*. 4 vols. Leiden: Brill, 1959–1973.

IV. *Sectarian.* Literature among the Dead Sea Scrolls from the Qumran community, which desired to set up a pure community. Examples are the Damascus Document, Rule of the Community, War Scroll, and Genesis Apocryphon. Many other fragments were also discovered at Qumran, including Old Testament scrolls.[15]

> Charlesworth, James H., et al., eds. *Graphic Concordance to the Dead Sea Scrolls.* Louisville: Westminster John Knox, 1991.
> Dupont-Sommer, A. *The Essene Writings from Qumran.* Translated by G. Vermes. Gloucester, UK: Smith, 1961. The book includes a Scripture index.
> Embry, Brad, Ronald Herms, and Archie T. Wright, eds. *Early Jewish Literature: An Anthology.* 2 vols. Grand Rapids: Eerdmans, 2018. The volumes contain books (categorized by genres) from the Apocrypha, Old Testament Pseudepigrapha, some biblical books such as Daniel, selections from Josephus, Philo, and the Dead Sea Scrolls, with introductions, glossaries, and subject indexes.
> García Martínez, Florentino, and Eibert J. C. Tigchelaar, eds. *The Dead Sea Scrolls Study Edition.* 2 vols. Grand Rapids: Eerdmans, 1997.
> García Martínez, Florentino, and Eibert J. C. Tigchelaar, eds. *The Dead Sea Scrolls Translated: The Qumran Texts in English.* 2nd ed. Grand Rapids: Eerdmans, 1996. Includes an online index.
> Vermes, Géza. *The Dead Sea Scrolls in English.* 3rd ed. Sheffield: JSOT Press, 1987.

References for the Literature of the Ancient Greco-Roman World

The Hellenistic context may help the Bible interpreter by providing historical background, language, literary forms, and cultural and geographical information.[16] Contemporary Greek writers of significance for New Testament study

---

15. Between 1947 and 1956, approximately nine hundred manuscripts, dated from 250 BC to AD 68, were discovered in caves around Qumran near the Dead Sea. Between the 1950s and 1960s, more ancient scrolls were found in the Judean Desert. Over two hundred scrolls from Qumran are portions of the Bible, including the oldest known copy of the book of Isaiah (c. 125 BC). Many of these ancient scrolls confirm the accuracy of the Masoretic Text. Many of the manuscripts are named by the cave in which they were found, such as 1Q15, which was found in cave 1 at Qumran. See Jeremy D. Lyon, "The Dead Sea Scrolls and the Reliability of the Bible," *Bible Study Magazine* 14, no. 2 (January–February 2022): 29–31. For a general introduction, see James C. VanderKam, *The Dead Sea Scrolls Today,* rev. ed. (Grand Rapids: Eerdmans, 2010).

16. See subject indexes to Loeb Classical Library editions and online *TLG* and Perseus. Maria C. Pantelia, *Thesaurus Linguae Graecae: A Bibliographic Guide to the Canon of Greek Authors and Works* (Oakland: University of California Press, 2022), lists more than twenty thousand works in *TLG* as of 2022. See the shortened list of references in ch. 5 Appendix.

190 | In-Depth Study of the Text

include Stoic philosopher Epictetus, *Discourses as Reported by Arrian*; Strabo of Amaseia, *Geography*; Lucian, *How to Write History*; rhetoric teacher Dionysius Halicarnassus, *Roman Antiquities*; Demetrius, *On Style*; Lucian, *Selected Satires*; Plutarch, *Parallel Lives*; and Hippocrates, *Ancient Medicine*. Latin writers include Cicero, *Letters to Atticus*; Tacitus, *Histories, Annals*; Pliny the Elder, *Natural History*; Livy, *History of Rome*; and Quintilian, *Institutio Oratoria*. Earlier influential writers include Aristotle and Plato. There are also many collections of papyri with their own indexes of words used, including the following:

> Deissmann, Adolf. *Light from the Ancient East: The New Testament Illustrated by Recently Discovered Texts of the Graeco-Roman World*. Translated by Lionel R. M. Strachan. Rev. ed. New York: Doran, 1927. Includes indexes.
>
> Grenfell, B., and A. Hunt, eds. *Oxyrhynchus Papyria*. 18 vols. London: Egypt Exploration, 1898–1994.
>
> Horsley, G. H. R., ed. *New Documents Illustrating Early Christianity: A Review of the Greek Inscriptions and Papyri*. 10 vols. North Ryde, Australia: Ancient History Qumran Documentary Research Centre, Macquarie University, 2012.
>
> Hunt, A. S., and C. C. Edgar, trans. *Select Papyri*. 3 vols. Loeb Classical Library. London: Heinemann, 1959.
>
> Moulton, James H., and G. Milligan. *The Vocabulary of the Greek Testament: Illustrated from the Papyri and Other Non-Literary Sources*. Peabody, MA: Hendrickson, 1997 (reprint).

Excellent secondary references include the following:

> Bromiley, G. W., ed. *International Standard Bible Encyclopedia*. 4 vols. Grand Rapids: Eerdmans, 1988.
>
> Daniel-Rops, Henri. *Daily Life in the Time of Jesus*. Translated by Patrick O'Brian. Ann Arbor, MI: Servant, 1961. This book includes indexes.
>
> Evans, Craig A., and Stanley E. Porter, eds. *Dictionary of New Testament Backgrounds*. Downers Grove, IL: InterVarsity Press, 2000.
>
> Frank, Harry Thomas, ed. *Atlas of the Bible Lands*. 2nd ed. Maplewood, NJ: Hammond, 1984.
>
> Hammond, N. G. L., and H. H. Scullard, eds. *The Oxford Classical Dictionary*. 2nd ed. Oxford: Clarendon, 1970.
>
> Keener, Craig S. *The IVP Bible Background Commentary: New Testament*. 2nd ed. Downers Grove, IL: InterVarsity Press, 2014.
>
> McRay, John. *Archaeology and the New Testament*. Grand Rapids: Baker, 1991.[17]

---

17. BDAG may also suggest parallel Jewish and Greco-Roman references under word meanings.

References for the Literature of the Early Church

"Background" refers to the history, culture, and geography of the people referred to in the book or letter you are studying. "History" includes the events leading up to the occurrences or events in the book or letter. In a picture, "background" is the surroundings, especially behind the central image, that provide harmony or contrast. The "foreground" would be the part of a scene or landscape nearest the viewer. In biblical studies, you may seek the foreground as well, for example, by asking, "What are the results of an event? What are the events that follow? How were the New Testament writer's words interpreted after the first century?" The way a later Christian interpreted a New Testament word might shed light on its developing meaning.

For instance, was Onesimus ever mentioned in the early church writings? Possibly, yes. The Onesimus of the letter to Philemon may be the same Onesimus who became the pastor and overseer at Ephesus at the end of the first century. (See "Larger Historical and Literary Context" in chapter 8, "Sample Exegesis Paper: Philemon 4–6.")

How was Paul's letter to the Romans received? The New Testament itself gives us some hints. The letter was likely received well because the Christians of Rome traveled over thirty miles to greet Paul after his long sea journey (Acts 28:15). The letter to the Philippians, written approximately four years later from Rome, indicated that most Roman Christians approved of Paul's imprisonment (Phil. 1:13–14). Paul had asked the Roman church to donate and they became famous as a church that aided other churches (Eusebius, *Church History* 4.23).[18]

The following outline summarizes the process of checking the foreground of a text.

Study Further Contextual Resources: Foreground

1. *Check the New Testament* to see if it gives any indication of any events or people following the text studied. What was the result of the letter? Use a New Testament concordance to trace the city/province or people from among the readers of the letter. Use also your knowledge of the chronology of New Testament books and letters.

2. *Check concordances* citing Christians living in the second through fourth centuries. The material after Emperor Constantine's proclamation of freedom of religious beliefs (AD 313; Eusebius, *Church History* 10.5) presents another important stage in Christian history.

3. *Check the indexes* in Eusebius's *Church History*.

---

18. See Aída Besançon Spencer, *Paul's Literary Style: A Stylistic and Historical Comparison of II Corinthians 11:16–12:13, Romans 8:9–39, and Philippians 3:2–4:13* (Lanham, MD: University Press of America, 1984), 82, 92.

192 | In-Depth Study of the Text

If time allows, finding further information about a church, person, event, or interpretation may bring light to your New Testament passage. However, an early church interpreter may be affected by his or her philosophical beliefs, such as neoplatonism, which would affect the resulting interpretation.

Here are further resources in addition to *TLG* (which indexes Greek words in Eusebius, Clement, Ignatius, Justin Martyr, Irenaeus, and others) and *Perseus*. Except for word studies, most of these resources do not require a knowledge of Greek.

Allenbach, J., A. Benoit, D. A. Bertrand, A. Hanriot-Coustet, P. Maraval, A. Pautler, and P. Prigent. *Biblia Patristica: Index des Citation et Allusions Bibliques dans la Litteratur Patristique.* 6 vols. Paris: Recherche Scientifique, 1975.

The Apostolic Fathers. Edited and translated by Bart Ehrman. 2 vols. Loeb Classical Library 24 and 25. Cambridge, MA: Harvard University Press, 2003. Volume 1 includes 1 and 2 Clement, Ignatius, Polycarp, and Didache.

The Apostolic Fathers: Greek Texts and English Translations. Edited and translated by Michael W. Holmes. 3rd ed. Grand Rapids: Baker, 2007. Includes 1 and 2 Clement, Letters of Ignatius, Letter of Polycarp to the Philippians, Martyrdom of Polycarp, Didache, Barnabas, Shepherd of Hermas, Diognetus, Papias, and indexes of Scripture and ancient writers.

Barrett, C. K. *The New Testament Background: Selected Documents.* New York: Harper & Row, 1961.

Eusebius. *The Ecclesiastical History.* Translated by Kirsopp Lake and J. E. L. Oulton. 2 vols. Loeb Classical Library. New York: Putnam, 1926–1932. Volume 2 has an index of names.

Eusebius. *Eusebius: The Church History: A New Translation with Commentary.* Edited and translated by Paul L. Maier. Grand Rapids: Kregel, 1999. Has subject indexes. Eusebius is a third-century historian who collected many earlier traditions. Moreover, Eusebius's work is worth reading for its many interesting stories.

Eusebius. *The History of the Church from Christ to Constantine.* Translated by G. A. Williamson. Rev. ed. New York: Penguin, 1989. Indexes people.

Goodspeed, Edgar. *Index Patristicus.* Peabody, MA: Hendrickson, 1993. Has Greek word indexes for 1 and 2 Clement, Barnabas, Papias, Diognetus, Ignatius, Polycarp, Shepherd of Hermas, and Didache.

Kraft, Henricus. *Clavis Patrum Apostolicorum.* Munich: Kösel, 1964. Indexes Greek words (in German).

Quasten, Johannes. *Patrology.* 3 vols. Westminster, MD: Christian Classics, 1986.

Riesenfeld, Harald, and Blenda Riesenfeld. *Repertorium Lexicographicum Graecum: A Catalogue of Indexes and Dictionaries to Greek Authors.* Stockholm, Sweden: Almquist & Wiksells, 1954.

Stevenson, J., and W. H. C. Frend, eds. *A New Eusebius: Documents Illustrating the History of the Church to AD 337*. Grand Rapids: Baker, 2013.

HOW TO AVOID COMMON ERRORS

1. The ancient references cited should be sufficiently complete to be understood in the context of your essay.
2. The ancient references should be integrated into the essay, not presented in list form only. However, the appendix can include lists of ancient references if you think that is helpful for the reader.
3. The ancient references need to be compared to the New Testament reference to show how they illustrate or amplify the significance of or contrast with the New Testament reference.
4. The ancient references must be cited by title, book, and chapter number, not by page number. Readers use different editions of primary sources, and the page numbers will be different from edition to edition.
5. The bibliography should include the editions used of the primary sources. This also allows the professor to know you have looked at the primary sources and helps you find the appropriate edition if you need to consult it in the future.
6. The context of the ancient source must be read in order to understand the meaning of the quotation.
7. Think about how the different ancient references relate to the text so as to present a consistent message in your paper.
8. Chronology is very important; however, remember that source derivation is very difficult to prove. Do not say a later reference is the source for an earlier New Testament reference.
9. Primary ancient references cited by secondary references should be double-checked whenever possible (or indicate the name of the primary reference "as cited by X"). Misquoting does occur.
10. If the ancient primary reference is long, summarize or cite a portion or footnote it. The main content of your paper should be your own thoughts and explanations and deductions. A lot of quotations are difficult for your readers to digest. Quote especially well-written or important references.
11. Use abbreviations for titles of books as directed in *The SBL Handbook of Style* or another approved reference book. Do not use the ones in *TLG* or *Perseus* or a concordance. Italicize or underline book titles if the author is known. Use standard English titles for books unless otherwise directed.

The following cover sheet may be used for self evaluation of the cultural background study.

COVER SHEET FOR CULTURAL BACKGROUND STUDY

Exegesis_____   To:_____
Assignment: Cultural Background Study   (student's name)
Date:_____   Box/email: _____

The following items are rated according to the following symbols:
I=Inadequate   A=Adequate   G=Good   S=Superior

RESEARCH METHODOLOGY:
Comprehensive/Exhaustive ....I A G S
Accurate...I A G S
Thoughtful...I A G S
Insightful ....I A G S
Conclusions proved ....I A G S
Original (primary references).......................................I A G S
Clarity in defining issues...I A G S
Categorized different views (compare and contrast)...I A G S
Awareness of how dates might affect conclusions......I A G S

COMPLETENESS:
Other references compared to own..............................I A G S
References (quantity)..I A G S
Reference Awareness (variety, pivotal).......................I A G S

WRITTEN PRESENTATION:
Well-organized paper...I A G S
Literary Style—clear and succinct...............................I A G S
Spelling and grammar—correct ....I A G S
Print is readable..I A G S

The following items need attention if checked:
_____ The pages should be numbered consecutively throughout.
_____ Cite primary sources by chapter and paragraph number
(not by page number).
_____ Cite Greek words out of context in their lexical entry form.
_____ Accent Greek words in Greek font.
_____ Use a consistent and/or correct form in footnotes, bibliography, and primary citations.

Comments:

APPENDICES

Philemon: Examples of the Place of Slaves in the Rabbinic and Greco-Roman Worlds *(for use in exegesis paper of Philemon 4–6)*

1. "Women and slaves and minors are exempt from reciting the Shema and from wearing phylacteries; but they are not exempt from saying the Teffilah, from the law of the Mezuzah or from saying the Benediction after meals" (Ber. 3:3). Slaves and women were often in the same category in rabbinic teaching.
2. Slaves are "goods." Nevertheless, a slave who inherits all "goods" can become free (Pe'ah 3:8). Slaves could be set free.
3. "Women, slaves and minors are exempt from [the law of] the Sukkah" (Suk. 2:8).
4. "These are they that are ineligible [to declare new moon]: a dice-player, a usurer, pigeon-flyers, traffickers in Seventh Year produce, and slaves. This is the general rule: any evidence that a woman is not eligible to bring, these are not eligible to bring" (Ros Has. 1:8). Slaves and women are not included in Sanhedrin 3:3 witnesses.
5. "Women and slaves may vow the Nazirite-vow. Greater stringency applies to women than to slaves, since one may compel his slave [to break the vow], but he cannot compel his wife. Greater stringency applies to slaves than to women, since a man may revoke his wife's vow, but he cannot revoke those of his slave. If he revoked his wife's [Nazarite-] vow he has revoked it for all time; but if he revoked that of his slave and the slave was set free, he must complete his Nazarite-vow" (Naz. 9:1).
6. "If a man is minded not to provide for his slave, this is his right; but if he is minded not to provide for his wife, this is not his right. . . . [The slave] is his chattel" (Git. 1:6). Onesimus is Philemon's property according to Jewish and Greco-Roman laws.
7. "A proselyte is regarded as of like standing to freed slaves even to ten generations, until such time as his mother is of Israelitish stock" (Qidd. 4:7 [vs. Hor. 3:8]). Even freed slaves had limited rights.
8. "If he wounded a Hebrew bondman . . . [or] Canaanitish bondman belonging to others he is liable on all the counts. R Judah says: [Damages for] indignity are not paid for bondmen" (B. Qam. 8:3).
9. "He that wounds [a bondman or a woman] is culpable, but if they wound others they are not culpable; yet they may need to make restitution afterward" (B. Qam. 8:4).
10. "What is found by . . . minors, what is found by his Canaanitish bondman or bondwoman, and what is found by his wife, belong to him" (B. Mes. 1:5).

11. Pharisees say: "If my bondman or my bondwoman have done an injury they are not culpable" because the master must make restitution (Yad. 4:7).
12. "Slaves who have escaped to you from their owners shall not be given back to them. They shall reside with you" (Deut. 23:15–16 NRSV). The Old Testament law supported Paul not returning Onesimus to Philemon.
13. "Epaphroditus owned a certain cobbler whom he sold because he was *useless*; then by some chance the fellow was bought by a member of Caesar's household and became a cobbler to Caesar. You should have seen how Epaphroditus honoured him! . . . Why, had he not sold him as being *useless*?" (Epictetus, *Discourses as Reported by Arian* 1.19.19–23; Barth and Blanke, *Letter to Philemon*, 339). Being "useless" might signify being "unprofitable" and therefore cause for selling a slave.
14. About Moses's laws: "And if another man's slave, it may be with two generations of slavery behind him, takes refuge with you to obtain protection in fear of his master's threats or through consciousness of some misdeed, or because without having committed any offense, he has found his master generally cruel and merciless, do not disregard his plea. For it is a sacrilegious act to surrender a suppliant and the slave is a suppliant who has fled to your hearth as to a temple, where he has a right to obtain sanctuary, and protected from treachery may preferably come to an honest and open agreement, or if that is not possible, be sold as a last resort. For though in changing masters there is no certainty which way the scale will turn, the uncertain evil is not so grave as the acknowledged" (Philo, *On the Virtues* 24.124). Philo supports the Old Testament law.
15. "A slave is a live article of property," "the slave wholly belongs to the master," "one who is a human being belonging by nature not to himself but to another is by nature a slave, and a person is a human being belonging to another if being a human he is an article of property" (Aristotle, *Politics* 1.2.4–7).
16. *Lex Fabia de Plagiariis* (*Digesta* 48.15) (first century) prohibited the harboring of fugitive slaves and imposed heavy fines on trespassers (Barth and Blanke, *Philemon*, 22). The Roman laws supported Onesimus being returned to Philemon.
17. "I am the slave of archdeacon Felix: hold me so that I do not flee" (engraved on a bronze collar fifth/sixth century) (Horsley, *New Documents Illustrating Early Christianity*, par. 91, 140.)
18. "To Sabinianus. Your freedman, whom you lately mentioned as having displeased you, has been with me; he threw himself at my feet and clung there with as much submission as he could have done at yours. He earnestly requested me with many tears, and even with the

eloquence of silent sorrow, to intercede for him; in short, he convinced me by his whole behavior, that he sincerely repents of his fault. And I am persuaded he is thoroughly reformed, because he seems entirely sensible of his delinquency. I know you are angry with him, and I know too, it is not without reason; but clemency can never exert itself with more applause, than when there is the justest cause for resentment. You once had an affection for this man, and, I hope, will have again: in the meanwhile, let me only prevail with you to pardon him. If he should incur your displeasure hereafter, you will have so much the stronger plea in excuse for your anger, as you show yourself more exorable to him now. Allow something to his youth, to his tears, and to your own natural mildness of temper: do not make him uneasy any longer, and I will add too, do not make yourself so; for a man of your benevolence of heart cannot be angry without feeling great uneasiness. I am afraid, were I to join my entreaties with his, I should seem rather to compel, than request you to forgive him. Yet I will not scruple to do it; and so much the more fully and freely as I have very sharply and severely reproved him, positively threatening never to interpose again in his behalf. But though it was proper to say this to him, in order to make him more fearful of offending, I do not say it to you. I may, perhaps, again have occasion to entreat you upon his account, and again obtain your forgiveness; supposing, I mean, his error should be such as may become me to intercede for, and you to pardon. Farewell" (Pliny the Younger, *Epistles* 9.21). Pliny interceded for a freed slave, comparable to Paul's intercession for Onesimus, a runaway slave.

Summary

In rabbinic teaching, slaves were often in the same category as women and minors: all were exempt from reciting the *Shema,*' wearing phylacteries, the law of the Sukkah, declaring the new moon, and all they found belonged to the master. The slave is the master's property. For Greeks, too, the slave was a "live article of property," who "wholly belongs to the master." Even though the Old Testament did not allow escaped slaves to be returned to their masters, the first century Lex Fabia de Plagiariis prohibited the harboring of fugitive slaves, imposing heavy fines on trespassers.

Why might Onesimus have left Philemon? Maybe Onesimus had ceased to be "profitable" (v. 11). For instance, the philosopher Epictetus described a master by the name of Epaphroditus who had employed a slave Felicio to make shoes and when he considered him "unprofitable" (*achrestos*) sold him. An able-bodied adult could be sold for the yearly income of a free artisan. Buyers also had to pay any private debts the slave may have incurred plus taxes. Possibly instead of selling him for a generous profit, Paul wanted Philemon to receive Onesimus as a beloved "useful/profitable" guest (vv. 16, 17).

198 | In-Depth Study of the Text

Early Church Fathers and Mothers Who Wrote in the First Four Centuries[19]

1st Cent. AD	30–101	**Clement** of Rome* in *Apostolic Fathers*, vol. 1	
	50–115	**Ignatius** of Antioch* in *Apostolic Fathers*, vol. 1	
	60–135	Papias of Hierapolis* in *Apostolic Fathers, vol. 2*	
	69–156	Polycarp of Smyrna* in *Apostolic Fathers*, vol. 1	
2nd Cent.	75–145	(Quadratus*)	
	100–160	Aristo(n) of Pella*	*ANF*
	100–165	**Justin Martyr***	*ANF* 1
	100–180	Hegesippus*	
	110–180	Dionysius of Corinth*	
	115–185	Tatian the Syrian*	*ANF* 2
	115–185	(Melito of Sardis*)	
	140	Aristides of Athens*	*ANF* 9
	140–202	**Irenaeus** of Lyons*	*ANF* 5, 9?
	160–180	(Apollinaris of Hierapolis)*	
	160–193	(Miltiades)*	
	177	Athenagoras of Athens	*ANF* 2
	180	Theophilus of Antioch*	*ANF* 2
3rd Cent.	202/3	Perpetua in *Martyrdom of Perpetua and Felicitas*	*ANF* 3
	150–212	**Clement** of Alexandria*	
	160–221	Quintus Septimus Florens Tertullian*	*ANF* 3, 4
	160–235	Hippolytus of Rome*	*ANF* 5
	170–245	Julius Africanus*	*ANF* 6
	185–253/4	**Origen** (E)* of Alexandria and Caesarea	
	190–264	Dionysius of Alexandria*	
	200–258	Thrascius Caecilius **Cyprian** of Carthage (W)*	*ANF* 5
	213–275	Gregory Thamaturgus (Wonder-Worker)*	*ANF* 6
	240–309	Pamphilus of Caesarea*	
	240–317	Lucius Cecilius Firmianus Lactantius (W)	*ANF* 7
	250	Novatian*	*ANF* 5
	265–340	**Eusebius** of Caesarea	
	268	Firmilian of Caesarea	*ANF* 5
	282	(Theognostus of Alexandria)	
	295–373	**Athanasius** of Alexandria	
4th Cent.	300	(Hesychius)	
	304	Victorinus of Pettau	*ANF* 7
	311	Methodius of Olympus	*ANF* 6
	311	(Peter of Alexandria)*	
	330	Arnobius	*ANF* 6

---

19. *ANF* stands for *Ante-Nicene Fathers*; primary writers are in bold; and asterisks (*) mark persons quoted in Eusebius and parentheses are (less important writers).

340–420	**Jerome**
344–407	**Chrysostom** of Constantinople
351	Falconia Proba of Rome *Cento*
363	Egeria (Etheria) *Pilgrimage*

Bible Reading Plan That Highlights Chronological Order

Old Testament Reading Plan in 13 Weeks		New Testament Reading Plan in 10 Weeks	
Week 1:	*Patriarchal Age* Genesis Job	Week 1:	*New Covenant Related to Old Covenant* Matthew (50–57?)
Week 2:	*From Egypt to Canaan* Exodus Leviticus	Week 2:	*Birth of John the Baptist to Jesus's Ascension* Luke (57–59?)
Week 3:	Numbers Deuteronomy	Week 3:	*Paul at Rome (Main New Testament Events)* Acts (60–61)
Week 4:	Joshua	Week 4:	*Earliest Letters after Stoning of Stephen (c. 34)* James (34–48) Galatians 1 Thessalonians (51–52) 2 Thessalonians
	Time of the Judges Judges Ruth	Week 5:	1 Corinthians (56) 2 Corinthians (56–57) Romans (57)
Week 5:	*Samuel, Saul, David, and Beginning of the Kings* 1 Samuel 2 Samuel	Week 6:	*Prison Letters (59–61)* Philippians Colossians Philemon Ephesians
Week 6:	*Writings of David and His Time* Psalms (optional: read 2–3 psalms while reading 1–2 chs. in 1 and 2 Samuel)	Week 7:	*Pastoral Letters (61–64)* 1 Timothy (61–64) Titus 2 Timothy (64–68)
Week 7:	*Solomon-- Ahaziah and Jehoshaphat* 1 Kings		Mark (53–57?)
	Solomon's Writings Song of Songs Proverbs Ecclesiastes	Week 8:	*Events after Death of James (62) and Nero's Persecution (64–68)* 1 Peter (64–67) 2 Peter Jude
Week 8:	*Ahaziah—Captivity of Israel and Judah* 2 Kings	Week 9:	Hebrews

200 | In-Depth Study of the Text

Old Testament Reading Plan in 13 Weeks		New Testament Reading Plan in 10 Weeks	
Week 9:	*Writings of Prophets during the Time of 2 Kings and before Captivity (in Israel or Judah)* Joel Jonah Amos Hosea Isaiah Micah Zephaniah Nahum Obadiah	Week 10:	*Writings of John during Domitian's Reign (90–100)* John (75–95?) 1 John 2 John 3 John Revelation (95–96?)
Week 10:	Jeremiah Habakkuk Lamentations	27 books in New Testament; read 5–10 pages per night	
Week 11:	*Exile Prophets* Daniel Ezekiel		
Week 12:	1 Chronicles: *Adam–David*	AIM	
	Solomon–end of Exile 2 Chronicles	1. To have a historical sweep of Bible events. 2. To read the Bible as an exciting historical account.	
Week 13:	*After First Jews Allowed to Return to Jerusalem* Ezra Haggai Zechariah Esther Malachi Nehemiah	© 1977 Aída Besançon Spencer	
39 books in Old Testament; read 10–20 pages per night to cover indicated books each week			

CHAPTER 8

SAMPLE EXEGESIS PAPER: PHILEMON 4–6

PRESENT FINDINGS IN AN ESSAY[1]

I. Present findings on what the author intended the original readers to understand.
   A. Introduce topic, thesis, and scope of paper.
   B. Summarize how the text fits in the wider context of the letter.
      1. Summarize the historical context of the letter.
      2. Explain how the text fits in with the purpose, overall outline, and immediate context.
   C. Present the true text and why it is true text. (This can also be inserted in an appendix.)
   D. Present your own translation of the text.
   E. Explain the meaning of the text.
      1. Explain the grammar of the text.
         a. Analyze the structure of the sentence and paragraph.
         b. Analyze the grammar of important words, phrases, and clauses.
      2. Explain the meaning of important words and phrases.
      3. Explain the stylistic features of the text.
         a. Recognize any effect from the kind of writing (such as letter or narrative format).
         b. Recognize and explain the effect of any figures of speech.
   F. Explain any significance from further contextual resources (background and foreground).

---

1. This is not the only format for an exegesis paper, but it moves from the general to the specific. Another format might be to begin with the introduction (A) and then move immediately to present the text (D and C), then the meaning of the text, (E), the literary and historical contexts (B, F), and finally the application (II). II A also serves as the summary.

201

1. Study and explain important biblical background and, if time and space allows, foreground.
2. Present any helpful extrabiblical references (Jewish, Greek, Roman) and their relevance to the text.

II. Make the application to life.
   A. Derive principles and summarize the type of people or situation to which the text is addressed.
   B. Make the direct application.

INTRODUCTION

The overall goal in exegesis is to explain the meaning of the text. Each interpreter has some flexibility in terms of presenting the different components, so long as all the parts are included in an organized fashion. This sample exegesis paper uses a simple format (eleven pages, double-spaced, size 12 font, plus an appendix).

Pray for the Lord's help. Do your translation of the passage and all the traditional components of an exegesis paper: text criticism and the grammatical, semantic, stylistic, and Jewish and Greco-Roman cultural aspects of the text.

Determine the primary meaning of your text and summarize it in one sentence. This statement will become your thesis. Write a tentative introduction to your paper that includes your thesis and how you will develop the paper. Write a summary of the conclusions of your historical context, emphasizing any aspects that enlighten your text. Include your purpose sentence for the whole letter. Show how your text fits within the overall purpose and the main headings of your outline. Show how the sentence flow explains the flow of thought in your text and how your text fits in its immediate context. At the end, see what themes in your text may also be in the overall letter and can be shared here or under "Larger Historical and Critical Context."

Present your text critical study in essay form, showing the variants and which one you think is most likely the original text written by the author. Tell the readers why the external evidence (listing sample MSS) is superior for that variant, why the external evidence (citing sample MSS) is inferior for the other variants, and make a guess from likely changes made by scribes for the inferior variants.

Present your own translation of the text. Present your findings from the studies on grammar, semantics, style, and historical-cultural background either verse by verse or topic by topic. Select parsing that enlightens your text. Present your full word study. Identify style features and explain possible effects from the stylistic elements. Show how some information from the Old Testament and/or the Jewish and/or Greco-Roman background enlightens your text. Make sure you give examples for each point in the text and footnote less important ones.

Summarize all that you have shown about your text in a paragraph. Include in the summary, in one sentence, the main theological point of your text and the type of audience to which this message is especially relevant. Pick one application option and elaborate in one to two pages (personal, preaching, teaching, artistic, or corporate). Type your references cited, including primary sources. In the appendix include your original sentence flow or diagram. If necessary, have someone check your grammar when done.

EXEGESIS OF PHILEMON 4-6

According to many commentators on Philemon, verses 4–7 "are the most difficult part of the letter," and verse 6 has "baffled interpreters more than any other part of this letter."[2] Indeed, when I first read Philemon, I too was baffled by verses 4–6. How could Paul make a request (v. 6) when thanking God (v. 4)? What does the *"koinōnia* of your faith" mean (v. 6)? We will answer these questions by looking at the historical and literary contexts; verifying the text; studying the sentence's grammar, semantics (especially *mneia, energēs, koinōnia*), and literary aspects; and concluding with an application. We learn that a prayer of thanksgiving can indeed include a request in bold confidence, as *Victor Bartling says: "Gratitude then leads to confident intercession (v. 6) in the assurance that God will further secure and extend His victories."*[3] We also learn that faith needs to flow outward in "sharing" with the Lord and with other believers.

---

2. Victor A. Bartling in H. Armin Moellering and Victor A. Bartling, *Concordia Commentary: 1 Timothy, 2 Timothy, Titus, Philemon* (St. Louis: Concordia, 1970), 252, 255; John Calvin, *Calvin's Commentaries: Ephesians–Jude* (Wilmington, DE: Assoc. Publishers, n.d.), 2293; Andrew D. Clarke, "'Refresh the Hearts of the Saints': A Unique Pauline Context?," *Tyndale Bulletin* 47, no. 2 (1996): 295; William Barclay, *The Letters to Timothy, Titus, and Philemon*, Daily Study Bible Series (Philadelphia: Westminster, 1975), 278; Markus Barth and Helmut Blanke, *The Letter to Philemon*, Eerdmans Critical Commentary (Grand Rapids: Eerdmans, 2000), 280–81; Herbert M. Carson, *The Epistles of Paul to the Colossians and Philemon*, Tyndale New Testament Commentaries (Grand Rapids: Eerdmans, 1960), 105; William Hendrickson, *New Testament Commentary: Exposition of Colossians and Philemon* (Grand Rapids: Baker, 1964), 213–14; Alexander Maclaren, *The Epistles of St. Paul to the Colossians and Philemon* (New York: Hodder & Stoughton, n.d.), 433; Richard R. Melick Jr., *Philippians, Colossians, Philemon*, New American Commentary 32 (Nashville: Broadman, 1991), 353; Arthur G. Patzia, *Ephesians, Colossians, Philemon*, New International Biblical Commentary (Peabody, MA: Hendrickson, 1990), 109; Michael R. Weed, *The Letters of Paul to the Ephesians, the Colossians, and Philemon*, Living Word Commentary (Austin, TX: Sweet, 1971), 16.

3. Bartling, *Philemon*, 252.

204 | In-Depth Study of the Text

Double-space, one-inch margin on all sides

Material in italics was added in the final draft after secondary references study. Students may want to show their changes to the professor.

If a chapter is cited, do not use "verses" (e.g., 1:4–7).

Use a readable font (12 point or larger).

Papers need an introduction.

Overview plan of essay follows "We will answer. . .
Place all footnotes at bottom of page or gather as endnotes.
Thesis begins "We learn that. . .

This paper begins with the larger context, then moves to the text, then returns back to the context of the letter and ancient references.

Headings can help clarify the content of the paper.

Historical Context

The letter of Philemon was sent from Paul and Timothy (v. 1). Paul wrote the letter.[4] Timothy's name is included possibly to serve as a cowitness of Paul's affection for the readers and as a supporter of Paul's appeal. Paul, an "elder," was a prisoner at the time because of his testimony for Christ Jesus (vv. 1, 9).

The letter is addressed to Philemon, Apphia, Archippus, and the church in their home (vv. 1–2). Philemon is called a "dear [friend] and coworker" (or "beloved coworker," v. 1) and "brother" (vv. 7, 20). Apphia is called "sister" (v. 2), and Archippus "our fellow soldier." *Many commentators think Philemon and Apphia were husband and wife and Archippus was their son.*[5] "Our" indicates Philemon was a friend and coworker of both Paul and Timothy. Verses 4–21 give information only on Philemon, the first person addressed in the heading.[6]

Since Archippus was noted as being in Colossae and Onesimus was on the way there (Col. 4:9, 17), we know the readers were in Colossae. Timothy, Epaphras, Mark, Aristarchus, Demas, and Luke were with Paul (Philem. 1, 23–24). They were also with him when he wrote the letter to the Colossians

---

4. Verses 4–24 use only the first person ("I, my"), including the sentence "I, Paul, am writing this with my own hand" (v. 19 NRSV).

5. E.g., J. B. Lightfoot, *Saint Paul's Epistles to the Colossians and to Philemon* (Grand Rapids: Zondervan, 1959), 303.

6. "You" is plural in verses 3, 22, 25, but "you" is singular in verses 2, 4–21, 23.

(Col. 4:10, 12, 14). Aristarchus and Luke had accompanied Paul to Rome (Acts 27:2). Thus, Philemon was written about the same time as Colossians. Both letters were written during Paul's two-year imprisonment in Rome, most likely near the end, since he expected to be released soon (Philem. 22; Acts 28:16, 30).

> Number every page, even if by hand.
>
> Shorten the historical context to about one page.
>
> Double-check all references at the end.
>
> Use standard New Testament abbreviations.
>
> Use a style manual for correct and consistent format.
>
> In footnotes the first name precedes the last name; a comma is used instead of a period between author and title of book; a semicolon is placed between entries.
>
> Shorten the name and the title after the first reference.

Literary Context

In this handwritten letter, Paul appealed to his beloved Christian friend Philemon to welcome Onesimus as a beloved brother on the basis of the love and faith Philemon had extended to others. Verses 1–3 are opening greetings. Even though much of the letter is addressed only to Philemon ("you" is singular in vv. 2, 4–21, 23), the household (Apphia and Archippus) and the church gathering in their home (v. 2) also received this letter ("you" is plural in vv. 3, 22, 25).[7] They would all see Paul shortly, and they would all learn how Philemon decided to act. The individual exhortation was set in a Christian communal setting. Not only did the household and the church form the listening environment, but also Timothy, the Christian brother, and all those at Rome who greeted the church (Epaphras, Mark, Aristarchus, Demas, and Luke). And the most expectant listener of all was Onesimus, the slave whose relationship with his master had been ruptured (v. 15).[8]

---

7. Craig S. de Vos points out that first-century Mediterranean people lived in strongly collectivist cultures. "Once a Slave, Always a Slave? Slavery, Manumission and Relational Patterns in Paul's Letter to Philemon," *Journal for the Study of the New Testament* 82 (2001): 92–93.

8. Allen Dwight Callahan, in contrast, suggests "as a slave, but more than a slave" is a simile. "Paul's Epistle to Philemon: Toward an Alternative Argumentum," *Harvard Theological Review* 86, no. 4 (1993): 369.

206 | In-Depth Study of the Text

> Purpose sentence with brief information from scope begins "In this hand-written letter. . .
>
> Use of the historical context to enlighten the meaning of text begins "They would all see. . .

This brief letter covers four themes. In verses 4–7, Paul remembered in his prayers two broad categories: what he heard about Philemon's love and faith and what he wanted to happen. Paul then encouraged Philemon on the basis of love to receive Onesimus as a beloved brother (vv. 8–16). Verse 17 begins "therefore," with an imperative, "welcome." The conjunction (*oun*) and imperative (*proslambanomai*) suggest a change of approach. Now Paul used a series of shorter imperatival sentences exhorting Philemon on the basis of partnership in the faith to receive Onesimus as he would receive Paul himself (vv. 17–20). Paul was confident Philemon would do what he asked and gave Philemon an opportunity to receive him (Paul) soon (vv. 21–22). The prayers of the whole church were needed for Paul to be released from prison (v. 22). In the closing greetings, Paul's coworkers greeted the church and Paul prayed the church would receive the Lord's grace (vv. 23–25).

The text to be studied is one long sentence in Greek (vv. 4–6). In it is a microcosm of the message of the whole letter. From it we learn that Philemon was a Christian growing in love and faith who still had more to do in order to energize his faith by acting on the ramifications of his faith for social relationships (vv. 6, 17). Many English translations punctuate verse 6 as a new sentence (e.g., NRSV, NIV); however, as an adverbial clause it cannot syntactically be separated from verses 4–5.

> Use the outline and notes from chapter 1, "Discern the Wider Context," in the "Literary Context."
>
> Transliterate all Greek (using italics) or use all Greek font, not both.
>
> How text fits in letter begins "In it is a microcosm. . .
>
> The thesis is restated ("From it we learn. . .
>
> Have the essay flow between sections.

Textual Verification

One significant textual variation unit is in verse 6. Did Paul write "among you," "among us," or neither? "Among you" (*en hymin*) has somewhat better early attestation. It is the reading in the earliest Greek manuscript

(א, fourth century) and the only papyrus (p[61] [AD 700]). Codex Sinaiticus (א) is an important Alexandrian text type. The second-person pronoun is also attested in the earliest Syriac and Coptic versions (syr[p] [fifth century]; cop[sa] [sixth–seventh century, third–fourth-century original]). It also has an early variety of text types: Alexandrian (א, cop[sa]); Caesarean (arm [887, 400s original]; 075 [ninth century]); early Byzantine (syr[p], syr[h], slav [ninth century]); Chrysostom [d. 407]; and Western (F, G, ninth century). Omitting the phrase altogether has only late support. The earliest Greek manuscript evidence is fourteenth century.

> Present variations.
>
> Choose the best variant.
>
> AD is written in front of the date; BC follows behind the date.
>
> Present proof.
>
> Early versions are important too.
>
> Note the date of the earliest version MSS.

"Among us" (*en hēmin*) has good support. It has the earliest Western texts (it[d], D [fifth–sixth centuries]). It also has support from a variety of text types (Alexandrian, Western, Byzantine [C (fifth century), Chrysostom], and Caesarean (0150 [ninth century], geo [897]). It has good (but not the earliest) Alexandrian support (A [fifth century], 048 [fifth century], ψ [eighth–ninth century]).

"Among you" fits the context well since Paul was addressing the faith of Philemon (*sou*, vv. 6, 7), not the faith of the writers. However, some later scribes may have thought that "among us" makes the prayer more inclusive of all Christians.[9] Or the error may have occurred accidentally because of the closeness in sound.

Philemon 4–6 may be translated literally: "I am giving my God thanks always while making remembrance of you at the time of my prayers, because of hearing of your faithful love, which you have toward the Lord Jesus and toward all the saints, with the result that the sharing of your faith might become active in knowledge of every good, the (good) among you toward Christ."

---

9. "You" is also chosen as the correct reading for verse 6 by KJV, NASB, and NTME. In verse 5, the preposition *eis* has almost as strong attestation as *pros*, where "Lord Jesus" is the object. *Pros* is supported by fourth-century Alexandrian א. *Eis* is supported by fifth-century Alexandrian A and 048. The earlier D has *eis*; the later D has *pros*.

208 | In-Depth Study of the Text

> Decide based on external evidence ("Among you [*en humin*]. . .
>
> Explain how the error(s) might have occurred ("However, some later. . .
>
> Present your finished translation. For interpretation, a more literal rendering is helpful.

Grammatic, Semantic, and Stylistic Analysis

Philemon 4–6 has one main clause ("I am giving my God thanks always while making remembrance of you at the time of my prayers because of hearing of your love and faith") with two subordinate clauses (adjectival and adverbial). What kind of faith did Philemon have? He had a faith "toward the Lord Jesus and toward all the saints." "I am giving thanks," the main verb, is modified by two participial phrases ("making . . . hearing") and an adverbial result clause ("so that the sharing of your faith might become active in knowledge of every good, the one among you toward Christ"). (See appendix to chapter 4 for sentence flow.) The final adverbial clause is expressed in expectation but with some element of doubt[10] since *ginomai* is in the aorist subjunctive. Consequently, the final clause must be tied to the main clause: "I thank . . . so that your faith might become."

Is it possible, then, that Paul was making "mention" rather than "remembering"? *Mneia*, the noun, is related to the verb *mimnēskomai*, "I remember." For example, Peter "remembered" what Jesus had said (Matt. 26:75). The Thessalonians always had a good "remembrance" of Paul and his coworkers (1 Thess. 3:6). Paul used *mneia* plus *poieō* ("I make") several times when describing his prayers.

> These three areas can be presented separately or together, but all must be included.
>
> Use the flow to clarify meaning in the grammatical section
>
> Do not just repeat grammatical information; draw out the significance for the meaning of your text.
>
> Use any parsing that helps interpretation.
>
> Above occurs a word (semantic) study ("*Mneia*. . .")

---

10. A. T. Robertson, *A Grammar of the Greek New Testament in the Light of Historical Research* (Nashville: Broadman, 1934), 926.

Of Paul's six references to prayer that use *mneia*, three of them end with a request. "I thank" (*eucharisteō*) is used four times. In Ephesians Paul thanked God for the remembered listeners while making a request of God (just as in Philemon):

Ephesians 1:16–17: "I am thanking in behalf of you, making remembrance at the time of my prayers that God . . . may give you . . . a spirit of wisdom."

Romans 1:9–10: "I am making remembrance of you always at the time of my prayers, . . . asking to see you."

1 Thessalonians 1:2–3: "We are thanking God always concerning . . . you, making remembrance at the time of our prayers, . . . remembering your walk of faith."

Philippians 1:3–5: "I am thanking my God because of remembrance of you always in every prayer, . . . because of your fellowship in the gospel."

2 Timothy 1:3: "I have remembrance concerning you in my prayers."

Therefore, because of the close derivative connection between *mneia* and *mimnēskomai* and because Paul elsewhere tied thanks and requests together, "making *remembrance*," even if harder to interpret, is more likely than "making *mention*." Paul thanked God for his listeners as he *remembered* them in his prayers. Philemon 4–6 is not unique in having a desire for change encased in appreciation, as we saw.

Normally use only essay form, except when clarity calls for another.

Indent quotations over 4–5 lines and single-space in a student paper (double-space for published books and journals). Use the same size font as you do in the rest of the paper.

I did my own translation of these New Testament quotations. If you choose to use a translation, indicate in a footnote "these quotations are all from the __ version unless otherwise indicated."

Italicize transliterated Greek words. Transliterated words are easy to print and can be read by all readers.

Also italicize any word you are studying.

Cite the Greek lexical form, not the text form, normally.

Poieō is probably a temporal adverbial participle. At the time Paul thanked God, he was praying. *Akouō* is a causal adverbial participle. The reason for Paul's thankfulness was Philemon's love and faith toward Jesus and toward the saints. Probably "love and faith" is a hendiadys[11] and is best rendered "faithful love" (v. 5). *Pros* entails a sense of intimacy: "face-to-face converse with the Lord."[12] *Pros* plus "lord" is almost an oxymoron. How can one have intimacy with a master? That is the paradox facing the Christian who is redeemed. That is the problem Onesimus had to face. *Eis* has a sense of aim or purpose.[13] Philemon's love and faith were intimate and personal with Jesus, purposeful toward believers. Moreover, Philemon's love and faith extended not to some believers but to "all" believers (v. 5).

How may we reconcile the request to follow? Paul's request is embedded in thanksgiving because of his confidence in the faith of Philemon. Therefore, the final adverbial clause functions as a result clause: "I am thanking God . . . with the result that," not "with the purpose that." A "result" clause is consequent upon or issues from the action of the main verb.[14] Paul's thanksgiving was not contingent on Philemon's change (that would be more of a purpose clause). Paul's thanksgiving was because he prayed in confidence.

> Above includes the grammatical study ("*Poieō* is probably. . .)
>
> Define any technical terms, for example "hendiadys. . .
>
> Use a style that helps interpretation.
>
> Grammar and sentence flow explain the flow of thought ("How may we. . .)

What was the result Paul wanted? The subject is "your faith's sharing" (v. 6). "Faith" (genitive case) is probably a subjective genitive. "Faith," the noun in the genitive case, produces the action (or functions as subject). "Faith" is the attribute Paul praised in the earlier adjectival clause, yet more was needed. In the final clause, Paul moved the complement/object (*energēs*) before the verb for emphasis. *Energēs* may signify "to be at work, produce, or be powerful." *Energēs* may have a sense of power, as "the Word of God is living and powerful and sharper than any two-edged sword and piercing" (Heb.

---

11. A hendiadys is an expression of an idea by two nouns connected by "and" instead of a noun and its qualifier. See Richard A. Lanham, *A Handlist of Rhetorical Terms*, 2nd ed. (Berkeley: University of California Press, 1991), 82.

12. Robertson, *Grammar of the Greek New Testament*, 624–25.

13. Robertson, *Grammar of the Greek New Testament*, 594.

14. H. E. Dana and Julius R. Mantey, *A Manual Grammar of the Greek New Testament* (Toronto: Macmillan, 1955), 285.

4:12).[15] The Word of God is powerful because it functions like a powerful and effective two-edged sword. Ephesus had a "great and *powerful*" opened door and many adversaries (1 Cor. 16:9). Since Paul had many opportunities to speak, he had a powerfully opened door. The verb *energeō*, a popular word for Paul, more frequently means "to be at work" than "to be powerful." For example, faith should "work through" love (Gal. 5:6).[16] Yet Paul struggled with all Christ's "energy," "the one working powerfully" in Paul "in power" (Col. 1:29). *Energeō* may simply refer to "produce," as the "comfort, the one producing in patience" (2 Cor. 1:6).[17] Thus, if we use the more common meaning for *energēs/energeō*, Paul wanted the sharing of Philemon's faith to become more "at work" or "more active." More active in what? More active in his knowledge of good. Paul himself was an example of activated faith when he shared his faith with Onesimus, treating him as a full Christian family member (v. 10).

Grammatical analysis begins "what was the result. . .

Cite English words in quotation marks.

No quotation marks are needed to cite words in Greek font or transliterated Greek words.

Show effect of style begins "Paul moved. . .

Give proof or examples for points ("Word of God is. . .)

Do a study of the word family, and focus on meaning, not form, for semantics ("The verb *energeō*. . .)

Extended examples can be footnoted for smother reading (see note 16).

What should become more "active"? It is the "*koinōnia* of his faith." *Koinōnia/koinōnos/koinōneō* has a strong economic literal base, referring to sharing financially. It can refer to business partners, as Simon, James, and John were in the fishing business (Luke 5:10). As a verb, it can refer to giving financially to another (e.g., Rom. 12:13; Gal. 6:6; Phil. 4:15) or to the gift itself (noun: Rom. 15:26; 2 Cor. 8:4; 9:13; Heb. 13:16). Thus, hospitality is at its core. In that sense, it signifies welcoming (Gal. 2:9; 2 John 11). It includes the idea of having in "common" (*koinos*). It does not refer to opposites that cannot mix, such as light and dark (2 Cor. 6:14). Taking on the same physical nature

---

15. Unless otherwise indicated, all New Testament quotations are by the author.
16. "To be at work" can be positive (Matt. 14:2; 1 Cor. 12:6, 11; Gal. 2:8; 3:5; 5:6; Eph. 3:20; Phil. 2:13; 1 Thess. 2:13) or negative (Rom. 7:5; 2 Cor. 4:12; Eph. 2:2; 2 Thess. 2:7).
17. See also Eph. 1:11; James 5:16.

212 | In-Depth Study of the Text

is a type of *koinōnia* (Heb. 2:14). It also has the literal sense of being a part of a group, doing the same action, as "participating" in killing together (Matt. 23:30) or in worshiping together (1 Cor. 10:18, 20).

> Relate the word study to your text.
>
> Use standard Greek transliteration and Bible abbreviations.
>
> Come to a conclusion ("If we use. . .)
>
> Make your own groupings of meanings after using a New Testament concordance (begins "what should. . .)
>
> Cite examples for each meaning ("It can refer to. . .)

In a metaphorical sense, *koinōnia* as "participation" can include participating in the gospel (Phil. 1:5); in sufferings, as Christ did (2 Cor. 1:7; Phil. 3:10; Heb. 10:33; 1 Peter 4:13); or in glory (Rom. 15:27; 1 Peter 5:1; 2 Peter 1:4). Participation or sharing also has an interpersonal sense, between humans with similar goals (Acts 2:42; 1 John 1:3); humans and Jesus/God (1 Cor. 1:19; 1 John 1:6); and humans and evil (1 Cor. 10:18, 20; 1 Tim. 5:22). Genuine *koinōnia* comes from the Holy Spirit (2 Cor. 13:13; Phil. 2:1).

So what does *koinōnia* mean in Philemon 6? In Philemon *koinōnia* is modified by "faith." Faith metaphorically has *koinōnia* (*subjective genitive*). It is oriented "toward Jesus and toward saints" (v. 5). As oriented toward Jesus, believers have an intimate sharing with the Lord. As oriented toward saints, believers have a material and relational sharing. Even though Philemon's love and faith were praiseworthy, the "sharing" of his faith could become more active.[18] The letter itself suggests how Philemon's faith could become more active. Paul considered Titus to be a true "partner" (2 Cor. 8:23, *koinōnos*), whereas Philemon was a conditional one. Philemon's partnership was conditioned on whether he welcomed Onesimus in the same way as he would Paul (Philem. 17).

> Stylistic analysis (begins "In a metaphorical sense. . .)
>
> Compare the figurative to the literal base.

---

18. Thus, since the eventual object of *koinōnia* is "you" and "Christ," *koinōnia* has both the idea of "fellowship" and economic generosity. Most commentators agree the *koinonia* flows from Philemon's faith (subjective genitive) rather than the *koinōnia* in his faith (objective genitive). For the former, see Bartling, *Philemon*, 255; Barclay, *Philemon*, 278; Lewis B. Radford, *The Epistle to the Colossians and the Epistle to Philemon*, Westminster Commentaries (London: Methuen, 1930), 352; Hendrickson, *Philemon*, 213–14. For the latter, see A. T. Robertson, *Word Pictures in the New Testament*, 6 vols. (Nashville: Broadman, 1931), 4:465.

> Use the immediate context (begins "So what does. . .")
>
> Come to a conclusion regarding the significance for the text (begins "As oriented toward. . .)

Thus, Philemon 6 should be interpreted in light of verse 17. Philemon's goodness and faith were laudable enough to reach Paul in Rome. However, when it came to *koinōnia*, Philemon still had a ways to grow. Paul prayed with thanksgiving, so Philemon's growth was likely. But Philemon's "faith sharing/participation" was not as active as it could be when it came to knowing and doing what was good. Goodness has a two-pronged character, as expressed by "among us, toward Christ" (v. 6), as faith is "toward the Lord Jesus and toward all the saints" (v. 5). How might Paul's prayer be answered? Paul's prayer would be answered if Philemon became Paul's "partner" by welcoming Onesimus in the same way as he would welcome Paul (v. 17). The letter includes one example of welcoming: if Philemon were to prepare a guest room for Paul (v. 22). Since *koinōnia* includes the idea and practice of hospitality, Philemon should prepare a guest room for Onesimus too.[19] "Prepare a guest room for me" is not a passing request, but the very heart of the letter.

> The historical context of the letter is important.

To prepare a guest room for Paul, an educated elder, was one thing. To be reconciled and treat as an equal a former runaway slave (v. 16) was quite another. In rabbinic teaching, slaves were often in the same category as women and minors: all were exempt from reciting the Shema or wearing phylacteries (m. Ber. 3:3), all were exempt from the law of the Sukkah (m. Sukk. 2:8), all were ineligible to declare the new moon (m. Ros Has. 1:8), and all they found belonged to the master (B. Mesi'a 1:5). The slave was the master's property (m. Git. 1:6; Pe'ah 3:8). For Greeks too the slave was a "live article of property" who "wholly belong[ed] to the master" (Aristotle, *Poetics* 1.11.4–7). Even though the Old Testament did not allow escaped slaves to be returned to their masters (Deut. 23:15–16), the first-century *Lex Fabia de Plagiariis* (Digesta 48.15) *prohibited the harboring of fugitive slaves and imposed heavy fines on trespassers.*[20]

Why might Onesimus have left Philemon? Maybe Onesimus had ceased to be "profitable" (v. 11). *Achrēstos* can mean "useless, unprofitable."[21] *For instance, the philosopher Epictetus described a master by the name of Epaphro-*

---

19. De Vos, "Slave," 103, agrees that Paul's language (v. 17) is "clearly drawn from the domain of hospitality, where receiving a guest meant that the one received becomes a friend. . . . Hospitality was only offered between social equals."

20. Barth and Blanke, *Philemon*, 22.

21. Henry G. Liddell and Robert Scott, *A Greek-English Lexicon*, ed. H. S. Jones and R. McKenzie, 9th ed. (Oxford: Clarendon, 1940), 297.

214 | In-Depth Study of the Text

ditus who had employed a slave, Felicio, to make shoes, and when he considered him "unprofitable" (achrēstos), he sold him (Discourses as Reported by Arrian 1.19.19–23). Maybe Philemon was going to sell Onesimus because he no longer needed him. He was going to be "useless" or unprofitable. And Onesimus did not want to be sold to a new slave owner. An able-bodied adult could be sold for the yearly income of a free artisan. Buyers also had to pay any debts the slave may have incurred, plus taxes.[22] Possibly instead of selling him for profit, Paul wanted Philemon to receive Onesimus as a beloved "useful/profitable" guest (Philem. 16, 17). This "good" deed, a sign of Philemon's activated sharing of faith, had to be voluntary (vv. 9, 14) because it signified outwardly an inward change. Onesimus was transformed, and now Philemon needed to be transformed as well.

> Compare the text to extrabiblical references (begins "to prepare a guest room. . .)
>
> "M." refers to Mishnah; "B." to Babylonian Talmud. Mishnah always has a number, colon, number, whereas Talmud has a number and a letter.
>
> Cite key references, not necessarily all of them.
>
> Use standard abbreviations.
>
> Page numbers are not used for ancient references (use book title, chapter, verse, and section numbers).
>
> Primary references suggested by others are checked ("*Discourses. . .*)

Larger Historical and Literary Context

Did Paul achieve this change? Possibly, yes, and an Onesimus did become a pastor and an overseer at Ephesus at the turn of the first century (Eusebius, *Church History* 3.36; Ignatius *To the Ephesians* 1.3). How did Paul achieve this example of the transforming social power of Christ's grace (Philem. 25)? In the first stage, he praised Philemon (vv. 4–5), prayed for him (v. 6), and praised him again (v. 7). Second, he exhorted him, explaining why he needed to welcome Onesimus (vv. 9–16). Third, he exhorted him more strongly, explaining the ramifications of his action (v. 17). He offered the means of restitution (v. 18) and reminded Philemon of his debts to Paul (v. 19). Finally, he closed, expressing his confidence in Philemon (v. 21). Transforming social

---

22. Barth and Blanke, *Philemon*, 6, 339.

change needs prayer, positive reinforcement, education, exhortation, and financial assistance. Christ's grace is not coercive.[23]

> "Larger historical and literary context" is an optional section, giving the result of the letter (if known) and new insights that flow from the study but that did not fit earlier. Fit the text into the structure of the overall letter, if that was not done earlier. But do not begin a new exegesis paper!

Summary

From Philemon 4–6, we have learned that Philemon was a Christian growing in love and faith, but he still had more to do to energize his faith by acting on the ramifications of his faith for social relationships. Paul's desire to move him to live out more of Christ's grace began with praise, remembering his positive qualities and praying in thankful confidence for change. This change was done in the setting of the Christian community. Despite the contrast to their cultures, Paul wanted Philemon to welcome Onesimus as a Christian brother.

> The exegesis paper should include an application (see chapter 9, appendix, "Sample Application Outlines") and a sentence flow (see chapter 4 appendix, "Sentence Flow of Philemon 4–6").
>
> Always summarize your findings.
>
> Reread your paper and jot down points accomplished.
>
> Add no new data in your summary.
>
> Repeat your thesis.
>
> Review your key points.
>
> Have someone check your grammar if necessary—if they do a lot of editing, give them credit in a footnote.
>
> Titles of books and journals are italicized.
>
> Footnote ideas and words of others.

---

23. Ben Witherington III explains some of the rhetorical features of Philemon in *The Letters to Philemon, the Colossians, and the Ephesians: A Socio-Rhetorical Commentary on the Captivity Epistles* (Grand Rapids: Eerdmans, 2007), 58–64.

216 | In-Depth Study of the Text

Bibliography

Aristotle. *Politics*, Translated by H. Rackham. Loeb Classical Library. Cambridge: Harvard University Press, 1932.

Barclay, William. *The Letters to Timothy, Titus, and Philemon*. Daily Study Bible Series. Philadelphia: Westminster, 1975.

Barth, Markus, and Helmut Blanke. *The Letter to Philemon*. Eerdmans Critical Commentary. Grand Rapids: Eerdmans, 2000.

Callahan, Allen Dwight. "Paul's Epistle to Philemon: Toward an Alternative *Argumentum*." *Harvard Theological Review* 86, no. 4 (October 1993): 357–76.

Calvin, John. *Calvin's Commentaries: Ephesians–Jude*. Wilmington, DE: Assoc. Publishers, n.d.

Carson, Herbert M. *The Epistles of Paul to the Colossians and Philemon*. Tyndale New Testament Commentaries. Grand Rapids: Eerdmans, 1960.

Clarke, Andrew D. "'Refresh the Hearts of the Saints': A Unique Pauline Context?" *Tyndale Bulletin* 47, no. 2, (1996): 277–300.

Dana, H. E., and Julius R. Mantey. *A Manual Grammar of the Greek New Testament*. Toronto: Macmillan, 1955.

Danby, Herbert. *The Mishnah*. Oxford: Oxford University Press, 1933.

Elwell, Walter A., and Robert W. Yarbrough, eds. *Readings from the First-Century World: Primary Sources for New Testament Study*. Grand Rapids: Baker, 1998.

Epictetus: The Discourses as Reported by Arrian. Vol. 1, translated and edited by W. A. Oldfather. Loeb Classical Library. Cambridge: Harvard University Press, 1925.

> *Book and journal titles are italicized or underlined. You can capitalize if you have neither.*
>
> *Check Style Manual. Last name goes first in the bibliography so books can be alphabetized. Periods come between entries.*
>
> *References cited format also needs full bibliography.*

Hendrickson, William. *New Testament Commentary: Exposition of Colossians and Philemon*. Grand Rapids: Baker, 1964.

Horsley, G. H. R. *New Documents Illustrating Early Christianity*. Ryde: Macquarie, 1981.

Lake, Kirsopp, trans. *Apostolic Fathers* Vol. 1. Loeb Classical Library. Cambridge, MA: Harvard University Press, 1912.

Lanham, Richard A. *A Handlist of Rhetorical Terms*. 2d ed. Berkeley: University of California Press, 1991.

Liddell, Henry George, and Robert Scott. *A Greek-English Lexicon*. Edited by Henry Stuart Jones and Roderick McKenzie. 9th ed. Oxford: Clarendon, 1940.

Lightfoot, J. B. *Saint Paul's Epistles to the Colossians and to Philemon*. Grand Rapids: Zondervan, 1959.

Maclaren, Alexander. *The Epistles of St. Paul to the Colossians and Philemon*. New York: Hodder & Stoughton, n.d.

Melick, Richard R., Jr. *The New American Commentary 32: Philippians, Colossians, Philemon*. Nashville: Broadman, 1991.

Moellering, H. Armin, and Victor A. Bartling. *Concordia Commentary: 1 Timothy, 2 Timothy, Titus, Philemon*. Saint Louis: Concordia, 1970.

Patzia, Arthur G. *Ephesians, Colossians, Philemon*. New International Biblical Commentary. Peabody, MA: Hendrickson, 1990.

Philo VIII. Translated by F. H. Colson. Loeb Classical Library. Cambridge: Harvard University Press, 1939.

Radford, Lewis B. *The Epistle to the Colossians and the Epistle to Philemon*. Westminster Commentaries. London: Methuen, 1930.

Robertson, A. T. *A Grammar of the Greek New Testament in the Light of Historical Research*. Nashville: Broadman, 1934.

Include grammar books. Include editions of ancient references cited.

_____. *Word Pictures in the New Testament*. Vol. 4. Nashville: Broadman, 1931.

Vos, Craig S. de, "Once a Slave, Always a Slave? Slavery, Manumission and Relational Patterns in Paul's Letter to Philemon." *Journal for the Study of the New Testament* 82 (2001): 89–105.

Weed, Michael R. *The Letters of Paul to the Ephesians, the Colossians, and Philemon*. Living Word Commentary. Austin, TX: Sweet, 1971.

Williamson, G. A., trans. *Eusebius: The History of the Church from Christ to Constantine*. New York: Penguin, 1989.

Witherington, Ben, III. *The Letters to Philemon, the Colossians, and the Ephesians: A Socio-Rhetorical Commentary on the Captivity Epistles*. Grand Rapids: Eerdmans, 2007.

PART 4

APPLICATION AND COMPLETION OF STUDY

CHAPTER 9

MAKE THE APPLICATION TO LIFE

I. *Derive the basic theological principles* of your passage. What is the author's theological intention? What are the universal principles?[1]

II. *Summarize* the people or situation to which the original text is addressed.

III. Prayerfully *decide what would be an analogous people* or situation today.

IV. *Choose one* specific application option (one to two pages).

    A. *Personal application.*

        1. What were and are your feelings about the appropriate application of your text? (Feelings? Memories?) In other words, what are you now like?

        2. Apply the principles of the passage to the will and direction of your life.

            a. What should you be like? What does it tell you about yourself? What should you do? What should you pray? Do you have an example to follow, sin to avoid, or promise to claim?

---

1. For further reading, see Haddon W. Robinson, *Biblical Preaching: The Development and Delivery of Expository Messages,* 3rd ed. (Grand Rapids: Baker Academic, 2014), chs. 4–9; Gordon D. Fee, *New Testament Exegesis: A Handbook for Students and Pastors,* 3rd ed. (Louisville: Westminster John Knox, 2002), 149–54; William W. Klein, Craig L. Blomberg, and Robert L. Hubbard Jr., *Introduction to Biblical Interpretation,* 3rd ed. (Grand Rapids: Zondervan, 2017), ch. 12; Roy B. Zuck, ed., *Rightly Divided: Readings in Biblical Hermeneutics* (Grand Rapids: Kregel, 1996), chs. 18–19, 22; A. Berkeley Mickelsen, *Interpreting the Bible* (Grand Rapids: Eerdmans, 1963), ch. 17; Jack Kuhatschek, *Applying the Bible* (Grand Rapids: Zondervan, 1990), esp. ch. 5; Paul E. Little, *How to Give Away Your Faith* (Downers Grove, IL: InterVarsity Press, 1966), ch. 9; Daniel M. Doriani, *Getting the Message: A Plan for Interpreting and Applying the Bible* (Phillipsburg, NJ: P&R, 1996), chs. 9–11; Richard J. Erickson, *A Beginner's Guide to New Testament Exegesis: Taking the Fear Out of Critical Method* (Downers Grove, IL: InterVarsity Press, 2005), 213–20; Michael J. Gorman, *Elements of Biblical Exegesis: A Basic Guide for Students and Ministers,* 3rd ed. (Grand Rapids: Baker Academic, 2020), ch. 8.

222 | Application and Completion of Study

        b. "Corner yourself." What changes do you want or not want to make? How will you make these changes possible? When will you do it?

B. *Sermon outline.*
1. Title of sermon.
2. Scripture text (plus other possible Bible readings).
3. Type of congregation for which sermon is intended.
4. Purpose of the sermon in one sentence. Basic theological principle.
5. What actions do you want your congregation/listeners to take?
6. Show in an outline how you will develop the purpose. Remember to use an interesting introduction and conclusion. Develop your purpose by explanations, definitions, illustrations, questions, narrations, factual information, restatement, describing the opposite or causes. Include one or two accompanying hymns or songs that develop the purpose.

C. *Lesson plan.*
1. Topic.
2. Type (and age) of students for which lesson is intended.
3. Goals/purposes of the lesson.
4. Total time for lesson.
5. An outline of class procedures and percentage of time allotted to each section. Include inductive questions that lead students to right answers and time for application and prayer. (Indicate what part of the outline can be omitted if time runs out.)
6. Materials needed.
7. Optional: Physical arrangement of room for accomplishment of goals.

D. *Artistic creation*: drama (dialogue, monologue), music, poem, fictional short story.

E. *Situational application*: develop the ramifications of the exegesis for a specific group of people, situation, or issue today.

F. *Theological motifs* (if time and sufficient space allows in an exegesis paper). What appropriate theological categories seem to lead out of the text you studied? Compare your passage with other crucial passages bearing on the same subject. Organize your material. Make a succinct statement of the teachings of your passage in everyday terms that can be applied to ministry or devotional understanding.

This step can be done by both Greek and translation readers.

INTRODUCTION

Renowned grammarian A. T. Robertson wrote, "A grammarian must admit that, however necessary and fundamental grammatical exegesis is, it forms only the basis for the spiritual exposition which should follow."[2] In formal education, learning cognitive information seems easier than learning how to correlate theory and practice. Yet the Bible exhorts us to do what we believe (James 1:22).

Everything we have done so far has been limited to exegesis—that is, discovering the meaning of a passage for the original readers. It is as if we were listening in on a conversation of someone telling other persons a story in order to affect and change their actions. Before we can tell others about this story and what it can mean for them, we should hear the whole story, know the meaning of all the phrases being used, and find out what point the speaker wanted to make. So many times there is a chasm between exegesis (clarifying the meaning of a text) and the application of the meaning today.

Text meaning → //
　　　　　// → application (The application one develops may be Christian, but its basis is not this specific Bible text.)

When the application does not flow from the text, it tends to be simple, bland, individualistic, and usually the same application we get from every other passage. For instance, I have noticed individual preachers tend to have a similar application to every sermon, depending often on their spiritual gift; for example, we should pray more or we should go to the mission field or we should go to church. But it takes courage and boldness to say what you discover is the proper application of your text, even if you never heard it before or it seems impossible to do. The Bible will become its dynamic, relevant, radical, and revolutionary self when we let it speak for itself.

More than one application may flow from a text, but they *all* must come from the text. We consequently ask, "What are the appropriate applications for this one text?"

$$\text{Text meaning} \;\; {\to \atop {\to \atop \to}} \;\; \text{applications}$$

This one text does not have to cover every part of the Christian life. The Bible has other texts that support other applications. However, every verse must have some application at some time today if it is indeed God's Word.

2.　A. T. Robertson, *A Grammar of the Greek New Testament in the Light of Historical Research* (Nashville: Broadman, 1934), 114–15.

But not every Scripture verse may necessarily apply to every situation and to every person at every time. While Paul commanded Timothy, "No longer drink water, but use a little wine on account of the stomach and your frequent sicknesses" (1 Tim. 5:23), Paul would not want everyone to drink wine for all ailments.[3] If someone were to be addicted to wine or other intoxicating substances, (s)he should avoid them all the time. God gave us historical situations in the Bible so we can use those teachings in similar historical situations. Although truths are timeless, it does not follow that they can be applied indiscriminately to all circumstances. We need prayerfully to discover the appropriate contemporary situation in which a Bible passage is applicable.

What is entailed in making an application? We as Bible interpreters need to correlate two poles: the Bible and what it means and the listeners, the situation of the person or people to whom we are seeking to interpret the Bible to fulfill their real needs. For instance, Paul, Silas, and Timothy wrote to the church at Thessalonica and said they prayed night and day with all earnestness to see them face-to-face so as to supply the needs of their faith (1 Thess. 3:10). Or as was popularized by the famous theologian Karl Barth, the preacher must have the Bible in one hand and the newspaper in the other and interpret the newspaper from the Bible.[4] Often parishioners come to church to be enlightened by the minister's interpretation of a momentous current event. Cadbury suggested a formula for the application of the biblical message:

$$\frac{\text{The author's message}}{\text{The author's environment}} = \frac{X}{\text{Our environment}}$$

The problem of the minister is to find X.[5] To do that, the minister needs to know his or her parishioners' current life situations, "our environment." Building relationships and refining interpretations of the Bible go hand in hand if we are to make appropriate applications. "Interpret" comes from the Latin *interpres,* which is an agent between two parties, a mediator. We are the agent between God's Word and our listeners. An interpreter is not a giver of advice but rather an interpreter or messenger of God's revelation. If a Bible text is first applied to oneself and then applied to others, we must apply it with the humility that is appropriate, not self-righteously. We need to learn to live according to Scripture ourselves as we apply it to others.

What is missing from the formula above? The means to learn X is not only knowledge of our environment but also the presence of the Holy Spirit,

---

3. For a further explanation of the passage, see Aída Besançon Spencer, *1 Timothy,* New Covenant Commentary Series (Eugene, OR: Cascade, 2013), 140–41.

4. E.g., Bobby Ross Jr., "Bible in One Hand, Newspaper in the Other," *Christian Chronicle* (February 27, 2021), https://christianchronicle.org/bible-in-one-hand-newspaper-in-the-other.

5. Robert M. Grant, "Commentaries," *Tools for Bible Study,* ed. Balmer H. Kelly and Donald G. Miller (Richmond, VA: John Knox, 1956), 105.

who was present during the writing of the author's message and the author's environment and is present today in our environment to help us figure out what our message should be for our environment. The Holy Spirit helps us comprehend the author's message and helps us apply that message to our listeners. As A. Berkeley Mickelsen reminded us: "The crucial question to ask oneself at the close of every sermon is: did the word (the proclaimed truth of God) become alive to me and to my hearers? . . . Closeness to God is essential for getting close to men and their needs."[6]

Holy Spirit		Holy Spirit
↓		↓
The author's message	=	X
The author's environment		Our environment

So how do we go about making an application for today?

1. *Pray.* As Proverbs 16:3 (RSV) exhorts, "Commit your work to the LORD, and your plans will be established."
2. *Reduce your text to basic principles*, timeless universal teaching that affects action.[7] You focus on your text, but you interpret it by means of the purpose of the book or letter and all you have learned about it. This step is the pivot that proceeds to direct application. For example, for the sample exegesis paper in chapter 8, I summarized the principle of Philemon 4–6 as "Christ's grace brings reconciliation and transformation," and the purpose of my sermon is to "encourage listeners to energize their faith by praying and acting on ruptured relationships." For the inductive study, the main theme is phrased in this way: "Transforming social change begins with prayer and praise." In the final point of the inductive study, I summarized: "Philemon's sharing of faith would become activated if he was reconciled and treated a former slave as an equal." In the paper, I wrote, "Philemon's goodness and faith were laudable. . . . However, when it came to *koinōnia*, Philemon still had a ways to grow. . . . Paul's prayer would be answered if Philemon became Paul's 'partner' by welcoming Onesimus, in the same way as he would welcome Paul."
3. *Summarize the people or situation* to which the original text is addressed. What were the original readers like? Aspects of the historical context should be summarized. In the sample inductive

---

6. Mickelsen, *Interpreting the Bible,* 366.
7. See further Henry A. Virkler, "A Proposal for the Transcultural Problem," in *Rightly Divided: Readings in Biblical Hermeneutics,* ed. Roy B. Zuck (Grand Rapids: Kregel, 1996), 232, 237–38, 243–44; Roy B. Zuck, "Application in Biblical Hermeneutics and Exposition," in *Rightly Divided,* 278–96; Kuhatschek, *Applying the Bible,* chs. 4–5.

226 | Application and Completion of Study

Bible study, I summarized Philemon and Onesimus's relationship as between two people who were not considered equal in their society and needed to be reconciled.

4. *Analyze the contemporary situation* in view of the biblical passage. The key is to discover similar people or situations as those encompassing the original people and their situations. We need to draw up appropriate analogies for today.

5. *Make the direct application.*

Applications can be direct and explicitly taken from the Bible if the historical situation is the same today as it was in the past. Or they can be implicit or analogous to the Bible. The principle for the text helps us make an appropriate application. The disciplines of preaching, educating, counseling, and so on develop this area of the study. Nevertheless, we all need at least to begin an application right away. Normally I ask my students to write a one-to-two-page outline of an application. I hope that professors in the practical division will allow students to develop what they began in the biblical division. In the preliminary outline for this chapter, I suggested six options. You can pick one: a personal application, sermon outline, lesson plan, artistic creation, situational application, or theological motif. Most students do the sermon outline, but other formats are fine to do as well.

TYPES OF DIRECT APPLICATION

Personal Application

A good place to begin is to analyze one's own reactions to a text, even if this aspect of a text is not developed in an essay.

Ask, "What is *my* gut reaction, my basic visceral response?" When first reading the Bible book, you should have jotted down your feelings. This is a time to remember what those feelings were. Ask, "What memories or associations do I have? How will my feelings affect my interpretation and application?" Everyone has feelings and a will. This is healthy and good, because God created us with a will and feelings. I remember a time when my regional religious leaders (the presbytery ministerial committee) required me (and all ministerial candidates) to be evaluated by a psychologist at a career center. The psychologist showed me different Rorschach inkblots, and I was to describe what I saw. But he never showed any emotion. Having a human being without emotional expression was so strange that I began trying to get him to smile. I made up the most outlandish interpretations of the different inkblots until—success!—he laughed. But I may have ruined his test! We cannot pretend to be completely objective, but if we recognize our feelings, we can be more objective.

Our first step is to analyze ourselves honestly. What are we now like? Where are we now as related to this passage? The second step is to apply the

Make the Application to Life | 227

principles of the passage to the will and direction of our life. This step has two subdivisions.

1. *Asking:* What should I be like in light of the properly interpreted Scripture? What does the passage tell me about myself? What does it tell me I should do, value, or be? What does it tell me I should encourage others to do, value, be? Or we might ask, "What should I pray? Is there an example for me to follow? Is there a sin for me to avoid? Is there a command for me to obey? Are there any promises for me to claim or to hope in?"[8]
2. *Applying:* We often forget the final step in a personal application. We need to make behavioral goals for changes in our life that are realistic and possible. We must corner ourselves. Thinking honestly, What changes do I *not* want to make that I should? How will I make these changes possible? What do I need to do to make these changes? When will I do them?

For example, let's say you decide that you need to be reconciled to someone. You may analyze why you are resistant, but after prayer you decide you must make the first step toward reconciliation. The final step is to determine when and how you will do it. An email is the worst way to reconcile with someone unless it is a very minor matter. There is no context for our words, and we can be easily misunderstood. The impact of email can readily spiral out of control. Even a telephone conversation leaves out a lot. Using Zoom might be better, but even then people can look quite different on a monitor. Once I had a student who looked as if she were fifty years old. I was shocked when I first saw her in person. She was only in her twenties! But she had been very ill. Face-to-face conversation is usually the best, but it may not be possible. Philemon's reconciliation with Onesimus was face-to-face and action oriented. Having a nice guest room prepared for Onesimus when he returned would be quite a shock to Onesimus and would communicate a great dramatic message, even without any words, but with a smile.[9]

---

8. Paul Little, in his classic study *How to Give Away Your Faith*, 125–26, suggested seven helpful questions for personally applying a text. To the five questions above, he added, "What does this particular passage teach me about God or about Jesus Christ?" and "Is there a difficulty here for me to explore?"
9. Many excellent books have been written on reconciliation. Matthew D. Kim and Paul A. Hoffman propose that preaching can be a means to reconciliation as well, but "preaching marked by unction" functions as a "double-edged sword. On the one hand, it often reaps transformation; on the other hand, confronting abusive authorities and unjust powers may arouse hostility." *Preaching to a Divided Nation: A Seven-Step Model for Promoting Reconciliation and Unity* (Grand Rapids: Baker, 2022), 69.

228 | Application and Completion of Study

Sermon Outline

In preaching you communicate to the will primarily and secondarily to the mind, but you include as much of the content as is necessary. Good preaching is *not* reading an exegesis paper. You are not parading your learning or stressing your points of uncertainty. You are not trying to solve every exegetical problem or answer every objection or present everyone's opinion. Sometimes you might say, "This is a well-known difficult text, but if this is the correct understanding, as I think it is, then it is going to mean such and such." If you feel comfortable with what you have studied, God has given you authority through the church to build up others so they might grow and minister. We must preach in a way that we think pleases God. The Lord told Jeremiah, "Is not my word like fire . . . and like a hammer that breaks a rock in pieces?" (Jer. 23:29 NRSV). After Cleopas and his companion heard Jesus's interpretation about himself with regard to the Old Testament, they responded: "Didn't our heart burn within us as [Jesus] spoke to us along the way, as he opened to us the Scriptures?" (Luke 24:32). If you simply reveal to others what God has already revealed to you, God's Word will again burn in their hearts, as it did in your heart, to convict, to cleanse, and to counsel. We must ask God to help us preach with conviction.

Sermons come in many formats: expository sermons in which the main points and subpoints come from the passage, textual sermons in which a particular text provides the main points, and topical sermons on a theme or subject in which the main points come from various parts of the Bible.[10] Or an exegesis paper might result in a series of sermons. When I first began to preach, my sermons were really long. I was content, but my listeners were not. They probably stopped listening after twenty or thirty minutes. A sermon might even be given as a creative monologue. Any format is fine. However, it should always end with an application of the text to your congregation's or hearers' situation. Without an application, your listeners have no hope!

The outline for a sermon should include a title, one that is accurate, but one that would attract listeners to come. My first sermon was based on Cain and Abel, and I thought a scintillating title would be "The Sins of Worship." Readers might puzzle over how something good like worship could have any sins. However, when I saw the title in the newspaper, I felt no one would want to come to hear such a depressing topic. The people did come, but I think it was more to hear their first female preacher than to hear the topic.

The Scripture text reading for our sample sermon is simply Philemon 4–6, but at other times I have included an Old Testament passage that is important for interpretation. Many times I have included the immediate context around the text in the public reading. I recommend using the pew Bible version in the read-

---

10. See also Mickelsen, *Interpreting the Bible*, 365. For examples of moving from exegesis to a sermon, see John D. Harvey, *Interpreting the Pauline Letters: An Exegetical Handbook* (Grand Rapids: Kregel, 2012), chs. 6–7.

Make the Application to Life | 229

ing so the congregation is not confused. Gauge how long a passage should be in light of contemporary listeners' ability to listen. Also, the types of illustrations should be chosen with the type of congregation you are addressing in mind.

The introduction is key to a sermon. You want to draw in/attract the interest of the listeners and, at the same time, get them to the heart of the passage.[11] You may ask yourself, "Why should my listeners find this subject important or relevant?" This is a challenge, and asking God for help is essential. Being contemporary is also essential. Developing your message can be enabled by looking at the different ways any topic is developed: explanations, definitions, illustrations, quotations, narrations, factual information, restatements, describing the opposite or cause.[12] You ask, "What do the listeners need to know about this subject?" When I was a student, I once had to develop a sermon at a time when my mind was filled with so many things I had to do that all I could do was present my main point and give three stories. My audience loved the stories!

Another key to a sermon is knowing when to stop. Some preachers are so charismatic that they can speak for an hour and a half and their listeners love to hear all of it. Other preachers can be excellent if they know when to stop. They present a fine message, and then, bit by bit, they go on to present another message. The listeners are satisfied with the first message, but their minds become distracted once the preacher starts the second message. Some churches tell me the congregation is used to ninety-minute sermons. I sat in one such church service and noticed that once the preacher reached forty-five minutes, there was a change in the listeners, and individuals in the congregation slowly began to fall asleep. Once we reached an hour and a half, almost half of the congregation was sleeping. Coming to a conclusion at the right time is essential. My own recommendation, for most Anglo churches, is that twenty to thirty minutes is enough. Preaching should be a tight genre.

In the conclusion, ask yourself, "How can my listeners use this information in everyday life? If my listeners put this information into practice, what will their lives look like?"[13]

Whatever length of sermon you craft, you need to be clear about the main point you want to communicate: your thesis. Experienced preacher, radio announcer, and professor Alice Mathews said:

---

11. E.g., see Robinson, *Biblical Preaching*, 119–33, 183.
12. For examples, see Robinson, *Biblical Preaching*, ch. 7. See also chapter 4, "Seek a Translation and Understand the Grammar of the Text," in this book.
13. Bonita Joyner Shields suggested these questions as ways to respond to different learning styles related to perceiving and processing. Some perceive life through their senses and feelings, others through their intellect by conceptualizing or thinking. Some people process new experiences though reflecting (observing), others through action (doing). She summarizes four learning styles that ask four learning questions: experiential doer (What if?), experiential reflector (Why?), intellectual doer (How?), and intellectual reflector (What?). "Growing Disciples through Transformational Learning," *Ministry*, May 2011, 6–9.

> One thing that can't be stated often enough is the reminder that the sermons with multiple points being made never really stick in listeners' minds. It's important to make one important point and continue to develop it through the sermon. Haddon Robinson recognized that listeners need to hear a core teaching being repeated in one way or another over and over. Making multiple points in a sermon dilutes the power of those points. In general nothing lands and stays with listeners. . . . So the expositor's task is to bridge from the biblical text to what has relevance to listeners' lives. So a good sermon sets up the biblical text but then deals with the "so what" question: "Why should I listen to you?"[14]

Praise songs or hymns are part of the communication process and should relate to your Scripture passage, whether in preparation or application. For Presbyterian ministers, the preacher has the right to choose the hymns or praise songs. Thus, if the church has a director of music, the preacher and the praise team need to work together.

Lesson Plan

Teaching is especially part of a relationship. Often the relationship is ongoing. We want to establish a climate of mutual respect, encouragement, security, warmth, supportiveness, and eagerness to learn. If preaching mainly affects the will, teaching mainly affects the mind. Jesus did both: he preached and he taught at different times. But he always was interested in transformation.[15] People have certain capacities to understand and also desire to respond, which is why teaching is often gradual. For example, Jesus taught the crowds about the necessity to persevere, but then privately he explained everything to his disciples (Mark 4:1–34). As teachers, we have messages to communicate and need to think prayerfully about how we can best simplify and clarify our messages. We also want to leave students with tools they can use by themselves.

We might begin preparation for the lesson plan with questions: What do I want the students to learn? Why do I want the students to learn this? When they have learned it, What do I want them to do with it? How long do I expect them to retain it? What provision will I make for varying learning abilities, such as rate, mode, motivation, and interpersonal variations?[16] After thinking about your students, study the Scripture passage, and then write down the main idea and your objectives, activities, and time allotment for each. For

---

14. Alice Mathews, email message to the author, June 15, 2023. Used by permission.
15. William David Spencer describes his graduate plan for educating seminarians in "Intentional Teaching," in *Empowering English Language Learners: Successful Strategies of Christian Educators*, ed. Jeanne C. DeFazio and William David Spencer (Eugene, OR: Wipf & Stock, 2018), 106–37. The entire book is full of excellent chapters on teaching strategies.
16. Kenneth O. Gangel, "Delivering Theological Education That Works," *Theological Education* 34, no. 1 (1997): 6.

every class I teach, I write a lesson plan. This helps me know my own goals for the class and, when rushing to get ready, helps me remember to bring what I need for the class.

Each lesson plan varies, depending on the audience. Young children love crafts as hands-on activities that might not interest older people. Calculating the time is important in planning, and, when time runs out, the teacher needs to know how to adjust: what can be omitted and what must be retained at the end of the lesson. An outline of class procedures is needed, and the tentative time allotted for each procedure must be marked. Teachers need to find a way to balance time for discussion and listening and time to move on to a new topic. I have found I cannot please every student. Some will think the teacher allowed too much flexibility, and others will think the flexibility for discussion was just right. Do not expect to please everyone, but if a teacher gets many complaints or many students who cannot complete the assignments, that teacher needs to adapt what to expect. The point in teaching is not to prove that we are rigorous, that no one can complete our assignments, but rather to help the maximum number of people learn and complete the course. God has called people to our classes, and we are there to prepare them as best as possible. We should not forget to include the physical arrangement that is best to meet our stated purpose. Prayer is a great way to start and end our classes.

Questions to ask yourself following each class include, "Did I estimate the time as accurately as possible? Did the plan fit together logically? Did it fit in with my plans for the unit? Did I pray for the class and for myself as its teacher?"[17] If your answer is no to any of these questions, do not despair but keep trying. If necessary, bring in a trusted colleague or friend or spouse to suggest how you can adapt the class if it is too long. Once I had a Sunday school class of sixth graders who were bored and uncooperative. I prayed for them and came up with the idea of reading a chapter from C. S. Lewis's *The Lion, the Witch, and the Wardrobe* to begin each class. Believe it or not, that quieted them, and I was able to proceed with our planned Scripture study. Some got so excited they looked forward to the class, and one student even began reading the book on her own during the week. What really made a difference was that I had established with them a relationship of love through the means of sharing a delightful treasure with them. I did not simply demand they rise to my interest level.

Inductive Bible Study

Inductive Bible study is an excellent way to format a Sunday school class. The goal is to write inductive questions that lead students to the right answers. In the study I wrote on Philemon 4–6, I began by asking questions that dealt more with content, and I indicated where the answers could be found in

---

17. Presbyterian and Reformed Educational Ministry, "Planning for Teaching/Learning," *Alert: For Leaders and Planners of the Church's Education Program,* May 1989, 5.

232 | Application and Completion of Study

the Bible. I also prepared my own parallel versions that helped the students answer some of my questions. Paul McReynolds's *Word Study Greek-English New Testament* is very helpful for students who do not know Greek but want to see the Greek and English translation.[18] I ended each class with an application question and prayer. The following are some guidelines for writing your own inductive Bible study.

How to Prepare an Inductive Bible Study (Summary)

I.   How to prepare an inductive Bible study. Your goal is to help your students look at the Bible and draw out information from it.

  A.   In the Bible, pick a paragraph or passage that is a complete thought unit. Use different translations if you do not know Greek.

  B.   After prayer, read and study the passage yourself. If time allows, read the whole book.

  C.   Develop the Bible study. Decide if you want to use the laissez-faire or the focused format.

   1.   *Laissez-faire:* Plan to have each person read a full sentence or thought unit and present any insights, applications, or feelings (s)he gets from the text. Begin and end with prayer. This format works well with students who are well versed already in Bible knowledge.

   2.   *Focused:*

    a.   Start with general points. Decide what main points you want the group to derive from the text. Ask questions that direct the group to answer by using the Bible. Always allow time for prayer (a brief time at the beginning of the study and a longer time at the end) and for application at the end. Look up any information you need as background. Do not jump all over the Bible, but if there is a reference to another passage, have the students look it up. Do not let them get side-tracked.

    b.   Pick an introductory activity students can do as they wait for the full class to arrive. In that way, students are encouraged to come on time, and those who are on time are rewarded.

    c.   Look at the passage. Summarize the content of each small thought unit with a question.

    d.   Close with questions. What applications did you draw from this passage? (See "Personal Application" above.)

---

18.   Paul R. McReynolds, *Word Study Greek-English New Testament* (Wheaton, IL: Tyndale House, 1999).

Make the Application to Life | 233

  e. Find helpful illustrations you can bring to illuminate any point.
  f. *Optional:* Find optional resources for students who want further study.
D. Write a lesson plan.
  1. Describe the students.
  2. List the goals of the lesson.
  3. Choose the best room arrangement. Come early to arrange the room if necessary.
  4. Open with prayer and an introduction.
  5. Write your inductive questions and expected answers. Decide the time for each part of the lesson.
  6. Leave time for applications, optional resources for further study, and prayer.
  7. Decide what materials are needed.
E. Present the Bible study.
  1. Encourage genuine dialogue.
  2. Find a way to include everyone without embarrassing anyone. Ask who wants to read. Be careful with persons who may not read well.
  3. Do not run the class over the scheduled time. Face a clock. Ask someone to warn you five minutes before the end.
  4. Do not talk too much or too little.

Artistic Creation

Preaching and teaching are the more traditional means by which to apply an exegetical study. However, you might preach a sermon, teach it, teach it, or create something artistic, such as a poem, drama, or song. I once received a painting as an application but decided I was not qualified to evaluate it! Sometimes sermons can be adapted into blogs, which may be like mini devotional studies. After doing a study of John 12:1–8 and a book review of Elisabeth Schüssler Fiorenza's *In Memory of Her,*[19] I wrote a blog monologue titled "In Memory of Them: Mary of Bethany's Recollections before Passover."[20] I not only studied John 12 but also compared and harmonized that passage with its gospel parallels in Matthew and Mark. Years later a church in Britain asked me if they could use the blog post as a monologue in a service.

Exegetical studies can also be transformed into poems or lyric poems. The following is a lyric poem I composed together with my husband, based on Luke 2:19 ("Mary treasured all these words and pondered them in her heart" NRSV):

---

19. Aída Besançon Spencer, review of *In Memory of Her,* by Elisabeth Schüssler Fiorenza, *Update II,* Summer 1987, 11–13.
20. See *Applying Biblical Truths Today,* March 25, 2017, https://aandwspencer.blogspot.com/2017/03/in-memory-of-them-mary-of-bethanys.html.

Secreted in Her Heart

In her arms lies the sweet Jesus, sleeping, helpless, Ruler of all,
Gift of love, sent from the Father, wondrous to behold.
Lord of all, Love of the universe, Lord of all that is.
Surely, he has borne my grief, surely born to grieve for me.

In her heart lies the sweet mystery, whispering, singing, lulling to sleep.
In her arms lies the sweet Jesus, wounded, given death.
Lord of all, Love of the universe, Lord of all that is.
Surely, I will see him exalted, as he exalted me.

In her arms lies the sweet Jesus, in her arms lies the sweet Jesus. . . .[21]

The Lord has inspired artists ever since God the Trinity created the world,[22] and some of those creations have flowed from exegetical studies.

Situational Application
Another type of application is one in which we apply an exegetical study for a situation, or issue, or group of people today. However, the one passage studied may not answer all questions related to our topic. If we do not study the issue, or situation, or people group first, we may not know what is most appropriate and helpful to apply from our Bible study findings. Instead, the danger is we will just wander around in the air never really touching down and landing anywhere.

Theological Motifs
Sometimes an exegesis of a passage may be the start of a theological study that continues in the Bible. For example, Philemon 4–6 might be part of a study on love or evangelism or church discipline. *Theologia* is literally "a word of God," or the study of God, the "science of things divine."[23] From an exegetical perspective, it is the expressing of what is in the Bible (mainly historical experiences) into general categories—in other words, either traditional categories or original ones. Often theological interpretation changes the format of Scriptures into doctrines. Justo González writes that one definition of theology is "the systematization of Christian doctrine on the basis of Scripture."[24] According to Fred Fisher, theological interpretation helps us give form and precision to faith and helps us understand and communicate our faith and

---

21. "Secreted in Her Heart," words and music by William David Spencer and Aída Besançon Spencer © 1973.
22. See further William David Spencer and Aída Besançon Spencer, eds., *God through the Looking Glass: Glimpses from the Arts* (Grand Rapids: Baker, 1998).
23. LSJ, 790.
24. Justo L. González, *Essential Theological Terms* (Louisville: Westminster John Knox, 2005), 170.

formulate and test our doctrines.[25] These categories help us comprehend what is in the Bible, although the categories will not be sufficient to contain the awesomeness of God or God's Word. They help immensely but can hinder if taken as authoritative in themselves. When we derive a theological principle for a text, we have begun the process from exegesis to theology.

The Process of Interpretation			
Begin	Particular, detail →	Categorize, systematize, generalize	End
Prayer →	Bible exegesis →	Theology and ethics →	Application

Some theological categories are explicitly stated in the Bible. For example, Paul ended his letter to Philemon, Apphia, Archippus, and the church: "The grace of the Lord Jesus Christ be with your [plural] spirit" (v. 25). This verse clearly states that Jesus Christ has grace. Romans 1:20 says that God has eternal power and divine nature. Other Bible passages imply or implicitly refer to theological categories. For example, Philemon 4–6 implies that communication with God is worthwhile (God is personal). We also learn that faith is not merely words stated but also actions (vv. 5–6).

After deriving theological categories from your text, you can compare the passage with other biblical passages bearing on the same subject. These passages can be organized under subcategories, such as the nature of God and nature of humans. Then, after studying these categories, state the basic teaching in complete sentences, summarizing what you learned. Sometimes marginal biblical references might help you to find related passages.[26]

Verbal cross-references have identical words or expressions in common or quotations or allusions to related Scripture, such as Philippians 2:29 as a marginal reference for Romans 16:2. Both passages have the word "receive": receive Phoebe and receive Epaphroditus. Or Philippians 1:5 may be a verbal marginal reference for Philemon 6 because both have the word *koinōnia*. Conceptual cross-references refer to passages of Scripture that, although not possessing identical wording, have very similar concepts, including fulfillment of prophecy and applications, such as Romans 14 and 1 Corinthians 8, as both deal with the weak brother or sister in the faith and eating. The idea of Paul thanking God may be found in Philemon 4 and Philippians 1:3.

Parallel cross-references refer to accounts of identical occurrences or historical background, such as Romans 16:1 and Acts 18:18, which both refer to Cenchreae, or Philemon 10 and Colossians 4:9, which both refer to

---

25. Fred L. Fisher, *How to Interpret the New Testament* (Philadelphia: Westminster, 1966), 151.
26. See Bernard Ramm, *Protestant Biblical Interpretation: A Textbook of Hermeneutics*, 3rd ed. (Grand Rapids: Baker, 1970), 140–42.

236 | Application and Completion of Study

Onesimus. In preparation for ordination, I had to write an exegetical study and the outline for a sermon in only three hours. I did that by not only translating my passage but also using the marginal references for additional information.

The positive side of this type of theological analysis is that it provides information on a topic more fully. The danger is to the time and space allotted to a paper. If your paper has limited space and time, you may not be able to do such a study, as worthy as it is. Therefore, normally I do not recommend that my students in a one-semester exegetical study do much in this area of theological analysis. It all depends on the time available. Also, the application may not be as specific as doing a sermon outline, lesson plan, or artistic piece.

A theological study might also be done from a broad perspective, beginning with a topic, then gathering everything that might remotely contribute to the topic. A topical concordance is very helpful.[27] Cross-references may help. Then the passages need to be read in their context, and sometimes more detailed exegetical work needs to be done. At this point, a chart with your findings may be made, concluding with a summary of the teachings on the topic. The danger of this approach is eisegesis (using Scripture to prove your own doctrine rather than extrapolating doctrine from Scripture). Again, always begin with Scripture, use sound exegetical methods, pay attention to the immediate context of each passage, and limit your interpretation to the evidence. The Bible is not written to satisfy our curiosity but to meet our needs (2 Tim. 3:16–17). Our study of the Scriptures should result in good action. That is why applying our text in some specific way is so important. At least a beginning step can be taken in the exegesis paper to be developed later.

How worthwhile is *The Exegetical Process* to the application of the Bible text? Some students concluded:

> My exegetical skills certainly improved. . . . This class helped me integrate technical exegetical skills (word studies, variants, sentence flow, etc.) into the body of the exegetical work so that the information made sense in the context of preparing a sermon. My sermon preparation has drastically changed due to the skills acquired in this class. I had a basic understanding of exegetical elements when I began this class but now know how to put the elements together to handle the study and preaching of God's Word to the best of my ability. Of course, I am still learning and will continue to execute the exegetical process. (Julie, 2022)
>
> I wanted to learn how to exegete and apply it to preaching. This objective was definitely met. Thank you for taking me through all

---

27. E.g., Orville J. Nave, *The New Nave's Topical Bible*, ed. Edward Viening (Grand Rapids: Zondervan, 1969); see also Edward Viening, ed., *The Zondervan Topical Bible* (Grand Rapids: Zondervan, 1969), https://www.biblestudytools.com/concordances/naves-topical-bible.

the assignments step-by-step. Hopefully this will become the bread and butter of my teaching and preaching ministry. The course helped me see how my Greek studies would benefit New Testament interpretation. (David, 2016)

I studied under Dr. Spencer decades ago, and to this day, I still remember and apply what I learned in her courses. More than anything, I love studying God's Word, and this manual prepared me well to do so whether I am preparing to teach or preach. (Rev. Dr. Leslie McKinney Attema, 2023)

Looking back over the past year and a half, I realized the gratitude I have for . . . Aída Spencer [who] taught me the way to interpret faithfully and then apply the New Testament. I was amazed at her ability to make me think about the richness of the Bible! (Jeffrey, 1986)

HOW TO AVOID COMMON ERRORS

1. Applying a text to today is a process that takes creative thought. Sometimes students begin a whole new topic in the application or add topics that were never covered earlier. If you find your application has ideas that are essentially in the passage but you have not included them, make sure you go back to the exegetical study and add them there.
2. Keep the application specific and not too broad.
3. Use illustrations in your sermon and lesson. Pastor Steven J. Lawson explains that "sermon illustrations are like open windows which allow outside light to be shed upon the passage, enlightening its meaning. A good illustration can create interest, capture attention, explain a truth, motivate powerfully or ensure that the message is unforgettable."[28] I have endured sermons with no illustrations. Maybe the preacher wants only to be biblical; however, Jesus used many illustrations while teaching and preaching on earth. Why should we not follow his example?
4. On the other hand, make sure your authority is the Bible text, not the illustration. I heard a sermon the other day that had a memorable illustration, but the main point of the illustration was different from the main point of the Bible text.
5. In the application, the main point must be the same as the Bible text. If a new issue or problem arises in the application, leave that issue

---

28. Steven J. Lawson, "The Ten How-To's of Expository Preaching," *The Tie* 65, no. 3 (1997): 12.

for another study. Your goal is to reinforce the Bible text with your exposition and application. Do not stray from it.

6. Do not use your Bible text as a diving board to dive into other issues, but begin in the shallow water of your text and look around carefully at the natural beauty there already where you stand.

7. Craft your sermon to communicate best with your audience. Do not simply copy the exegesis paper. Professor Patricia Morrison Batten reiterated:

> Regarding the jump from exegesis to homiletics: The journey from exegesis to homiletics can be rocky terrain. In some instances, students are tempted to preach an exegetical study of a passage or an exegetical paper. Their concern for the text is valid, but they've demonstrated a lack of concern for their listeners. The listener must also be "exegeted." Listeners want to know what the Bible says, but more importantly, they want to know how the truth of the Bible affects their particular lives on Monday morning and they want to hear it in a way that makes sense to them. Western preachers in particular tend to apply a biblical passage primarily in an individual sense rather than a communal sense. But preaching God's word can transform the whole body of Christ and move the whole body of Christ toward maturity.[29]

APPENDICES: SAMPLE APPLICATION OUTLINES

Sermon Outline of Philemon 4–6

Title: How to Become Partners of the Great Apostle Paul

Text: Philemon 4–6

Congregation: Middle-class urban Christians

Purpose: To encourage listeners to energize their faith by praying and acting on ruptured relationships

Principle: Christ's grace brings reconciliation and transformation.

Introduction: Relate the contemporary story of person who has not forgiven a family member for fifty years. (optional skit)

---

29. Patricia A. Morrison Batten, email message to the author, June 26, 2023. Used by permission.

I. Body:
    A. Explain what is known for certain about Philemon and Onesimus's ruptured relationship and why Onesimus may be "useless."
    B. Assess Philemon's strengths: love and faith.
    C. Explore Philemon's weakness: sharing of faith.
    D. Discuss:
        1. What is *koinōnia*? *Koinōnia* comes from the Holy Spirit.
        3. How is *koinōnia* related to faith?
    E. Illustrate how Paul's faith is activated in Philemon.
    F. Compare text to ancient times.

II. Application:
    A. Would you like to become Paul's partner?
        1. To whom should you be reconciled?
        2. Explain how to reconcile as Paul did.
    B. Close with illustrations of reconciliation.
        1. Onesimus probably became a bishop.
        2. Relate account of persevering faith of servant Blandina, a faith greater than her Christian mistress (Eusebius, *Church History* 5.1).
    C. Prayer: Praise the congregation. Ask the congregation to remember relationships that need reconciliation and to acknowledge that they have the strength of character to be reconciled.

Possible hymns: "Renew Thy Church, Her Ministries Restore" and "O to Be Like Thee!"

Lesson Plan of Philemon 1–7

Topic:	Inductive Bible Study of Philemon 1–7
Main Theme:	Transforming social change begins with prayer and praise.
Students:	Adult Christians who do not know Greek but who are interested in Bible study
Goals:	Communicate the main theme; enable students to use the Bible for the answers; help students see the Bible as worth studying; have at least two students think of a relationship that needs reconciliation.
Time:	Forty-five minutes, about five minutes for each question

240 | Application and Completion of Study

Materials: Paul R. McReynolds, *Word Study Greek-English New Testament,* 3rd ed., (Wheaton, IL: Tyndale House, 1983), 782–83; KJV text of Philemon and New Testament.

Arrangement: Seats around a table would be ideal for discussion.

Open with Prayer: Ask for God's enlightenment.

1. What was Philemon's relationship with Onesimus, and what had happened between them? Read verses 11, 14–16, 18.
2. What happened between Onesimus and Paul? What was their relationship like? Read verses 10, 12–13.
3. Where was Onesimus from? See Colossians 4:9. Therefore, where was Philemon?
4. Philemon can be divided into four sections. Present outline. Today we will study verses 1–7. Look at verses 4–6. How many sentences does the NRSV (left margin) have? How many sentences does the Greek have?
5. Read aloud verses 4–6. What is the first word in the Greek sentence? For what does Paul thank God (see vv. 4–6)? How does verse 6 relate to verses 4–5? Look at Ephesians 1:16–19. How is it similar to Philemon 4–6?
6. Look at verse 5 in the English versus the Greek. In Greek "faith" has two objects (also see KJV). What are they? In verse 6 (using KJV) "in" has two objects. What are they? Faith and goodness have both a vertical (Christ) and a horizontal (human) dimension.
7. What is the meaning of "the sharing of your faith may become effective"? For example, see verses 10, 17, 22. What must Philemon do to become Paul's partner (see v. 17)? "Partner" (*koinōnos*, v. 17) is in the same word family as "sharing" (*koinōnia*, v. 6). How then does verse 17 relate to verse 6? How do both relate to "grace" in the closing benediction (v. 25)?
8. Philemon's sharing of faith would become activated if he was reconciled and treated a former slave as an equal. Do you know of anyone who socially is not your "equal" and with whom you should be reconciled? Pray for guidance. Do you know any Christian who has not become reconciled to someone? Pray for them.
9. Closing prayer for application.

CHAPTER 10

FIND OTHER
INTERPRETATIONS OF TEXT

I. *Find* articles, essays, and books on one aspect of your text.[1]
   A. *Collect.* Check all commentaries on reserve in the library to see where most commentators agree and disagree. Take a sampling of other commentaries, contemporary and earlier. Make sure to note full bibliographical information of commentaries used.[2] (For a doctoral dissertation, you need to add some works in other languages.)
   B. *Find* all articles and essays on your text. See key indexes. Choose verses of immediate context.
II. *Decide* what one aspect or issue or problem (if there are many) you will report on in the "Summary of Interpretations" or as an introduction to the exegesis paper.
III. *Think.* As you read, notice what articles and books appear to be pivotal for certain viewpoints (e.g., by repetition of citation in the works you are reading), what articles and books appear to be unique for a certain viewpoint, and what articles and books appear to be helpful for you. Also pay attention to any presuppositions the authors may have that affect the final conclusion. With which presuppositions do you agree?
IV. Write a tentative *outline* clearly explaining and categorizing the interpretations of the issue you are studying and the reasons and

---

1. For further reading, see Gordon D. Fee, *New Testament Exegesis: A Handbook for Students and Pastors,* 3rd ed. (Louisville: Westminster John Knox, 2002), 32–34, ch. 5; Michael J. Gorman, *Elements of Biblical Exegesis: A Basic Guide for Students and Ministers,* 3rd ed. (Grand Rapids: Baker, 2020), ch. 11, app. D.
2. To save time, possibly photocopy or scan the title page and copyright year of the latest edition (often the page following the title page), *not* the latest printing, and the series title, if any, or bring in a style manual and copy over the data into the prospective bibliography.

presuppositions (if any) behind each interpretation. Briefly indicate which scholars support each interpretation. Make sure you accurately represent each scholar's thought. Where do you fit? Does anything you are reading change your view? Do you have additional reasons for your view? Do you need to answer problems raised against your view by others?

V. Write a paragraph or up to several pages *summarizing* clearly the different categories of interpretations of this one issue in your text. Cite examples for each view. Footnote additional examples. Conclude with how your interpretation relates to those of others. Answer briefly criticisms of your view. Have you provided any unique and/or helpful interpretations?

VI. Type a *bibliography* of the references you have read and quoted. I recommend a minimum of ten references for a short exegesis paper. Use a style manual for the correct format.

VII.*Change* your original exegesis paper to add helpful comments and strengthen your reasons for conclusions where others disagree. Consult the sample exegesis paper (chapter 8). Material in this sample paper that was added after looking at secondary material is in italics.

This step can be done by both Greek and translation readers.

INTRODUCTION

As I write this chapter, the current news Christians are discussing is Pastor Rick Warren's change of position on women's leadership in the church. Whatever our view is on the topic, his comments highlight dramatically the relevance of the topic of this book, the exegetical process:

My biggest regret in 53 years of ministry is that I didn't do my own personal exegesis sooner on the 4 passages used to restrict women. Shame on me.

I wasted those 4 yrs of Greek in college & seminary. When I finally did my proper "due diligence," laying aside 50 years of bias, I was shocked, chagrined, and embarrassed.

So many hermeneutical rules were being violated including: Never build a doctrine on a single word that is used *only once* in Scripture! There's nothing to compare it to (correlation). Do your own study of *authentein* in ancient Greek and you'll be shocked too.

I think maybe it was because I didn't WANT to know anything that might challenge the view I WANTED to believe for 50 yrs. But eventually, integrity required that I read over 70 commentaries by INERRANTIST scholars that blew apart my comfortable, traditional, and culture-based interpretation. No seminary told me that those commentaries even existed and Baptist Bookstores refused to carry them. (My mother managed a Baptist Bookstore.) So I accepted the interpretation that was most comfortable for me as a man with my background. . . .

We must live for an Audience of One [God].[3]

Pastor Warren's words are an encouragement to us to do our own study first and then compare our study of the Bible to those of other Christian interpreters from a variety of perspectives.

THEORIES FOR QUOTATIONS

I have categorized the basic theories on *why* to quote secondary references under two basic ones: (1) documentation from a guild or academy and (2) dialogue with a community of scholars.

In documentation, one believes an interpretation cannot be valid unless one can document or show that some past or contemporary "acceptable" scholar already has that interpretation or suggests it. The analogy would be legal precedence, the summoning of authorities.

Probably a rationale for documentation rests on the history of education. In medieval higher education (c. 1125–1225), a university (*universitas*) was a guild of scholars, a "voluntary association of individual masters rather than a single educational institution conducted by an organized staff. The *universitas* prescribed the studies which were to lead to the master's chair." A *universitas* formed a legally recognized self-governing association. The guild had the right to bestow an advanced degree and a license to teach.[4]

A vestige of the guild of scholars is the concept of documentation. A positive aspect of documentation is the demonstration to others of acquaintance with past scholarship. Past scholarship may show limitations or even errors of our interpretations that should be avoided. They can also refer us to primary references. Some Bible interpreters are gifted in collecting bibliographies and accessing their worth. But although legal studies must show precedence in legal decisions, in biblical studies our authority is *not* previous interpretation or interpreters but rather the Bible itself. Robert Grant explains:

---

3. Rick Warren, "My Apology to Christian Women," https://twitter.com/RickWarren/status/1667620086251925505, accessed June 16, 2023. Also cited in churchleaders.com/news/452917.

4. Jeremy Norman, "The Universitas Guild: Early Origin of What We Characterize as a University," *History of Information*, accessed June 19, 2023, https://www.historyofinformation.com/detail.php?id=4153, citing Christopher Beckwith, *Warriors of the Cloisters: The Central Asian Origins of Science in the Medieval World* (Princeton: Princeton University Press, 2012), 43–45.

244 | Application and Completion of Study

Interpretation means letting the text speak to you, in so far as this is possible; but there always remains an element of the individuality of the interpreter. We cannot simply add up commentators on this side as contrasted with those on that, and let the majority decide. To be sure, if most commentators agree that a passage means such and such, one or two individuals who say that it means thus and so are not likely to be right. But the possibility of their rightness remains. The church fathers are not infallible guides, nor are modern critics. We must concentrate first on the Bible itself before we can use commentaries to advantage. For we must judge for ourselves what is right.[5]

For instance, Robert M. Fowler criticizes a book, even though written for the "nonexpert," because the author "does not engage in dialogue with NT scholarship." He concludes that the "colleagues in the guild will have questions and doubts until such time as he addresses, specifically, such questions and doubts as we are wont to have."[6] Fowler demonstrates well an attitude of a panel of judges (the guild) that makes judgments on other works based on the guild's scholarship. Such an attitude fosters criticism, not encouragement, and blocks new ideas and new people with new ideas. Guilds have not been known to be always open-minded but rather often discriminatory. For instance, women, persons of color, Native Americans, new immigrants, and the poor have been marginal to much scholarly activity. They have not been members of "academic consensus."

I have heard the term *academic consensus* many times: "The academic consensus on this passage is . . ." But what is a consensus?[7] I have used this word in groups to signify unanimity. "Are we all in consensus about this decision? Then let's conclude." If one person disagrees, we do not have a consensus of opinion. But consensus may signify a *majority* opinion. But what is a majority? Is it 51 percent or 75 percent or 90 percent? Sometimes those holding a minority view are asked, "Shall we revote and all agree to a consensus [100 percent]?" The result becomes an enforced or fictionalized consensus. However, for some biblical interpreters, a "consensus" is simply an agreement by me and my buddies or those whom I befriend.[8] This is Rick Warren's complaint. He was not told about (and he did not seek) the differing views on women's leadership that yet agreed with his own stance on the reliability of the Bible.

---

5. Robert M. Grant, "Commentaries," in *Tools for Bible Study,* ed. Balmer H. Kelly and Donald G. Miller (Richmond, VA: John Knox, 1956), 101.

6. Robert M. Fowler, review of *The Silence of Jesus* by James Breech, *Journal of Biblical Literature* 104, no. 3 (September 1985): 535–38.

7. Lack of clarity with respect to defining "consensus" is even mentioned in the *Random House Webster's Unabridged Dictionary* (2001), s.v. "consensus."

8. On the principles and processes of consensus decision-making and dialogue, see Tim Hartnett, "The Basics of Consensus Decision Making," *Consensus Facilitation,* http://www.groupfacilitation.net; and Reuel L. Howe, *The Miracle of Dialogue* (New York: Seabury, 1963).

Marginal to the guild in the past include devout Christians. For example, Lisa M. Bowens, associate professor of New Testament at Princeton Theological Seminary, has documented that African Americans have been "studying and utilizing the Bible for hundreds of years," yet only recently have they been "entering the academy" in increasing numbers "to study Scripture in the guild." She cites Josiah Priest, author of *Slavery as It Relates to the Negro or African Race* (1843), who represented the "prevalent sentiments of the time" (i.e., academic consensus) that the African race was appointed by a "judicial act of God" to "servitude and slavery." However, even earlier, in 1774, enslaved Africans interpreted Ephesians 5 to argue their case for freedom and liberty to the civil leaders in Massachusetts: "By our deplorable situation we are rendered incapable of shewing our obedience to Almighty God."[9]

Bowens also cites early Black women preachers, such as Jarena Lee (c. 1783–1850) and Zilpha Elaw (c. 1790–1873) who advocated for female preaching based on Scripture. Lee asked, "Why should it be thought impossible, heterodox, or improper for a woman to preach? seeing the Saviour died for the woman as well as the man. If a man may preach, because the Saviour died for him, why not the woman? seeing he died for her also. Is he not a whole Saviour, instead of a half one?"[10]

Elaw, in her autobiography, added arguments supporting women in ministry that we also find still being written today. She often encountered interpretations opposing her preaching ministry based on 1 Corinthians 14:34–35 and 1 Timothy 2:12, but she responded, "The Scriptures make it evident that this rule [that females should not speak in the church, nor be suffered to teach] was not intended to limit the extraordinary directions of the Holy Ghost, in reference to female Evangelists, or oracular sisters; nor to be rigidly observed in peculiar circumstances. . . . [The] Scriptures make it evident" that this rule is not binding since women preachers and ministers appear throughout the New Testament. In regard to Phoebe, Elaw stated, "St. Paul himself attests that Phoebe was a servant or deaconess of the Church at Cenchrea; and as such was employed by the Church to manage some of their affairs; and it was strange indeed, if she was required to receive the commissions of the church in mute silence." The apostle's words of silence in 1 Corinthians 14:34 were given to a church that, because of its "disorders and excesses," needed "stringent rules for its proper regulation."[11]

---

9.   Lisa M. Bowens, *African American Readings of Paul: Reception, Resistance, and Transformation* (Grand Rapids: Eerdmans, 2020), 7, 16, 21–22. See also Jarena Lee, *Religious Experience and Journal of Mrs. Jarena Lee Giving an Account of Her Call to Preach the Gospel* (Philadelphia: Pantianos, 1836).

10. Jarena Lee, *The Life and Religious Experience of Jarena Lee, a Coloured Lady, Giving an Account of Her Call to Preach the Gospel*, rev. Ed. (Philadelphia, 1836), quoted in Bowens, *African American Readings*, 73, 77, 83.

11. Zilpha Elaw, *Memoirs of the Life, Religious Experience, Ministerial Travels and Labours of Mrs. Zilpha Elaw, an American Female of Color: Together with Some Account of the Great Religious Revivals in America* (London, 1846), quoted in Bowens, *African American Readings*, 92–93. For similar

246 | Application and Completion of Study

My point is that the church has had significant voices of Spirit-led women and persons of color whose biblical interpretations have been significant, yet they have not been always part of the "documentation" or precedence process in the guild of New Testament interpreters.

In a similar vein, Francisco Lozada Jr. states that without Latino/Latina biblical interpretation, "the history of biblical interpretation is incomplete." Latino/Latina presence brings the scholarly guild "new questions and new ways of seeing text." Latinos'/Latinas' participation widens "the existing boundaries on how to do biblical interpretation."[12] For instance, Latinos/Latinas might highlight new texts or themes in the Bible, such as God as stranger, the "fiesta" (the comestible experience or hospitality, family, generosity, and giving), the arts, and time. For Latinos/Latinas, God's Word is often important as a reliable foundation, and God alone is sovereign in the midst of global diversity and change.[13] Reading the Bible from diverse cultural perspectives can highlight underemphasized biblical themes for the academy and produce more relevant themes for currently marginalized communities.[14]

The editors of *The IVP Women's Bible Commentary,* Catherine Clark Kroeger and Mary Evans, state that the commentary introduces new questions and issues to enrich the perspective of other commentaries (frequently written by "white, Western, classically educated, middle-class males") by adding more pertinent themes for women readers: "Women need the opportunity to have the Scriptures explained in ways that are relevant to their lives."[15] For instance, Kristen Plinke Bentley, in her commentary on the letter to Philemon, focuses on Apphia as possibly the wife of Philemon and mother of Archippus. Their home is the meeting place for a local church. Using feminine imagery, Paul introduced Onesimus as the son whom he had "birthed in bonds" (v. 10): "The reintroduction of Onesimus will disrupt the balance of established relationships, probably with particular implications for Apphia. Hers would have been the responsibility to manage a household stretched by the inclusion of a worshiping community. . . . The relationship between mistress and household slaves was frequently a close one; literary evidence reveals that much of a slave's

---

arguments, see Aída Besançon Spencer, *Beyond the Curse: Women Called to Ministry* (Grand Rapids: Baker, 1985), ch. 4.

12. Francisco Lozada Jr., *Toward a Latino/a Biblical Interpretation,* Resources for Biblical Study 91 (Atlanta: Society of Biblical Literature, 2017), 1–3.

13. Aída Besançon Spencer, "My Journey as a Latin American Feminist New Testament Scholar," in *Feminist New Testament Studies: Global and Future Perspectives,* ed. Kathleen O'Brien Wicker, Althea Spencer Miller, and Musa W. Dube (New York: Palgrave Macmillan, 2005), 118–26.

14. E.g., Aída Besançon Spencer, "2 Corinthians: An Egalitarian Ideology for the Latinx Church," in *Latinx Perspectives on the New Testament,* ed. Osvaldo D. Vena and Leticia A. Guardiola-Sáenz (Lanham, MD: Lexington/Fortress, 2022), 184–85.

15. Catherine Clark Kroeger and Mary J. Evans, eds., *The IVP Women's Bible Commentary* (Downers Grove, IL: InterVarsity Press, 2002), xiii.

treatment lay in the hands of the mistress."[16] This background information helps us understand why Apphia, as well as Philemon, was included in the letterhead.

K. K. Yeo advocates multicultural readings of the Bible as the fulfillment of the law to love one's neighbors and as part of the "eschatological drive/vision" of the global church to be multicultural. Global "multicultural reading is neither a luxury nor an option." The mission of the global church is to "empower and mobilize the local churches in the matrix of diversity in unity." We are all "uniquely gifted" by God. "Multicultural reading of the biblical text is geared toward a global biblical interpretation whose theological ethics is that of loving one's neighbor."[17]

Therefore, because of these difficulties, I posited a second basic theory for quoting secondary references that we might term "dialogue" to enhance each as part of a community of scholars. All biblical interpreters should be lovers of God's Word who are pooling our resources. Thus, before we confirm our own interpretation, we would do well to compare it with other interpreters. In this way, we quote secondary sources *not* to summon authorities but to enrich our own interpretation. This expanded viewpoint encourages original interpretation and thought. It is the primary one that I use. I also try to treat others with respect, even when I disagree. That is not easy, because reducing the views of those with whom we disagree is an easy and helpful ploy to defend our own view. But shouldn't we attempt to create an encouraging and supportive discussion in our writings, as we, hopefully, do in our teachings? A seminary colleague suggested wisely that we should write book reviews that could be sent to the authors themselves, because they are peers and we may know them personally someday. Therefore, we need to know an author's writings and position so well that we could ask a question we did not yet read and answer it as the author would. We should try to be sympathetic to contemporary authors even as we try to be sympathetic to Bible authors. Gordon Fee has reminded us, "Before you can say, 'I disagree,' you must be able to say, 'I understand.' It is axiomatic that before you level criticism you should be able to state an author's position in terms that he or she would find acceptable."[18]

Yet God is a God of grace *and* truth. Although we are kind, we must also be truthful. Secondary sources may have different theological perspectives (whether global or provincial) or may be incorrect, misinformed, inconsistent, or incomplete. I have noticed typographical errors copied from one commentary to another to another. "Speaking the truth in love" is a way to "grow up in every way into him who is the head, into Christ" (Eph. 4:15 NRSV).

---

16. Kristen Plinke Bentley, "Philemon, Commentary," in *The IVP Women's Bible Commentary*, ed. Catherine Clark Kroeger and Mary J. Evans (Downers Grove, IL: InterVarsity Press, 2002), 759–62.

17. K. K. Yeo, "Response: Multicultural Readings; A Biblical Warrant and an Eschatological Vision," in *Global Voices: Reading the Bible in the Majority World*, ed. Craig S. Keener and M. Daniel Carroll R. (Peabody, MA: Hendrickson, 2013), 31, 35–36.

18. Fee, *New Testament Exegesis*, 33.

248 | Application and Completion of Study

Our scholarly enterprises should also work on such a style of communication (truth in love) instead of a style of communication that disparages (truth in disrespect) or one that simply agrees (love without truth).

How might we then communicate to the guild? Writing a "summary of interpretations" (see the appendix in this chapter) is one way to appeal to a professor and audience who insist on the documentation theory of quotations. Do your original work first, and then add an introduction about secondary references.

What do you do when writing for a professor or an audience that does not treat the Bible as reliable? Again, present your and their interpretations fully and fairly. Maybe begin with your opponent's basis of authority and show how that might lead to his or her biblical view. Or cite those in the opponent's camp, ferreting out points of agreement in such a way as to present your own view. Or you might only choose texts to study that do not entail points of major disagreement with your professor.

Do not use coded conservative language when communicating with theological liberals. Instead, use words acceptable to your opponent. Rephrase your concept in their words. Find points of agreement, but never lose sight of or compromise the truth you are sharing. Never be ashamed of God. If you are ashamed of God, God will be ashamed of you (Mark 8:34–38; Luke 9:23–26). I try to remember that my primary goal is to be commended by God as a faithful servant (2 Cor. 10:18). What good is it if we are commended by narrow-minded humans, powerful in a small sphere, but not commended by the all-powerful, loving God, ruling over the whole universe? And keep in mind that, to our surprise, our "opponent" may be won over to our side! Or if our view is ridiculed or rejected, at least we may feel God's affirmation even now (as Stephen did; see Acts 7:55–56).

PROCEDURES FOR FINDING SECONDARY REFERENCES[19]

We have thought about the theory behind quotations. But what procedure do I recommend? I favor the four-step process of find, decide, think, and write, as shown in the opening outline of this chapter. The work begins with *finding* articles, essays, and books on one aspect of the text. Begin with a few critical commentaries to see what problems the authors discuss. Choose one issue to

---

19. Primary literature or evidence or source material is literature on a particular topic or person under study. It is original, first in importance, being direct evidence and therefore the most reliable. Secondary literature or evidence or source material is literature that is at least one step removed from the particular topic or person under study and therefore derivative, indirect evidence, and interpretation or evaluation of a topic and therefore less reliable. How one defines *primary* or *secondary* may vary, depending on one's view of the Bible. For me, what is canonical is fully reliable and therefore "primary evidence." Writings of the first century are in the same historical-cultural milieu (e.g., Josephus) and are primary literature but not necessarily as reliable as the Bible.

elaborate. For instance, in the summary essay on Philemon 4–6 (in the appendices to this chapter), I found two exegetical problems: (1) Why does "love" precede "faith" in verse 5, and (2) what is the meaning of *koinōnia* in verse 6? I chose to discuss the first issue. Better to do comprehensive work on a smaller topic than superficial work on many topics.

List of Commentary Series

Once you narrow your topic (*decide*) you can find more commentaries on that topic. If you are near a seminary library, begin in the reference section, where the librarian has already isolated the most important references. For exegetical studies, you are looking for historical-grammatical series.[20] There are many excellent series. The following is a sampling of various sources I have used.

Baker Exegetical Commentary on the New Testament (BECNT)
Cornerstone Biblical Commentary
Eerdmans Critical Commentary (ECC)
Evangelical Exegetical Commentary
International Critical Commentary (ICC)
IVP New Testament Commentary Series
Kregel Exegetical Library
New American Commentary (NAC)
New Covenant Commentary Series (NCCS)
New International Biblical Commentary on the New Testament (NIBCNT)
New International Commentary on the New Testament (NICNT)
New International Greek Testament Commentary (NIGTC)
Socio-Rhetorical Commentary
Two Horizons New Testament Commentary
Tyndale New Testament Commentaries (TNTC)
Word Biblical Commentary (WBC)
Zondervan Exegetical Commentary on the New Testament (ZECNT)
Zondervan Commentary

Finding articles is important to show you are up to date. Sometimes articles precede books. The electronic card catalog in a seminary library often includes the topic and the article itself. Resources are *New Testament Abstracts*, *ATLA* and *ATLAS* (American Theological Library Association, formerly Religion Index One and Two), *Christian Periodical Index*, *Elenchus*

---

20. For the exegetical process, I am not including fine homiletical, theological, devotional, application-oriented, or other commentaries (e.g., People's Bible Commentary). For further lists, see Gorman, *Elements of Biblical Exegesis*, 241–50; Fee, *New Testament Exegesis*, 173–74.

250 | Application and Completion of Study

Bibliographicus Biblicus, Dissertation Abstracts, and *Internationale Bibliographie der Zeitschriftenliteratur (IBZ).*[21]

Do not simply list all your references, citing a line from each, but *think* about which articles or books are pivotal. Which have a unique interpretation? What presuppositions does an author assume that affect the final conclusion? Categorize the different viewpoints and their reasons on the issue you are studying. Indicate where you agree and disagree and why. Be clear. Where does your interpretation fit? Do you have additional reasons for your view? Do you need to answer any problems raised against your view by others? In your summary of interpretations paper, *write* a summary of the different interpretations and cite an example for each view (footnoting the other views). Conclude with how your interpretation relates to those of others, and briefly answer criticisms of your view. Do you bring any new insights?

Many scholarly articles begin with or footnote a summary of past interpretations.[22] Type your bibliography in the correct format.[23] After looking at a sampling of secondary references, you can also add helpful comments to your paper. (Be careful that you don't add errors from the commentaries!) Strengthen your reasons for your conclusions where others disagree. And while you are looking at these commentaries, make a separate list of potential commentaries you may purchase for your personal library. Some commentaries are especially geared to help you understand the Bible in places where the text is difficult to understand. Other commentaries give you depth of interpretation, attention to detail that matters. In both cases, you should be aware of the basic assumptions of the author. Check critical and hard-to-understand Bible passages and issues, such as historical background (e.g., who the author is and when the letter was written). I found it helpful to pick one commentary series and supplement it with my favorite individual volumes for my own library. The ultimate value of a commentary is finding one written by someone you have come to trust and with whom you can compare your own

---

21. Articles published before 1957 may be found in Bruce M. Metzger, *Index to Periodical Literature on the Apostle Paul,* 2nd ed., New Testament Tools and Studies 1 (Leiden: Brill, 1970), and articles published before 1961 may be found in Bruce M. Metzger, *Index to Periodical Literature on Christ and the Gospels,* New Testament Tools and Studies 6 (Leiden: Brill, 1966).

22. E.g., Aída Besançon Spencer, "The Denial of the Good News and the Ending of Mark," *Bulletin for Biblical Research* 17, no. 2 (2007): 269–83.

23. You must use an approved style manual, such as Billie Jean Collins et al., *The SBL Handbook of Style,* 2nd ed. (Atlanta: SBL Press, 2014); Carole Slade and Robert Perrin, *Form and Style: Research Papers, Reports, Theses,* 13th ed. (Belmont, CA: Wadsworth, 2007); Kate L. Turabian et al., *Manual for Writers of Term Papers, Theses, and Dissertations,* 9th ed. (Chicago: University of Chicago Press, 2018); or *The Chicago Manual of Style,* 17th ed. (Chicago: University of Chicago Press, 2017). The *SBL Handbook of Style's* first edition is available free online: https://papyrusmagicalhandbook.files. wordpress.com/2016/04/the-sbl-handbook-of-stylesblhs.pdf (accessed June 21, 2023). Such earlier editions of style manuals are cheaper, but you should only use them if they are acceptable to your reader(s).

Find Other Interpretations of Text | 251

analysis of the primary data, your interpretation of Scripture, and your use of Jewish and Greco-Roman materials. Come to commentaries only *after* you have done your own work with questions on puzzling passages, to test your own conclusions and to be alerted to questions or interpretations or data you passed over. A. J. Gordon, in his final thoughts in 1895, summarizes well the priorities in the exegetical process:

> Let us reverence our teachers and seek to know how much the Lord hath taught us through them, let the words of commentators, who have prayed and poured over God's holy word to search out precious ore for us, be honored for all the wealth that they have brought to us, knowing that only *"with all saints,"* can we "comprehend what is the breadth and length and depth and height" of the love of Christ which passeth knowledge. Nevertheless, . . . while the vendors of learning are crying "Lo here," and "Lo there," the Good Shepherd speaks saying: "My sheep hear my voice"; and he is still in the fold to care for his own, to lead them into green pastures where the freshest and sweetest truth is found; to make them lie down by still waters in which they may see his own blessed face reflected. Only let not the sheep hear the voice of strangers who know not the truth: let them hear only Christ.[24]

HOW TO AVOID COMMON ERRORS[25]

1. Use others' interpretations as dialogue partners, not as slave masters. Do not let yourself become a slave to others' viewpoints, copying everything down as if they were the words of God. After you have done your own original work, then functionally you are a peer of the commentators.
2. If you use the "dialogue" style of quotation, you do not even need to do the entire summary of interpretations for every reader. However, summarizing other viewpoints is necessary in academic journals and for some professors. Certainly for preaching, the summary of views is rarely appropriate.
3. In the summary of interpretations, you will probably present others' viewpoints before your own, but in the body of the paper clarify your view before you compare it with others' views.
4. Categorize the different views; do not simply list them.

---

24. A. J. Gordon, *How Christ Came to Church: The Pastor's Dream; A Spiritual Autobiography, with an introduction by Scott M. Gibson* (Grand Rapids: Kregel, 2010), 56–57.
25. For a summary of suggestions to prevent errors by exegetes, see also Gorman, *Elements of Biblical Exegesis,* ch. 10; A. Berkeley Mickelsen, *Interpreting the Bible* (Grand Rapids: Eerdmans, 1963), ch. 19; William W. Klein, Craig L. Blomberg, and Robert L. Hubbard Jr., *Introduction to Biblical Interpretation,* 3rd ed. (Grand Rapids: Zondervan, 2017), ch. 5.

252 | Application and Completion of Study

5. Quote the Bible or primary source directly when you can find it, not simply the commentator's citation.
6. Make sure, when you quote someone, that you are aware of how it affects your own argument. Sometimes students naively quote someone who contradicts their own views or presuppositions.
7. Make sure you footnote references whose ideas or phrasing you have used. If not, you are stealing from them and can be accused of plagiarism. What value is there in stealing ideas while serving a God of truth? Even if you deceive your professor or editor, you never deceive God.
8. Use a different format for footnotes than for bibliographies. I copy and paste my footnotes into the bibliography to save time, but then I adapt them to the format of the bibliography. Be sure your footnotes are all in the same format. Do not use both author-date (footnote-bibliography) and MLA formats. Follow the style format used by your school or your prospective journal.
9. Your own view should take precedence in your essay. Do not quote many commentators simply for the sake of quantity of references. Quality of thought is more important than quantity by itself.
10. Include a few journal articles even if they take longer to find.
11. Cite dictionary, essay, and encyclopedia articles by the name of the writer of the article, not the name of the editors. Editors are included in the reference, but they did not write the article or chapter and should not get credit for what they did not write.
12. Italicize book titles and names of journals. If you abbreviate, explain the abbreviation the first time it is introduced.
13. Remember to double-check the wording of any quotation and of the bibliographic data. Check onscreen and also the printed page. I have often found typographical errors in the printed pages even after checking my writing on the monitor.

APPENDICES

Summary of Interpretations Paper of Philemon 4–6
Even though a number of commentators consider verses 4–7, and especially verse 6 the most difficult part of the Letter to Philemon,[1] surprisingly almost all commentators are agreed that thankfulness and request are naturally combined[2] and that the point of Paul's request is for Philemon to actualize his faith in regard to Onesimus.[3] Commentators differ on two aspects of the sentence. First, they find the sequence of topics unusual in verse 5: love . . . faith . . . Jesus . . . saints. Normally, faith would precede love since love appears to be a fruit of faith (e.g. Eph. 1:15; Col. 1:4.) Second, commentators differ somewhat on the interpretation of *koinōnia*. In this brief essay, we will look in more depth at the first point of disagreement.

Find Other Interpretations of Text | 253

> *Show where people disagree.*
>
> *Only one issue needs to be explained.*

Because "love" appears first as object of the participle "hearing," "love" is emphasized. Commentators group around three basic views: (1) "Love" refers to the saints and "faith" to Jesus (v. 5). This would be a chiastic sequence of ABBA (love [A], faith [B], Jesus [B], saints [A]).[4] (2) "Faith" refers both to Jesus and to the saints.[5] (3) Love and faith are intimately knit together as a unity.[6] This view is close to view #2.

> *Different interpretations are clearly grouped.*

My own interpretation would fall under #2. Because of the singular feminine relative pronoun (*hen*), verse 5b ("which you have toward the Lord Jesus and toward all the saints") appears all to refer back to "faith," not to both faith and love. Thus, "faith" seems to be an attribute that governs Philemon's relationship toward both Jesus *and* the saints. In that sense, "the love and the faith" functions like hendiadys as "the faithful love." This point is amplified in verse 6 because there it is Philemon's "faith," not "love," which needs to be shared. Thus, the argument about the lack of parallel presentation in verse 5 misses the request in v.6.

> *Present all views fairly.*
>
> *Other views are compared to writer's.*
>
> *Support for own view is given.*
>
> *If the exegesis paper were rewritten for a journal article, I would develop the idea that "faith" refers both to Jesus and to believers since this view is not common today.*
>
> *Check style manual for how to abbreviate numbers. Different professors have different criteria as to how far back in history one should go to seek interpretations. I think that when it comes to biblical interpretation, any worthwhile view is worthy of mention. But it is true that different centuries have different issues of concern.*

Endnotes

1   Victor A. Bartling, in H. Armin Moellering and Victor A. Bartling. *1 Timothy, 2 Timothy, Titus, Philemon*. Concordia Commentary. (Saint Louis: Concordia,

254 | Application and Completion of Study

1970), 252, 255; John Calvin, *Calvin's Commentaries: Ephesians-Jude* (Wilmington: Assoc. Publishers, n.d), 2293; Andrew D. Clarke, "'Refresh the Hearts of the Saints': A Unique Pauline Context?", *Tyndale Bulletin* 47, no. 2 (1996): 295; William Barclay, *The Letters to Timothy, Titus and Philemon*, Daily Study Bible Series (Philadelphia: Westminster, 1975), 278; Markus Barth and Helmut Blanke, *The Letter to Philemon*, Eerdmans Critical Commentary (Grand Rapids: Eerdmans, 2000), 280–81; Herbert M. Carson, *The Epistles of Paul to the Colossians and Philemon*, Tyndale New Testament Commentaries (Grand Rapids: Eerdmans, 1960), 105; William Hendrickson, *Exposition of Colossians and Philemon*. New Testament Commentary. (Grand Rapids: Baker, 1964), 213–214; Alexander Maclaren, *The Epistles of St. Paul to the Colossians and Philemon* (New York: Hodder & Stoughton, n.d.), 433; Richard R. Melick Jr., *The New American Commentary 32: Philippians, Colossians, Philemon* (Nashville: Broadman, 1991), 353; Arthur G. Patzia, *Ephesians, Colossians, Philemon*, New International Biblical Commentary (Peabody: Hendrickson, 1990), 109; Michael R. Weed, *The Letters of Paul to the Ephesians, the Colossians, and Philemon*, Living Word Commentary (Austin: Sweet, 1971), 16. Douglas J. Moo, *The Letters to the Colossians and to Philemon*, The Pillar New Testament Commentary (Grand Rapids: Eerdmans, 2008), 389.

2   Calvin, *Ephesians*, 2292; Bartling, *Concordia*, 252; Edward Lohse, *Colossians and Philemon*, Hermeneia, ed. H. Koester, trans. W. Poehlmann and R. Karris (Philadelphia: Fortress, 1971), 192–3; Jac. J. Muller, *The Epistles of Paul to the Philippians and to Philemon*, New International Commentary on the New Testament (Grand Rapids: Eerdmans, 1955), 176; Lewis B. Radford, *The Epistle to the Colossians and the Epistle to Philemon*, Westminster Commentaries (London: Methuen, 1930), 350.

3   Calvin, *Ephesians*, 2293; Lohse, *Colossians*, 194–95; Radford, *Colossians*, 351; Marvin Vincent, *A Critical and Exegetical Commentary on the Epistles to the Philippians and to Philemon*, The International Critical Commentary (Edinburgh: T&T Clark, 1897), 180; Andrew Wedson, "The Pragmatics of Politeness and Pauline Epistolography: A Case Study of the Letter to Philemon," *Journal for the Study of the New Testament* 48 (1992): 114.

4   In the sixth century some manuscripts varied the text to create a parallel structure (D, p61, 323). Bartling, *Concordia*, 254; Adam Copenhaver and Jeffrey D. Arthurs, *Colossians and Philemon*, Kerux Commentaries (Grand Rapids: Kregel, 2022), 281; Hendrickson, *Colossians*, 213; Lohse, *Colossians*, 193; J. B. Lightfoot, *Saint Paul's Epistles to the Colossians and to Philemon* (Grand Rapids: Zondervan, 1959), 334; Maclaren, *Colossians*, 435–6, 438; Ralph P. Martin, *Colossians and Philemon*, New Century Bible (Greenwood, SC: Attic, 1978), 160–61. Scot McKnight, *The Letter to Philemon*, The New International Commentary on the New Testament (Grand Rapids: Eerdmans, 2017), 63, 66–69; Melick, *Philippians*, 352–53; Moo, *Colossians and Philemon*, 387–89; John G. Nordling, *Philemon*, Concordia Commentary

(Saint Louis: Concordia, 2004), 198–203; David W. Pao, *Zondervan Exegetical Commentary on the New Testament,* Zondervan Exegetical Commentary Series: New Testament (Grand Rapids: Zondervan, 2012), 368–69; Patzia, *Ephesians,* 108–9; Weed, *Ephesians,* 16.

5   G. K. Beale, *Colossians and Philemon,* Baker Exegetical Commentary on the New Testament (Grand Rapids: Baker Academic, 2019), 384–87; Walter Kelly Firminger, *The Epistles of St. Paul the Apostle to the Colossians and to Philemon,* Indian Church Commentaries (London: SPCK, 1921), 262; Crete Gray, *The Epistles of St. Paul to the Colossians and Philemon,* Lutterworth Commentary (London: Lutterworth, 1948), 85–6; A.R.C. Leaney, *The Epistles to Timothy, Titus and Philemon,* Torch Bible Commentaries (London: SCM, 1960), 139; Radford, *Colossians,* 350. Marianne Meye Thompson, *Colossians and Philemon,* The Two Horizons New Testament Commentary (Grand Rapids: Eerdmans, 2005), 213; Stephen E. Young, *Our Brother Beloved: Purpose and Community in Paul's Letter to Philemon* (Waco: Baylor University Press, 2021), 106.

6   Carson, *Colossians,* 105–6; Barth and Blanke even suggest a hendiadys, *Philemon,* 272; James D. G. Dunn, *The Epistles to the Colossians and to Philemon,* New International Greek Testament Commentary (Grand Rapids: Eerdmans, 1996), 317. Brian Wintle and Bruce Nicholls allow for both possibilities (*Colossians and Philemon,* Asia Bible Commentary Series (Cumbria, CA: Langham Global Library, 2019), 189, while McKnight, *Philemon,* 66, claims "The consensus sees here a chiasm."

Bibliography

Barclay, William. *The Letters to Timothy, Titus, and Philemon.* Daily Study Bible Series. Philadelphia: Westminster, 1975.

Barth, Markus, and Helmut Blanke. *The Letter to Philemon.* Eerdmans Critical Commentary. Grand Rapids: Eerdmans, 2000.

Beale, G. K. *Colossians and Philemon,* Baker Exegetical Commentary on the New Testament Grand Rapids: Baker Academic, 2019.

Calvin, John. *Calvin's Commentaries: Ephesians–Jude.* Wilmington, DE: Assoc. Publishers, n.d.

Carson, Herbert M. *The Epistles of Paul to the Colossians and Philemon.* Tyndale New Testament Commentaries. Grand Rapids: Eerdmans, 1960.

Clarke, Andrew D. "'Refresh the Hearts of the Saints': A Unique Pauline Context?" *Tyndale Bulletin* 47.2 (1996): 277–300.

Copenhaver, Adam, and Jeffrey D. Arthurs. *Colossians and Philemon.* Kerux Commentaries. Grand Rapids: Kregel, 2022.

Dunn, James D. G. *The Epistles to the Colossians and to Philemon.* New International Greek Testament Commentary. Grand Rapids: Eerdmans, 1996.

Firminger, Walter Kelly. *The Epistles of St. Paul the Apostle to the Colossians and to Philemon.* Indian Church Commentaries. London: Society for Promoting Christian Knowledge, 1921.

256 | Application and Completion of Study

Gray, Crete. *The Epistles of St. Paul to the Colossians and Philemon*. Lutterworth Commentary. London: Lutterworth, 1948.

Hendrickson, William. *New Testament Commentary: Exposition of Colossians and Philemon*. Grand Rapids: Baker, 1964.

Leaney, A. R. C. *The Epistles to Timothy, Titus and Philemon*. Torch Bible Commentaries. London: SCM, 1960.

Lightfoot, J. B. *Saint Paul's Epistles to the Colossians and to Philemon*. Grand Rapids: Zondervan, 1959.

Lohse, Edward. *Colossians and Philemon*. Hermeneia. Edited by H. Koester. Translated by W. Poehlmann and R. Karris. Philadelphia: Fortress, 1971.

Maclaren, Alexander. *The Epistles of St. Paul to the Colossians and Philemon*. New York: Hodder & Stoughton, n.d.

Martin, Ralph P. *Colossians and Philemon*. New Century Bible. Greenwood, SC: Attic, 1978.

McKnight, Scot. *The Letter to Philemon*. The New International Commentary on the New Testament. Grand Rapids: Eerdmans, 2017.

Melick, Richard R., Jr. *Philippians, Colossians, Philemon*. The New American Commentary 32. Nashville: Broadman, 1991.

Moellering, H. Armin, and Victor A. Bartling. *1 Timothy, 2 Timothy, Titus, Philemon*. Concordia Commentary. Saint Louis: Concordia, 1970.

Moo, Douglas J. *The Letters to the Colossians and to Philemon*. The Pillar New Testament Commentary. Grand Rapids: Eerdmans, 2008.

Muller, Jac. J. *The Epistles of Paul to the Philippians and to Philemon*. New International Commentary on the New Testament. Grand Rapids: Eerdmans, 1955.

Nordling, John G. *Philemon*. Concordia Commentary. Saint Louis: Concordia, 2004.

Pao, David W. *Zondervan Exegetical Commentary on the New Testament*. Zondervan Exegetical Commentary Series: New Testament. Grand Rapids: Zondervan, 2012.

Patzia, Arthur G. *Ephesians, Colossians, Philemon*. New International Biblical Commentary. Peabody: Hendrickson, 1990.

Radford, Lewis B. *The Epistle to the Colossians and the Epistle to Philemon*. Westminster Commentaries. London: Methuen, 1930.

Thompson, Alan J. *Colossians and Philemon*. Tyndale New Testament Commentaries. Downers Grove: InterVarsity, 2022.

Thompson, Marianne Meye. *Colossians and Philemon*. The Two Horizons New Testament Commentary. Grand Rapids: Eerdmans, 2005.

Vincent, Marvin. *A Critical and Exegetical Commentary on the Epistles to the Philippians and to Philemon*. International Critical Commentary. Edinburgh: T&T Clark, 1897.

Weed, Michael R. *The Letters of Paul to the Ephesians, the Colossians, and Philemon*. Living Word Commentary. Austin, TX: Sweet, 1971.

Wilson, Andrew. "The Pragmatics of Politeness and Pauline Epistolography: A Case Study of the Letter to Philemon." *Journal for the Study of the New Testament* 48 (1992): 107–19.

Wintle, Brian, and Bruce Nicholls. *Colossians and Philemon*. Asia Bible Commentary Series. Cumbria, CA: Langham Global Library, 2019.

Young, Stephen E. *Our Brother Beloved: Purpose and Community in Paul's Letter to Philemon*. Waco: Baylor University Press, 2021.

A cover sheet I employ for this topic follows.

SUMMARY OF INTERPRETATIONS COVER SHEET

Exegesis of _____ To: _____
                                [student's name]

Assignment: Summary of Interpretations
Date: _____Box/email: _____
From: _____
       [professor's name]   Grade: _____

I. The following items are rated according to the following symbols:
I = Inadequate   A = Adequate   G = Good   S = superior

RESEARCH METHODOLOGY:

Comprehensive/exhaustive ....I A G S

Accurate..I A G S

Thoughtful..I A G S

Insightful ....I A G S

Conclusions proved ....I A G S

Original (primary references read)...................................I A G S

Clarity in defining issues..I A G S

Categorized different views (compared and contrasted) I A G S

COMPLETENESS:

Other references compared to own view ....I A G S

References (quantity)...I A G S

Reference awareness (variety, pivotal)...............................I A G S

WRITTEN PRESENTATION:

Well-organized paper...I A G S

Literary style: clear and succinct ....I A G S

Spelling and grammar correct ....I A G S

Legible..I A G S

II. The following items need attention if checked:

☐ The paper needs to be a unified essay on the meaning of the text rather than a series of research notes.
☐ The paper needs balance; do not give too much space to a less significant item but too little space to a major item.
☐ The paper is too long.
☐ The pages should be numbered consecutively throughout.
☐ Cite dictionary and encyclopedia articles by the author and title of the article.
☐ Cite primary sources by chapter and paragraph number (not by page number).
☐ Cite Greek words out of context in their lexical entry form.
☐ Excessive use of the first and/or second person for a formal paper.
☐ Excessive use of passive verbs and "it is" without a clear antecedent.
☐ Use a consistent and/or correct form in footnotes, bibliography, and primary citations.

Comments:

CONCLUSION

In the forty-five years I have been teaching as of the time this book was published, I have developed at least seventy-two explanatory tables, outlines, charts, and sample papers for my students (and myself). These are contained in this book. Why did I bother? I have loved and will continue to love to do exegesis—in other words, to interpret the Bible—because no matter how long I study, I always find something new, something true, and something worthwhile and wholesome. As the prophet Isaiah recorded, "The grass withers and the flowers fall, but the word of our God endures forever" (40:8 NIV). People are like beautiful flowers that eventually fall, but God's Word never falls. God's Word, like God, is everlasting, trustworthy, deep, and rich in meaning. These have been worthwhile years. To help others delve into God's Word is such a valuable goal.

And from time to time, I remember my biblical heroine, the prophet Huldah, who stood before the rulers of her day prepared to interpret to them the meaning of God's Word for their times so they could obey it (2 Kings 22). The book of Deuteronomy was found, and it was read, but that was not enough. Huldah was needed to interpret it. And she was ready.

Much of interpretation is common sense. Of course we must understand a word in its paragraph, a paragraph in its chapter, a chapter in its book, and a book or letter in its historical and cultural times. Context determines meaning.

"Context" is an interweaving cloth. Our fabric begins at the literary level: a book or letter. Our text is set in that cloth. We must be sure we have the true text (not a patch that has been added later), understand with what kind of material we are dealing, find the appropriate thread, enjoy its pattern, be enriched with the history behind its making, begin to wear that attire ourselves, and compare our finished product with those of others. For years, preachers, teachers, translators, missionaries, and students of the New Testament have been assuring me that this methodology has been helpful and worthwhile for them.

Now the time has come for these tables, outlines, charts, sample papers, and explanations to travel everywhere to assist others in their own study of God's Word so that they may apply it in their own lives. My goal is to help others dwell on the Bible with the intent of understanding more deeply and more accurately what God has communicated so as to obey God more accurately.

Although this material can be used by those who read the New Testament in its own ancient Koine Greek, many of these steps can also be used by those who read the New Testament in translation. If even the Greek letters are learned, many tools for interpretation become available.

May this book on the exegetical process be a tool for all its readers to present themselves approved to God, workers who do not need to be ashamed, rightly handling God's truthful word (2 Tim. 2:15) as a prerequisite to having more godly thoughts, words, and actions.

BIBLIOGRAPHY

Aland, Barbara, Kurt Aland, Johannes Karavidopoulos, Carlo M. Martini, and Bruce Metzger, eds. *The Greek New Testament.* 5th rev. ed. New York: United Bible Societies, 2014.

Aland, Barbara, Kurt Aland, Johannes Karavidopoulos, Carlo M. Martini, and Bruce Metzger, eds. *Novum Testamentum Graece.* 28th ed. Stuttgart: Deutsche Bibelgesellschaft, 2012.

Aland, Kurt, and Barbara Aland. *The Text of the New Testament: An Introduction to the Critical Editions and to the Theory and Practice of Modern Textual Criticism.* Rev. ed. Grand Rapids: Eerdmans, 1989.

Allenbach, J., A. Benoit, D. A. Bertrand, A. Hanriot-Coustet, P. Maraval, A. Pautler, and P. Prigent. *Biblia Patristica: Index des Citation et Allusions Bibliques dans la Litteratur Patristique.* 6 vols. Paris: Recherche Scientifique, 1975.

Anstey, Martin. *How to Understand the Bible.* New York: Revell, 1916.

The Apostolic Fathers. Edited and translated by Bart D. Ehrman. 2 vols. Loeb Classical Library 24–25. Cambridge, MA: Harvard University Press, 2003.

The Apostolic Fathers. Translated by Kirsopp Lake. 2 vols. Loeb Classical Library. New York: Macmillan, 1912–1913.

The Apostolic Fathers: Greek Texts and English Translations. Edited and translated by Michael W. Holmes. 3rd ed. Grand Rapids: Baker, 2007.

Aristotle. *Art of Rhetoric.* Translated by J. H. Freese. Revised by Gisela Striker. Loeb Classical Library 193. Cambridge: Harvard University Press, 2020.

Aristotle. *Politics.* Translated by H. Rackham. Cambridge: Harvard University Press, 1932.

Aristotle, Longinus, Demetrius. Poetics, On the Sublime, On Style. Translated by Stephen Halliwell, W. Hamilton Fyfe, Doreen C. Innes, and Rhys Roberts. Revised by Donald A. Russell. Loeb Classical Library 199. Cambridge: Harvard University Press, 1995.

Athanasius. *The Incarnation of the Word of God.* New York: Macmillan, 1946.

Barclay, William. *The Letters to Timothy, Titus, and Philemon.* Daily Study Bible Series. Philadelphia: Westminster, 1975.

Barrett, C. K. *The New Testament Background: Selected Documents.* New York: Harper & Row, 1961.

Barth, Markus, and Helmut Blanke. *The Letter to Philemon.* Eerdmans Critical Commentary. Grand Rapids: Eerdmans, 2000.

Bauer, Walter, William F. Arndt, and F. Wilbur Gingrich, eds. *A Greek-English Lexicon of the New Testament and Other Early Christian Literature.* 1st ed. Chicago: University of Chicago Press, 1957.

Bauer, Walter, Frederick William Danker, W. F. Arndt, and F. W. Gingrich, eds. *A Greek-English Lexicon of the New Testament and Other Early Christian Literature.* 3rd ed. Chicago: University of Chicago Press, 2000.

Beale, G. K. *Colossians and Philemon.* Baker Exegetical Commentary on the New Testament. Grand Rapids: Baker Academic, 2019.

Beekman, John, and John Callow. *Translating the Word of God with Scripture and Topical Indexes.* Grand Rapids: Zondervan, 1974.

Beekman, John, John C. Callow, and Michael F. Kopesec. *The Semantic Structure of Written Communication.* 5th ed. Dallas: Summer Institute of Linguistics, 1981.

Bentley, Kristen Plinke. "Philemon, Commentary." In *The IVP Women's Bible Commentary,* edited by Catherine Clark Kroeger and Mary J. Evans, 759–62. Downers Grove, IL: InterVarsity Press, 2002.

Berkowitz, Luci, Karl A. Squitier, and William A. Johnson. *Thesaurus Linguae Graecae Canon of Greek Authors and Works.* 3rd ed. New York: Oxford University Press, 1990.

Black, David Alan, with Katharine Barnwell and Stephen Levinsohn, eds. *Linguistics and New Testament Interpretation: Essays on Discourse Analysis.* Nashville: Broadman, 1992.

Blass, F., A. Debrunner, and Robert W. Funk. *A Greek Grammar of the New Testament and Other Early Christian Literature.* Chicago: University of Chicago Press, 1961.

Blomberg, Craig L. *Interpreting the Parables.* Downers Grove, IL: InterVarsity Press, 1990.

Blomberg, Craig L., with Jennifer Foutz Markley. *A Handbook of New Testament Exegesis.* Grand Rapids: Baker, 2010.

Borgen, Peter, Kåre Fuglseth, and Roald Skarsten. *The Philo Index: A Complete Greek Word Index to the Writings of Philo of Alexandria.* Grand Rapids: Eerdmans, 2000.

Bowens, Lisa M. *African American Readings of Paul: Reception, Resistance, and Transformation.* Grand Rapids: Eerdmans, 2020.

Brenton, Lancelot C. L. *The Septuagint: Greek and English.* Grand Rapids: Zondervan, 1970.

Bromiley, G. W., ed. *International Standard Bible Encyclopedia.* 4 vols. Grand Rapids: Eerdmans, 1988.

Brown, A. Philip, II, and Bryan W. Smith. *A Reader's Hebrew Bible.* Grand Rapids: Zondervan, 2008.

Brown, Robert K., Philip Wesley Comfort, and J. D. Douglas. *The New Greek-English Interlinear New Testament: A New Interlinear Translation of the Greek New Testament.* 3rd ed. Wheaton, IL: Tyndale House, 1990.

Bullinger, E. W. *Figures of Speech Used in the Bible.* 1898. Reprint, Grand Rapids: Baker, 1968.

Burer, Michael H., and Jeffrey E. Miller. *A New Reader's Lexicon of the Greek New Testament.* Grand Rapids: Kregel, 2008.

Caird, George B. *The Language and Imagery of the Bible*. London: Duckworth, 1980.

Callahan, Allen Dwight. "Paul's Epistle to Philemon: Toward an Alternative *Argumentum.*" *Harvard Theological Review* 86, no. 4 (October 1993): 357–76.

Calvin, John. *Calvin's Commentaries: Ephesians–Jude.* Wilmington, DE: Assoc. Publishers, n.d.

Caragounis, Chrys C. *The Development of Greek and the New Testament: Morphology, Syntax, Phonology, and Textual Transmission.* Grand Rapids: Baker Academic, 2006.

Carson, Herbert M. *The Epistles of Paul to the Colossians and Philemon.* Tyndale New Testament Commentaries. Grand Rapids: Eerdmans, 1960.

Chapman, David W., and Andreas J. Köstenberger. "Jewish Intertestamental and Early Rabbinic Literature: An Annotated Bibliographic Resource Updated (Part 1)." *Journal of the Evangelical Theological Society* 55, no. 2 (June 2012): 235–72.

———. "Jewish Intertestamental and Early Rabbinic Literature: An Annotated Bibliographic Resource Updated (Part 2)." *Journal of the Evangelical Theological Society* 55, no. 3 (September 2012): 457–88.

Charles, R. H. *The Apocrypha and Pseudepigrapha of the Old Testament in English.* 2 vols. Oxford: Clarendon, 1913.

Charlesworth, James H., ed. *The Old Testament Pseudepigrapha.* 2 vols. Garden City, NY: Doubleday, 1985.

Charlesworth, James H., et al., eds. *Graphic Concordance to the Dead Sea Scrolls.* Louisville: Westminster John Knox, 1991.

The Chicago Manual of Style. 17th ed. Chicago: University of Chicago Press, 2017.

Clarke, Andrew D. "'Refresh the Hearts of the Saints': A Unique Pauline Context?" *Tyndale Bulletin* 47, no. 2 (1996): 277–300.

Collins, Billie Jean, et al. *The SBL Handbook of Style.* 2nd ed. Atlanta: SBL Press, 2014.

Comfort, Philip Wesley. *Early Manuscripts and Modern Translations of the New Testament.* Grand Rapids: Baker, 1990.

———. *The Quest for the Original Text of the New Testament.* Grand Rapids: Baker, 1992.

Copenhaver, Adam, and Jeffrey D. Arthurs. *Colossians and Philemon.* Kerux Commentaries. Grand Rapids: Kregel, 2022.

Corbett, Edward P. J. "A Method of Analyzing Prose Style with a Demonstration Analysis of Swift's *A Modest Proposal.*" In *Style in English.* Ed. John Nest. Bobbs-Merrill Series on Composiion and Rhetoric. New York: Bobbs-Merrill, 1969.

Dana, H. E., and Julius R. Mantey. *A Manual Grammar of the Greek New Testament.* Toronto: Macmillan, 1955.

Danby, Herbert. *The Mishnah.* Oxford: Oxford University Press, 1933.

Daniel-Rops, Henri. *Daily Life in the Time of Jesus*. Translated by Patrick O'Brian. Ann Arbor, MI: Servant, 1961.

DeFazio, Jeanne C., and William David Spencer, eds. *Empowering English Language Learners: Successful Strategies of Christian Educators*. Eugene, OR: Wipf & Stock, 2018.

Deissmann, Adolf. *Light from the Ancient East: The New Testament Illustrated by Recently Discovered Texts of the Graeco-Roman World*. Translated by Lionel R. M. Strachen. Rev. ed. New York: Doran, 1927.

Delamarter, Steve. *A Scripture Index to Charlesworth's The Old Testament Pseudepigrapha*. New York: Sheffield, 2002.

Dockery, David S., Kenneth A. Mathews, and Robert B. Sloan. *Foundations for Biblical Interpretation: A Complete Library of Tools and Resources*. Nashville: B&H, 1994.

Doriani, Daniel M. *Getting the Message: A Plan for Interpreting and Applying the Bible*. Phillipsburg, NJ: P&R, 1996.

Dover, Kenneth James. *Greek Word Order*. Cambridge: Cambridge University Press, 1960.

Dunn, James D. G. *The Epistles to the Colossians and to Philemon*. New International Greek Testament Commentary. Grand Rapids: Eerdmans, 1996.

Dupont-Sommer, A. *The Essene Writings from Qumran*. Translated by G. Vermes. Gloucester: Smith, 1961.

Elwell, Walter A., and Robert W. Yarbrough, eds. *Readings from the First-Century World: Primary Sources for New Testament Study*. Grand Rapids: Baker, 1998.

Embry, Brad, Ronald Herms, and Archie T. Wright, eds. *Early Jewish Literature: An Anthology*. 2 vols. Grand Rapids: Eerdmans, 2018.

Epictetus. *The Discourses as Reported by Arrian, the Manual and Fragments*. Translated and edited by W. A. Oldfather. 2 vols. Loeb Classical Library. New York: Putnam, 1926–1928.

Epstein, Isidore, and Judah Slotki, eds. *The Babylonian Talmud*. 18 vols. London: Soncino, 1935–1990.

Erickson, Richard J. *A Beginner's Guide to New Testament Exegesis: Taking the Fear Out of Critical Method*. Downers Grove, IL: InterVarsity Press, 2005.

Eusebius. *The Ecclesiastical History*. Translated by Kirsopp Lake and J. E. L. Oulton. 2 vols. Loeb Classical Library. New York: Putnam, 1926–1932.

_____. *Eusebius: The Church History; A New Translation with Commentary*. Edited and translated by Paul L. Maier. Grand Rapids: Kregel, 1999.

_____. *The History of the Church from Christ to Constantine*. Translated by G. A. Williamson. Rev. ed. New York: Penguin, 1989.

Evans, Craig A. "How Long Were Late Antiquity Books in Use? Possible Implications for New Testament Textual Criticism." *Bulletin for Biblical Research* 25, no. 1 (2015): 23–37.

Evans, Craig A., and Stanley E. Porter, eds. *Dictionary of New Testament Backgrounds*. Downers Grove, IL: InterVarsity Press, 2000.

Fee, Gordon D. *New Testament Exegesis: A Handbook for Students and Pastors.* 3rd ed. Louisville: Westminster John Knox, 2002.

Firminger, Walter Kelly. *The Epistles of St. Paul the Apostle to the Colossians and to Philemon.* Indian Church Commentaries. London: Society for Promoting Christian Knowledge, 1921.

Fisher, Fred L. *How to Interpret the New Testament.* Philadelphia: Westminster, 1966.

Fitzmyer, Joseph A. *An Introductory Bibliography for the Study of Scripture.* Subsidia Biblica 3. Rome: Istituto Biblico, 1990.

Fowler, Robert M. Review of *The Silence of Jesus,* by James Breech. *Journal of Biblical Literature* 104, no. 3 (September 1985): 535–38.

Frank, Harry Thomas, ed. *Atlas of the Bible Lands.* 2nd ed. Maplewood, NJ: Hammond, 1984.

Gangel, Kenneth O. "Delivering Theological Education That Works." *Theological Education* 34, no. 1 (Autumn 1997): 1–9.

García Martínez, Florentino. *Dead Sea Scrolls.* Electronic ed. Leiden: Brill, 1994.

———. *The Dead Sea Scrolls Translated: The Qumran Texts in English.* 2nd ed. Grand Rapids: Eerdmans, 1996. Has a computer index.

García Martínez, Florentino, and Eibert J. C. Tigchelaar, eds. *The Dead Sea Scrolls Study Edition.* 2 vols. Grand Rapids: Eerdmans, 1997.

Gianotti, Charles R. *The New Testament and the Mishnah: A Cross-Reference Index.* Grand Rapids: Baker, 1983.

González, Justo L. *Essential Theological Terms.* Louisville: Westminster John Knox, 2005.

Goodspeed, Edgar. *Index Patristicus.* Peabody, MA: Hendrickson, 1993.

Gordon, A. J. *How Christ Came to Church: The Pastor's Dream; A Spiritual Autobiography.* With an introduction by Scott M. Gibson. Grand Rapids: Kregel, 2010.

Gorman, Michael J. *Elements of Biblical Exegesis: A Basic Guide for Students and Ministers.* 3rd ed. Grand Rapids: Baker, 2020.

Grant, Robert M. "Commentaries." In *Tools for Bible Study,* edited by Balmer H. Kelly and Donald G. Miller, 99–109. Richmond, VA: John Knox, 1956.

Gray, Crete. *The Epistles of St. Paul to the Colossians and Philemon.* Lutterworth Commentary. London: Lutterworth, 1948.

The Greek-English New Testament: UBS Fifth Revised Edition and New International Version. Grand Rapids: Zondervan, 2015.

Green, Gene. "Lexical Pragmatics and Biblical Interpretation." *Journal of the Evangelical Theological Society* 50, no. 4 (December 2007): 799–812.

Grenfell, B., and A. Hunt, eds. *Oxyrhynchus Papyri.* 18 vols. London: Egypt Exploration, 1898–1994.

Guggenheimer, Heinrich, ed. *The Jerusalem Talmud.* 22 vols. New York: de Gruyter, 2000–2020.

Guthrie, Donald. *New Testament Introduction*. 3rd ed. Downers Grove, IL: InterVarsity Press, 1974.

Hammond, N. G. L., and H. H. Scullard, eds. *The Oxford Classical Dictionary*. 2nd ed. Oxford: Clarendon, 1970.

Harrison, Everett F. *Introduction to the New Testament*. Grand Rapids: Eerdmans, 1964.

Harrison, R. K. *Introduction to the Old Testament*. Grand Rapids: Eerdmans, 1969.

Hartnett, Tim. "The Basics of Consensus Decision Making." *Consensus Facilitation*. Accessed August 26, 2023. https://www.groupfacilitation.net/Articles%20for%20Facilitators/The%20Basics%20of%20Consensus%20Decision%20Making.pdf.

Harvey, John D. *Interpreting the Pauline Letters: An Exegetical Handbook*. Handbook for New Testament Exegesis. Grand Rapids: Kregel, 2012.

Hatch, Edwin, and Henry Redpath. *A Concordance to the Septuagint*. 2 vols. Grand Rapids: Baker, 1983.

Head, Peter M. "The Date of the Magdalen Papyrus of Matthew (P. Magd. 17 = P64): A Response to C. P. Thiede." *Tyndale Bulletin* 46, no. 2 (November 1995): 251–85.

Hendrickson, William. *New Testament Commentary: Exposition of Colossians and Philemon*. Grand Rapids: Baker, 1964.

Hoebel, E. Adamson. *Anthropology: The Study of Man*. New York: McGraw-Hill, 1966.

Horsley, G. H. R., ed. *New Documents Illustrating Early Christianity: A Review of the Greek Inscriptions and Papyri*. 10 vols. North Ryde, Australia: Ancient History Qumran Documentary Research Centre, Macquarie University, 2012.

Howe, Reuel L. *The Miracle of Dialogue*. New York: Seabury, 1963.

Jacobs, Philip Walker. *A Guide to the Study of Greco-Roman and Jewish and Christian History and Literature*. Lanham, MD: University Press of America, 1994.

Josephus. *Jewish Antiquities*. Translated by Louis H. Feldman, Ralph Marcus, and H. St. J. Thackeray. 10 vols. Loeb Classical Library. Cambridge: Harvard University Press, 1930–1965.

———. *The Jewish War*. Translated by H. St. J. Thackeray, R. Marcus, A. Wikgren, and L. H. Feldman. 10 vols. Loeb Classical Library. New York: Putnam, 1926–1981.

———. *The Life. Against Apion*. Translated by H. St. J. Thackeray. Loeb Classical Library 186. Cambridge, MA: Harvard University Press, 1926.

———. *The New Complete Works of Josephus*. Translated by William Whiston. Edited by Paul L. Maier. Rev. ed. Grand Rapids: Kregel, 1999.

———. *The Works of Josephus: Complete and Unabridged*. Translated by William Whiston. Peabody, MA: Hendrickson, 1987.

Keener, Craig S. *The IVP Bible Background Commentary: New Testament*. 2nd ed. Downers Grove, IL: InterVarsity Press, 2014.

Kelly, Balmer H., and Donald G. Miller, eds. *Tools for Bible Study*. Richmond, VA: John Knox, 1956.

Kenyon, F. G. *The Text of the Greek Bible*. 3rd ed. London: Duckworth, 1975.

Kim, Matthew D., and Paul A. Hoffman. *Preaching to a Divided Nation: A Seven-Step Model for Promoting Reconciliation and Unity*. Grand Rapids: Baker Academic, 2022.

Kittel, Gerhard, and Gerhard Friedrich, eds. *Theological Dictionary of the New Testament*. Translated by Geoffrey W. Bromiley. 10 vols. Grand Rapids: Eerdmans, 1964–1976.

Klein, William W., Craig L. Blomberg, and Robert L. Hubbard Jr. *Introduction to Biblical Interpretation*. 3rd ed. Grand Rapids: Zondervan, 2017.

Kohlenberger, John R., III, ed. *The Greek New Testament: UBS4 with NRSV and NIV*. Grand Rapids: Zondervan, 1993.

——————. *The Precise Parallel New Testament*. New York: Oxford University Press, 1995.

Kohlenberger, John R., III, Edward W. Goodrick, and James A. Swanson. *The Exhaustive Concordance to the Greek New Testament*. Grand Rapids: Zondervan, 1995.

——————. *The Greek-English Concordance to the New Testament*. Grand Rapids: Zondervan, 1997.

Kohlenberger, John R., III, and James A. Swanson. *The Hebrew-English Concordance to the Old Testament*. Grand Rapids: Zondervan, 1998.

Kraft, Henricus. *Clavis Patrum Apostolicorum*. Munich: Kösel, 1964.

Kroeger, Catherine Clark, and Mary J. Evans, eds. *The IVP Women's Bible Commentary*. Downers Grove, IL: InterVarsity Press, 2002.

Kubo, Sakae. *A Reader's Greek-English Lexicon of the New Testament*. Grand Rapids: Zondervan, 1975.

Kuhatschek, Jack. *Applying the Bible*. Grand Rapids: Zondervan, 1990.

Lanham, Richard A. *A Handlist of Rhetorical Terms*. 2nd ed. Berkeley: University of California Press, 1991.

——————. *Style: An Anti-Textbook*. New Haven, CT: Yale University Press, 1974.

Lanier, Gregory R., and William A. Ross. *Septuaginta: A Reader's Edition*. 2 vols. Peabody, MA: Hendrickson, 2018.

Larkin, William J. "Approaches to and Images of Biblical Authority for the Postmodern Mind." *Bulletin for Biblical Research* 8 (1998): 129–38.

Lauterbach, Jacob Z, trans. *Mekhilta de-Rabbi Ishmael*. 3 vols. Philadelphia: Jewish Publication Society, 1961.

Lawson, Steven J. "The Ten How-To's of Expository Preaching." *The Tie* 65, no. 3 (July 1997): 3.

Leaney, A. R. C. *The Epistles to Timothy, Titus and Philemon*. Torch Bible Commentaries. London: SCM, 1960.

268 | Bibliography

Lee, Jarena. *Religious Experience and Journal of Mrs. Jarena Lee Giving an Account of Her Call to Preach the Gospel*. Philadelphia: Pantianos, 1836.

Lewis, C. S. "Introduction." In *The Incarnation of the Word of God*, by Athanasius. New York: Macmillan, 1946.

Liddell, Henry George, and Robert Scott. *A Greek-English Lexicon*. Edited by H. S. Jones. 9th ed. Oxford: Clarendon, 1968.

Lightfoot, J. B. *Saint Paul's Epistles to the Colossians and to Philemon*. Grand Rapids: Zondervan, 1959.

Little, Paul E. *How to Give Away Your Faith*. Downers Grove, IL: InterVarsity Press, 1966.

Lloyd-Jones, H., and P. Parsons. *Supplementum Hellenisticum*. Berlin: de Gruyter, 1983.

Lohse, Edward. *Colossians and Philemon*. Edited by H. Koester. Hermeneia. Translated by W. Poehlmann and R. Karris. Philadelphia: Fortress, 1971.

Louw, Johannes P., and Eugene A. Nida, eds. *Greek-English Lexicon of the New Testament Based on Semantic Domains*. 2nd ed. 2 vols. New York: United Bible Societies, 1989.

Lozada, Francisco, Jr. *Toward a Latino/a Biblical Interpretation*. Resources for Biblical Study 91. Atlanta: SBL Press, 2017.

Lyon, Jeremy D. "The Dead Sea Scrolls and the Reliability of the Bible." *Bible Study Magazine* 14, no. 2 (January–February 2022): 29–31.

Lyons, John. *Introduction to Theoretical Linguistics*. Cambridge: Cambridge University Press, 1968.

Machen, J. Gresham. *New Testament Greek for Beginners*. Toronto: Macmillan, 1951.

Maclaren, Alexander. *The Epistles of St. Paul to the Colossians and Philemon*. New York: Hodder & Stoughton, n.d.

Martin, Ralph P. *Colossians and Philemon*. New Century Bible. Greenwood, SC: Attic, 1974.

Mattingly, Harold. *The Man in the Roman Street*. New York: Norton, 1966.

Mayer, Günter. *Index Philoneus*. Berlin: de Gruyter, 1974.

McKnight, Scot. *The Letter to Philemon*. New International Commentary on the New Testament. Grand Rapids: Eerdmans, 2017.

McRay, John. *Archaeology and the New Testament*. Grand Rapids: Baker, 1991.

McReynolds, Paul R., ed. *Word Study Greek-English New Testament*. Wheaton, IL: Tyndale House, 1999.

Melick, Richard R., Jr. *Philippians, Colossians, Philemon*. New American Commentary 32. Nashville: Broadman, 1991.

Metzger, Bruce M. *The Early Versions of the New Testament: Their Origin, Transmission, and Limitations*. Oxford: Clarendon, 1977.

_____. *Index to Periodical Literature on the Apostle Paul*. New Testament Tools and Studies. Leiden: Brill, 1970.

_____. *Index to Periodical Literature on Christ and the Gospels*. New Testament Tools and Studies 6. Leiden: Brill, 1966.

_____. *An Introduction to the Apocrypha*. New York: Oxford University Press, 1957.

_____ *A Textual Commentary on the Greek New Testament*. 2nd ed. New York: American Bible Society, 2002.

Metzger, Bruce M., and Bart D. Ehrman. *The Text of the New Testament: Its Transmission, Corruption, and Restoration*. 4th ed. New York: Oxford University Press, 2005.

Mickelsen, A. Berkeley. *Interpreting the Bible*. Grand Rapids: Eerdmans, 1963.

Mickelsen, A. Berkeley, and Alvera M. Mickelsen. *Understanding Scripture: How to Read and Study the Bible*. Rev. ed. Peabody, MA: Hendrickson, 1992.

Moellering, H. Armin, and Victor A. Bartling. *Concordia Commentary: 1 Timothy, 2 Timothy, Titus, Philemon*. St. Louis: Concordia, 1970.

Moo, Douglas J. *The Letters to the Colossians and to Philemon*. Pillar New Testament Commentary. Grand Rapids: Eerdmans, 2008.

Moon, Sun Myung. *The Kingdom of God on Earth and the Ideal Family*. New York: Holy Spirit Association for the Unification of World Christianity, 1977.

Moulton, James H., and G. Milligan. *The Vocabulary of the Greek Testament: Illustrated from the Papyri and Other Non-Literary Sources*. Peabody, MA: Hendrickson, 1930.

Mounce, William D. *The Analytical Lexicon to the Greek New Testament*. Grand Rapids: Zondervan, 1993.

Muller, Jac. J. *The Epistles of Paul to the Philippians and to Philemon*. New International Commentary on the New Testament. Grand Rapids: Eerdmans, 1955.

Nave, Orville J. *The New Nave's Topical Bible*. Edited by Edward Viening. Grand Rapids: Zondervan, 1969.

Neusner, Jacob. *The Mishnah: A New Translation*. New Haven, CT: Yale University Press, 1988.

_____, ed. *The Talmud of Babylonia: An American Translation*. 36 vols. Chico, CA: Scholars Press, 1984–1990.

_____, ed. *The Talmud of the Land of Israel*. 35 vols. Chicago: University of Chicago Press, 1982–1994.

_____. *The Tosefta Translated from the Hebrew*. 6 vols. New York: KTAV, 1977–1981.

Newman, Barclay M. *A Concise Greek-English Dictionary of the New Testament*. Rev. ed. Stuttgart: Deutsche Bibelgesellschaft, 2014.

Nordling, John G. *Philemon*. Concordia Commentary. St. Louis: Concordia, 2004.

Pantelia, Maria C. *Thesaurus Linguae Graecae: A Bibliographic Guide to the Canon of Greek Authors and Works*. Oakland: University of California Press, 2022.

270 | Bibliography

Pao, David W. *Colossians and Philemon.* Zondervan Exegetical Commentary on the New Testament 12. Grand Rapids: Zondervan, 2012.

Parker, Margaret. *Unlocking the Power of God's Word.* Downers Grove, IL: InterVarsity Press, 1991.

Patzia, Arthur G. *Ephesians, Colossians, Philemon.* New International Biblical Commentary. Peabody, MA: Hendrickson, 1990.

Philo. *On the Special Laws, Book 4. On the Virtues. On Rewards and Punishments.* Translated by F. H. Colson. Loeb Classical Library 341. Cambridge: Harvard University Press, 1939.

_____. *The Works of Philo: Complete and Unabridged.* Translated by C. D. Yonge. Peabody, MA: Hendrickson, 1993.

Plummer, Alfred. *A Critical and Exegetical Commentary on the Second Epistle of St. Paul to the Corinthians.* International Critical Commentary. Edinburgh: T&T Clark, 1915.

Poirier, John C. "Scripture and Canon." In *The Sacred Text: Excavating the Texts, Exploring the Interpretations, and Engaging the Theologies of the Christian Scriptures,* edited by Michael Bird and Michael Pahl, 83–98. Piscataway, NJ: Gorgias, 2010.

Presbyterian and Reformed Educational Ministry. "Planning for Teaching/ Learning." *Alert: For Leaders and Planners of the Church's Education Program,* May 1989.

Quasten, Johannes. *Patrology.* 3 vols. 1754. Reprint, Westminster, MD: Christian Classics, 1986.

Radford, Lewis B. *The Epistle to the Colossians and the Epistle to Philemon.* Westminster Commentaries. London: Methuen, 1930.

Rahlfs, Alfred, and Robert Hanhart, eds. *Septuaginta.* Stuttgart: Deutsche Bibelgesellschaft, 2006.

Ramm, Bernard. *Protestant Biblical Interpretation: A Textbook of Hermeneutics.* 3rd ed. Grand Rapids: Baker, 1970.

Random House Webster's Unabridged Dictionary. New York: Random House, 2001.

Rengstorf, Karl Heinrich, ed. *A Complete Concordance to Flavius Josephus.* 4 vols. Leiden: Brill, 1973.

Richards, E. Randolph. "The Codex and the Early Collection of Paul's Letters." *Bulletin for Biblical Research* 8 (1998): 151–66.

Riesenfeld, Harald, and Blenda Riesenfeld. *Repertorium Lexicographicum Graecum: A Catalogue of Indexes and Dictionaries to Greek Authors.* Stockholm, Sweden: Almquist & Wiksells, 1954.

Robertson, A. T. *A Grammar of the Greek New Testament in the Light of Historical Research.* Nashville: Broadman, 1934.

_____. *Word Pictures in the New Testament.* 6 vols. Nashville: Broadman, 1931.

Robertson, A. T., and W. H. Davis. *A New Short Grammar of the Greek Testament.* Grand Rapids: Baker, 1977.

Robinson, Haddon W. *Biblical Preaching: The Development and Delivery of Expository Messages*. 3rd ed. Grand Rapids: Baker, 2014.

Ross, Bobby, Jr. "Bible in One Hand, Newspaper in the Other." *Christian Chronicle*, February 27, 2021. https://chronicle.org/bible-in-one-hand-newspaper-in-the-other.

Sandmel, Samuel. "Parallelomania." *Journal of Biblical Literature* 81, no. 1 (March 1962): 1–13.

Schürer, Emil. *The History of the Jewish People in the Age of Jesus Christ (175 B.C.–A.D. 135): A New English Version*. Revised and edited by Géza Vermes, Fergus Millar, Pamela Vermes, and Matthew Black. 3 vols. Edinburgh: T&T Clark, 1973.

Select Papyri. Translated by A. S. Hunt, C. C. Edgar, and Denys L. Page. 3 vols. Loeb Classical Library. Cambridge, MA: Harvard University Press, 1934–1940.

Shields, Bonita Joyner. "Growing Disciples through Transformational Learning." *Ministry*, May 2011.

Silva, Moisés. *Biblical Words and Their Meaning*. Grand Rapids: Zondervan, 1983.

Slade, Carole, and Robert Perrin. *Form and Style: Research Papers, Reports, Theses*. 13th ed. Belmont, CA: Wadsworth, 2007.

Smith, Bob. *Basics of Bible Interpretation*. A Discovery Bible Study Book. Waco, TX: Word, 1978.

Spencer, Aída Besançon. *1 Timothy*. New Covenant Commentary Series. Eugene, OR: Cascade, 2013.

———. *2 Corinthians*. People's Bible Commentary. Oxford: Bible Reading Fellowship, 2001.

———. "2 Corinthians: An Egalitarian Ideology for the Latinx Church." In *Latinx Perspectives on the New Testament*, edited by Osvaldo D. Vena and Leticia A. Guardiola-Sáenz, 167–72. Lanham, MD: Lexington/Fortress, 2022.

———. *2 Timothy and Titus*. New Covenant Commentary Series. Eugene, OR: Cascade, 2014.

———. *Beyond the Curse: Women Called to Ministry*. Nashville: Nelson, 1985.

———. *A Commentary on James*. Kregel Exegetical Library. Grand Rapids: Kregel Academic, 2020.

———. "Critical Notes: Šərîrût as Self-Reliance." *Journal of Biblical Literature* 100 (June 1981): 247–48.

———. "The Denial of the Good News and the Ending of Mark." *Bulletin for Biblical Research* 17, no. 2 (2007): 269–83.

———. "Does James 'Show Thee Christ'? A Comparison of the Content and Communication Styles of Jesus and James (Matthew 7:7–27 vs. James 1:2–27)." *Journal of Language, Culture, and Religion* 3, no. 1 (2022): 63–88.

_____. "Eve at Ephesus: Should Women Be Ordained as Pastors according to the First Letter of Timothy 2:11–15?" *Journal of the Evangelical Theological Society* 17 (Fall 1974): 215–22.

_____. "God the Stranger: An Intercultural Hispanic American Perspective." In *The Global God: Multicultural Evangelical Views of God*, edited by Aída Besançon Spencer and William David Spencer, 89–103. Grand Rapids: Baker, 1998.

_____. "My Journey as a Latin American Feminist New Testament Scholar." In *Feminist New Testament Studies: Global and Future Perspectives*, edited by Kathleen O'Brien Wicker, Althea Spencer Miller, and Musa W. Dube, 115–29. New York: Palgrave Macmillan, 2005.

_____. "'Parallelomania' and God's Unique Revelation." *Africanus Journal* 1, no. 1 (April 2009): 31–40.

_____. *Paul's Literary Style: A Stylistic and Historical Comparison of II Corinthians 11:16–12:13, Romans 8:9–39, and Philippians 3:2–4:13*. Lanham, MD: University Press of America, 1998.

_____. Review of *In Memory of Her*, by Elisabeth Schüssler Fiorenza. *Update II*, Summer 1987.

Spencer, William David. "Intentional Teaching." In *Empowering English Language Learners: Successful Strategies of Christian Educators*, edited by Jeanne C. DeFazio and William David Spencer, 106–37. House of Prisca and Aquila Series. Eugene, OR: Wipf & Stock, 2018.

_____. *Mysterium and Mystery: The Clerical Crime Novel*. Carbondale, IL: Southern Illinois University Press, 1989.

Spencer, William David, and Aída Besançon Spencer, eds. *God through the Looking Glass: Glimpses from the Arts*. Grand Rapids: Baker, 1998.

Sperber, A., ed. *The Bible in Aramaic*. 4 vols. Leiden: Brill, 1959–1973.

Spicq, Ceslas. *Theological Lexicon of the New Testament*. Translated and edited by James D. Ernest. 3 vols. Peabody, MA: Hendrickson, 1994.

Sterrett, T. Norton, and Richard L. Schultz. *How to Understand Your Bible*. 3rd ed. Downers Grove, IL: InterVarsity Press, 2010.

Stevenson, J., and W. H. C. Frend, eds. *A New Eusebius: Documents Illustrating the History of the Church to AD 337*. Grand Rapids: Baker Academic, 2013.

Stobbe, Les. "Earning the Right to Be Published." *Africanus Journal* 10, no. 2 (November 2018): 4–11.

Strack, Hermann L., and Paul Billerbeck. *A Commentary on the New Testament from the Talmud and Midrash*. Edited by Jacob N. Cerone. Translated by Andrew Bowden and Joseph Longarino. 3 vols. Bellingham, WA: Lexham, 2022.

Streeter, B. H. *The Four Gospels: A Study of Origins*. Rev. ed. London: Macmillan, 1930.

Strong, James. *The Strongest Strong's Exhaustive Concordance of the Bible.* Edited by John R. Kohlenberger III and James A. Swanson. Grand Rapids: Zondervan, 2001.

Sturz, Harry A. *The Byzantine Text-Type and New Testament Textual Criticism.* Nashville: Nelson, 1984.

Terry, Milton. "The Use of Words in Various Contexts." In *Rightly Divided: Readings in Biblical Hermeneutics*, edited by Roy B. Zuck, 133–42. Grand Rapids: Kregel, 1996.

Thayer, Joseph H. *Thayer's Greek-English Lexicon of the New Testament.* Unabridged. Marshallton, DE: National Foundation for Christian Education, 1889.

Thiede, Carston Peter. "Papyrus Magdalen Greek 17 (Gregory-Aland p[64]): A Reappraisal." *Tyndale Bulletin* 46, no. 1 (May 1995): 29–42.

Thompson, Alan J. *Colossians and Philemon.* Tyndale New Testament Commentaries. Downers Grove, IL: InterVarsity Press, 2022.

Thompson, Marianne Meye. *Colossians and Philemon.* Two Horizons New Testament Commentary. Grand Rapids: Eerdmans, 2005.

Titrud, Kermit. "The Function of *Kai* in the Greek New Testament and an Application to 2 Peter." In *Linguistics and New Testament Interpretation: Essays on Discourse Analysis*, edited by David Alan Black, with Katharine Barnwell and Stephen Levinsohn, 240–70. Nashville: Broadman, 1992.

Traupman, John C. *The New College Latin and English Dictionary.* New York: Bantam, 1966.

Trimmer, Joseph F. *The New Writing with a Purpose.* 14th ed. Boston: Houghton Mifflin, 2004.

Turabian, Kate L., et al. *Manual for Writers of Term Papers, Theses, and Dissertations.* 9th ed. Chicago: University of Chicago Press, 2018.

VanderKam, James C. *The Dead Sea Scrolls Today.* Rev. ed. Grand Rapids: Eerdmans, 2010.

Vermes, Géza. *The Dead Sea Scrolls in English.* 3rd ed. Sheffield: JSOT Press, 1987.

Viening, Edward, ed. *The Zondervan Topical Bible.* Grand Rapids: Zondervan, 1969.

Vincent, Marvin. *A Critical and Exegetical Commentary on the Epistles to the Philippians and to Philemon.* International Critical Commentary. Edinburgh: T&T Clark, 1897.

Vos, Craig S. de. "Once a Slave, Always a Slave? Slavery, Manumission and Relational Patterns in Paul's Letter to Philemon." *Journal for the Study of the New Testament* 82 (2001): 89–105.

Wallace, Daniel B. "Challenges in New Testament Textual Criticism for the Twenty-first Century." *Journal of the Evangelical Theological Society* 52, no. 1 (March 2009): 79–100.

———. *Greek Grammar beyond the Basics: An Exegetical Syntax of the New Testament.* Grand Rapids: Zondervan Academic, 1996.

. "Medieval Manuscripts and Modern Evangelicals: Lessons from the Past, Guidance for the Future." *Journal of the Evangelical Theological Society* 60, no. 1 (March 2017): 5–34.

Weed, Michael R. *The Letters of Paul to the Ephesians, the Colossians, and Philemon*. Living Word Commentary. Austin, TX: Sweet, 1971.

Wilson, Andrew. "The Pragmatics of Politeness and Pauline Epistolography: A Case Study of the Letter to Philemon." *Journal for the Study of the New Testament* 48 (1992): 107–19.

Winter, S. C. "Philemon." In *Searching the Scriptures: A Feminist Commentary*, edited by Elizabeth Schüssler Fiorenza, 2:309–11. 2 vols. New York: Crossroad, 1993–94.

Wintle, Brian, and Bruce Nicholls. *Colossians and Philemon*. Asia Bible Commentary Series. Cumbria, CA: Langham Global Library, 2019.

Witherington, Ben, III. "'Almost Thou Persuadest Me . . .': The Importance of Greco-Roman Rhetoric for the Understanding of the Text and Content of the NT." *Journal of the Evangelical Theological Society* 58, no. 1 (2015): 63–88.

. *The Letters to Philemon, the Colossians, and the Ephesians: A Socio-Rhetorical Commentary on the Captivity Epistles*. Grand Rapids: Eerdmans, 2007.

Yeo, K. K. "Response: Multicultural Readings; A Biblical Warrant and an Eschatological Vision." In *Global Voices: Reading the Bible in the Majority World*, edited by Craig Keener and M. Daniel Carroll R., 27–37. Peabody, MA: Hendrickson, 2013.

Young, Robert. *Young's Analytical Concordance to the Bible*. Rev. ed. (with index lexicons). Nashville: Nelson, 1982.

Young, Stephen E. *Our Brother Beloved: Purpose and Community in Paul's Letter to Philemon*. Waco, TX: Baylor University Press, 2021.

Zahn, Theodor. *Introduction to the New Testament*. Translated by John Moore Trout et al. 2nd ed. 3 vols. New York: Scribner, 1917.

Zerwick, Max, and Mary Grosvenor. *A Grammatical Analysis of the Greek New Testament*. Rome: Editrice Pontificio Istituto Biblico, 1996.

Zuck, Roy B., ed. *Rightly Divided: Readings in Biblical Hermeneutics*. Grand Rapids: Kregel, 1996.